JUN   2018

Praise for Remembering the Stars of the NFL Glory Years

"I consider my era to be the glory days of the NFL, a true Golden Age, and this book provides a detailed inside look at many of the greatest players of that time period—of all time, actually. Wayne Stewart gives readers the opportunity to go behind the scenes and learn so much about the game, and in many cases, through the words of the greats themselves—men such as Lenny Moore, Gino Marchetti, and Mike Ditka. It's a must-read for any pro football fan."—**Raymond Berry, Hall of Fame receiver, Baltimore Colts**

"Remembering the Stars of the NFL Glory Years recalls the 1950s and 1960s, covering everything from the Hall of Famers of the day to the way the league has changed from that era to now. Fans of superstars such as Gale Sayers, Jim Brown, Johnny Unitas, and many more will enjoy reliving the Golden Age of football."—**Mike Ditka, Hall of Fame tight end**

"Wayne Stewart conducted exclusive interviews with a slew of NFL players from the Golden Age of the NFL to come up with Remembering the Stars of the NFL Glory Years. I was glad to contribute some of my memories, including those of stars such as Dick Butkus, Sam Huff, and Paul Hornung. As a running back for the New York Giants, Green Bay Packers, and New York Jets, I played with and against many of the greats featured in this excellent, nostalgic book that provides some laughs, along with a ton of facts, stats, and inside stories. It's a must-read for any football fan."—**Chuck Mercein, NFL running back and Super Bowl II champion, Green Bay Packers**

"Wayne Stewart has done a fine job of capturing the glory days of the NFL, back when I played for the Baltimore Colts with stars such as Raymond Berry and Johnny Unitas. The book is packed with anecdotes and a ton of inside information gained through exclusive interviews with many of us players from that era. Anyone who watched the NFL in the 1950s and 1960s will want to read this book!"—**Tom Matte, All-Pro running back, Baltimore Colts**

REMEMBERING THE STARS OF THE NFL GLORY YEARS

REMEMBERING THE STARS OF THE NFL GLORY YEARS

An Inside Look at the Golden Age of Football

Wayne Stewart

ROWMAN & LITTLEFIELD
Lanham • Boulder • New York • London

Published by Rowman & Littlefield
A wholly owned subsidiary of The Rowman & Littlefield Publishing Group, Inc.
4501 Forbes Boulevard, Suite 200, Lanham, Maryland 20706
www.rowman.com

Unit A, Whitacre Mews, 26-34 Stannary Street, London SE11 4AB

British Library Cataloguing in Publication Information Available

Library of Congress Cataloging-in-Publication Data

Names: Stewart, Wayne, 1953- author.
Title: Remembering the stars of the NFL glory years : an inside look at the golden age of football / Wayne Stewart.
Other titles: Remembering the Stars of the National Football League Glory Years
Description: First Atria Books Hardcover edition. | Lanham, Maryland : Rowman & Littlefield, 2017. | Includes bibliographical references and index.
Identifiers: LCCN 2016054867 (print) | LCCN 2017004309 (ebook) | ISBN 9781442274235 (cloth : alk. paper) | ISBN 9781442274242 (electronic)
Subjects: LCSH: National Football League—History—20th century. | National Football League—Biography. | Football players—United States—Biography. | Football players—United States—Anecdotes. | Football—United States—History—20th century—Anecdotes.
Classification: LCC GV955.5.N35 S73 2017 (print) | LCC GV955.5.N35 (ebook) | DDC 796.3320922 [B] —dc23
LC record available at https://lccn.loc.gov/2016054867

Printed in the United States of America

To those closest to me—
my wife Nancy, my sons and their spouses, Sean and
Rachel, Scott and Katie, and to my grandson Nathan

CONTENTS

ACKNOWLEDGMENTS

Sincere and huge thanks go out to the following people: Stephen Russell, Mid Mon Valley All Sports Hall of Fame General Chairman; Ron Paglia, a longtime newsman and writer from Charleroi, Pennsylvania; Chad Unitas; Paige Unitas; John Ziemann, former deputy director of the Sports Legends and Babe Ruth Birthplace Museum and president of Baltimore's Marching Ravens (formerly the Baltimore Colts Marching Band); Rich Erdelyi, Carnegie Mellon University football coach; Ron Main, chairman of the Larry Bruno Foundation at Carnegie Free Library of Beaver Falls, Pennsylvania; Pete Fierle and Chris Schilling of the Pro Football Hall of Fame; and John Vorperean, host and executive producer, *Beyond the Game*.

A final thanks goes out to all of the people who gave up their time to do interviews with the author, with special appreciation extended to the former players and coaches who generously did repeated and/or lengthy interviews with the author: Chuck Mercein, Manny Fernandez, Gino Marchetti, Sam Havrilak, Fred Cox, Myron Pottios, Doug Crusan, George Belu, Bob Hyland, Tom Matte, Rick Volk, John Isenbarger, Lenny Moore, Mike Ditka, Chuck Bryant, Mike Lucci, Joe Walton, Andy Nelson, Bill Malinchak, and Raymond Berry. All of the quotes in the book, unless otherwise noted, are from interviews conducted by the author.

INTRODUCTION

The genesis for this book is my roots in western Pennsylvania. I grew up in Donora, which is nestled in the Mon Valley area, not far from Pittsburgh. The town proclaims itself as The Home of Champions, and it has been a hotbed for a slew of marvelous athletes. Donora natives proudly point to the incredible fact that such a small town—at its peak the population hit around fifteen thousand—produced two baseball Hall of Famers in Stan Musial and Ken Griffey Jr. Coincidentally, the two were born on the same date.

I happen to have graduated from the same high school class as another great athlete, a lifetime .296 major league hitter, Ken Griffey Sr., who became a member of the famed Big Red Machine Cincinnati Reds. Further, yet another native of the town, one of four to make it to the NFL, "Deacon" Dan Towler, led the league in rushing in 1952. He also averaged 6.8 yards per carry that season, which still puts him at number fifteen all-time in this department, even though he didn't lead the NFL in that category—Tobin Rote did (6.9).

At any rate, across the river from my hometown is Monessen, which produced, according to the pro football reference website, a staggering fourteen NFL players, despite having a population that peaked at roughly twenty thousand. Other neighboring towns such as Mononga-hela produced almost ten NFL players, including an excellent kicker, Fred Cox, and Hall of Fame quarterback Joe Montana. The noteworthy coincidence involving these two men is that they not only were raised in the same town, they also grew up on the same block, though years apart.

The list of men who played their high school ball in the Mon Valley area and then went on to play in an NFL title game, either in or before the era of Super Bowls, includes not only Cox and Montana, who together played in eight Super Bowls, but also Towler, Doug Crusan, Myron Pottios, Sam Havrilak, and Bert Rechichar.

Hard to believe, but almost one-fourth of the twenty-five quarterbacks from the modern era who are enshrined in the Pro Football Hall of Fame hail from within a radius of about sixty miles around Pittsburgh, a veritable football factory. The six men from this cradle of quarterbacks are John Unitas, Joe Namath, and George Blanda, all three featured in this book, and Montana, Jim Kelly, and Dan Marino.

Growing up in such an area inspired this book, and so did working on my previous book, coauthoring Raymond Berry's autobiography, *All the Moves I Had: A Football Life* (Lyons Press, 2016). The western Pennsylvania thread runs throughout this book, with many other stars, from Mike Ditka to Joe Walton, featured heavily.

To be honest, though, I suspect that even if I had grown up in an area that never produced a pro athlete, I still would have turned my living room into a bunker on Sunday afternoons. I vividly remember the Glory Years as I sat in front of my parents' black-and-white Zenith television set (which, I think, measured about a minuscule thirteen or fifteen inches diagonally). It may have been difficult for me to make out the numbers of, say, John Unitas as he launched a pass to favorite target Raymond Berry, but that didn't seem to matter—these guys were larger than life regardless of their Lilliputian appearance on the screen. They were heroic figures in glorious black and white—as for color, you can't miss what never existed (and my family didn't own a color TV set until the 1970s).

Football through the eyes of a boy was wonderful. So much so that even now the stars of that era shine with much more luminescence than today's.

Finally, it should be noted that this book is the first of two companion books about the wonderful era of the 1950s and 1960s in the NFL. The second book will be released in 2018 and will likely be titled *Remembering the Best Coaches of the NFL Glory Years: An Inside Look at the Golden Age of Football*. One part of that book will explore several select great games of the era and examine the coaches' roles in those games. It will include Super Bowl III, the "Heidi" game, the "Ice Bowl" game, and the contest still referred to as "The Greatest Game Ever Played," the 1958 title clash between the Baltimore Colts of John Unitas and company, and the New York Giants of Frank Gifford and many others. The second part of the book will look at Hall of Fame coaches such as Paul Brown, Don Shula, Tom Landry, and Vince Lombardi.

I

THE BEST OFFENSIVE PLAYERS

Fans always want to know who the experts consider to be, say, the best quarterback ever, but Mike Ditka knows how foolish such inquiries are. "Somebody asked me, 'Who are the four top quarterbacks?' And I said, 'There is no such thing as the best quarterbacks.' But I think when you mention guys like Dan Marino and Johnny Unitas, and I go back to Y. A. Tittle, John Brodie, and a lot of guys in my era, those guys were very, very good football players.

"Now, were they the best? Was it Sammy Baugh or Sid Luckman? I don't know. You have to understand that the game has changed so much today. The things based on numbers of the passing game—there was no passing game in those days. You threw the ball, maybe, what, eighteen or twenty times a game? And you ran. The advent of the forward pass being *really* a weapon was with Johnny Unitas more than anybody. Throwing out numbers doesn't mean anything, and your contribution to the game is what counts."

To many fans, coaches, players, and members of the media, the time period from the 1950s through the 1960s remains the Glory Years of the NFL. A slew of all-time greats roamed the league's gridirons, creating history along the way.

It's nearly impossible to determine exactly which NFL players deserve to be labeled "great," as opposed to those who were very good or were borderline great players; and, without compiling a list, which would turn a readable book into a tome, it's impossible to cover every single one of the greats.

With that in mind, there are three ground rules for this chapter: First, it will cover Hall of Famers only. Secondly, this chapter will focus exclusively on quarterbacks, running backs, wide receivers, and tight ends. Finally, it does not attempt to cover every single player of this golden age who is enshrined in Canton, Ohio; rather, it's a sort of NFL Whitman-like sampler of many of the elite of the era.

By the way, through the 2016 induction ceremonies, there were a total of 260 players in the Hall of Fame, and more than half of them, 138, a whopping 53 percent to be exact, come from the Glory Years. Men who played in that time period are, for the purposes of this book, those who played at least briefly in the 1950s or 1960s. In the book *The NFL's Top 100*, more of the players selected as the best of all time debuted in the 1960s (a total of 21) than in any other decade. Plus, an additional 13 of them began their careers in the 1950s, meaning more than one-third of the top 100 greats came from the golden era.

Start any list of NFL greats from this era with a name such as Johnny Unitas or Jim Brown, and you can't go wrong. In fact, in 2002, *Sporting News* pulled no punches, calling Brown the greatest football player ever. His credentials bear that out, especially considering he played almost half of his career during years with schedules of twelve games and the rest of his tenure was played in fourteen-game seasons. In addition, he put up his unparalleled stats in just nine seasons.

Despite those drawbacks, his accomplishments still reverberate, and some of today's best runners, unborn when Brown departed from the game, still agree with the evaluation of *Sporting News*. His rapid ascension to stardom was a skyscraper's express elevator ride to the penthouse. He led the NFL in rushing and touchdowns as a rookie, led the league in those departments in his final season, and did the same and much more in many seasons in between.

Brown's 12,312 rushing yards still rank number nine all-time; his 106 touchdowns on runs and his average of 5.2 yards per run are number five all-time; and, get this, he averaged 104.3 yards per game played on runs for his entire career—nobody else has ever averaged 100+ yards.

With Brown in the backfield, any time, *anywhere* Cleveland had the ball, they were in scoring position—no need to use the term "red zone" in connection to him. Trying to tackle Brown single-handedly was like trying to bring down a polar bear with a popgun.

Hall of Fame defensive end Gino Marchetti looked back on some of the toughest opponents he had to tackle. "You know who I really admired as a back? The first two are no question—Jim Brown and Jim Taylor. Brown was a hard hitter. He could do everything but block—he didn't like to. He couldn't block a lick. Didn't want to block a lick. Didn't *have* to block a lick.

"He had great balance. He was fast; he could dodge; he could catch the ball. They just gave him the ball thirty times.

"Let me tell you, though, when I tackled him, wow. I used to tell the story at banquets: I played against him in a Pro Bowl and he was coming off tackle. I was able to get rid of the tackle and there was Jim Brown and there was me. So here he comes and I kinda grabbed him, sidearm a little bit, and then I made the tackle. I got up and I felt pretty damned good about it, you know. There he is, down, and there I am, my first Pro Bowl and all that bullshit. Then I heard the announcement say, 'Tackle by Marchetti. Ball carrier, Jim Brown. Second and one.' Second and one! He dragged me for nine yards. I had been happy as hell until I heard the announcer. And I wasn't the only guy Brown did that to."

Sam Huff, a Hall of Fame linebacker, once said this of trying to bring Brown down: "All you could do is grab hold, hang on, and wait for help."[1] Brown carried defenders on his back like a burly camper lugs a backpack, totally unconcerned about his load.

"I still think he's the greatest back of all time," opined former player and head coach Joe Walton. "He was a powerful guy. I played against him in college—Pitt played against Syracuse every year—and we played together in a college All-Star game. The first time I played against him was when I was on defense for the Redskins. The other defensive guys kept asking me about Brown. I told them, 'We hit him hard early in the game, and we had to concentrate on gang tackling to make sure he knew we're coming after him.' We never had any trouble with him at Pitt—he never gained a hundred yards against our class.

"So the game starts and we're getting after him pretty good, taking our shots against him—and he gained 160 yards, another 50 yards pass receiving, and scored four touchdowns. He killed us. After the game, the guys said to me, 'You dumb rookie.'

"If the Browns ran the ball three downs, Brown carried it twice at least. And if he wasn't running the ball, they'd throw to him. He had good hands. He could do everything."

Former NFL linebacker Myron Pottios said, "Jimmy had a knack of running that you, as a defensive ballplayer, had a hard time getting your arms around him because when he saw you coming, he would bend down and shove his forearm into you. He was strong enough to keep you away. If you can't get your arms around him, you can't get a hold of anything, and you just bounce off of him. And, if you went low, he would give you the thigh, and he was big enough and strong enough to hold you off. Unless you got the perfect hit on Jimmy, you weren't going to bring him down with just one guy tackling. And the biggest thing with him, you had to follow through to overcome his strength with yours. If he kept you off him, he would just pull away."

Marchetti spoke of another clever Brown tactic that "he was known for after he was tackled. He acted like he was tired, ready to quit." That way, if he really did get hurt or tired, opponents wouldn't know—to them it was just Brown wearily getting up off the turf once more.

Veteran coach and NFL scout George Belu added, "He had everything you needed as a great running back: size, speed, athletic ability. He could give you that limp leg, when you thought he was going to do that or try to avoid you, he could lower his shoulder and knock the hell out of you. He'd carry tacklers on his back, too."

Brown was so durable over his 118-game career that he led the NFL in total touches seven times while establishing the record for career touches; and, despite carrying the team on his broad shoulders, he never once missed a start.

Brown wound up leading the NFL in rushing in every one of his nine seasons except 1962 when his 962 yards was the fourth-highest total for rushing yardage. In 1963, Brown set a personal high with his 1,863 yards on runs. In all, there were five seasons in which he ran for 1,400+ yards and, again, for almost half of his career he played a twelve-game schedule. One year he accounted for a total of 2,131 yards gained from scrimmage. In five of his seasons he led the NFL in touchdowns on runs, and in almost half of his seasons, four, he was the NFL MVP according to at least one major poll.

At the age of twenty-eight, Brown was in his eighth and next-to-last season, and he was still in his prime. He led the league once again in a handful of major offensive categories. He scampered and pounded his way for 1,446 yards, an impressive total, but he was still capable of more. His stats the next year actually improved, up to 1,544 yards rushing, to complement his seventeen touchdowns, and he produced his fourth best single season average for rushing yards gained per game at 110.3. For that performance he was named to the First-Team All-NFL squad for the eighth time in nine seasons.

It took Hollywood to lure Brown off the NFL gridiron—he went on to appear in movies such as *The Dirty Dozen*. Doug Crusan, an offensive lineman for the Miami Dolphins, said, "To have him leave when he had years left in him—he still had a lot of gas left in his tank, and back then the Cleveland Browns teams were good. He controlled the game. It was kinda like, 'Oh, no. He's got the ball.' Watching him pick his way through holes—tremendous running back, my goodness! He was a fullback that ran like a halfback; that's the scariest part there. He was a good-sized guy, a big man." The 232-pound Brown went six feet, two inches, but he cast a ten-foot-long shadow.

Brown's credentials as an all-round superb athlete are sparkling. As a college freshman at Syracuse, where he would letter in four sports, he once came in fifth place in the decathlon. As a sophomore, he averaged fifteen points per game for the basketball team and he ran track as well. He is a member of both the College Football Hall of Fame and Pro Football Hall of Fame, and he is honored as well in the Lacrosse Hall of Fame. One source says only three athletes ever have been inducted into two or more different pro sport's halls of fame, with the other two being Ted Williams and Cal Hubbard.

Boxing champion George Foreman once said, "I had two heroes growing up, John Wayne and Roy Rogers. Then one day I saw Jim Brown." Those who had the opportunity to watch Brown know precisely what Foreman meant.[2]

If you start with Jim Brown in the backfield at fullback, then you positively must put John Unitas under center as the greatest of his era. In fact, Unitas, like Brown, has also been labeled the best player *ever*. For instance, in one poll based on the first fifty years of the NFL Unitas came out on top of all other stars since the league's inception. Lenny Moore opined, "I would say the publicity that was given to Unitas, and the grandeur of the things that he did were richly deserved, believe me."

Marchetti said of Unitas, a man who for more than five decades, from 1960 until 2012, held a record for firing at least one touchdown pass in forty-seven consecutive games: "First of all, I think he's the best. I don't think there's any doubt about it, and I think if they had the same rules today as they had yesteryear, he would be a much higher-rated passer than he is now. Nowadays, a receiver goes down the field and you can't touch him. In our day, we treated a receiver like a blocker. As long as he was running in the backfield, we could do whatever we wanted, as long as the ball wasn't thrown in the air."

Andy Nelson, a close friend of Unitas, said, "I knew he was good before I came to the Colts. He played for Louisville; I played for Memphis State. One day he completed about fifteen passes on us and somebody said, 'Who is that guy?' Another said, 'That's UNI-toss.' They called him that. But he was just the coolest guy on the field. Nothing bothered him. He just never got rattled."

Linebacker Jim Houston called Unitas a quarterback who was difficult to contain. *Impossible* to contain is more like it. When Unitas finally called it quits, he held twenty-two records and, as Marchetti pointed out, Unitas never played a sixteen-game season; most of his seasons had fourteen games, but in the first five of his eighteen total years in the NFL there were only twelve regular-season games staged. Marchetti continued, "When we first started, a season was twelve games, so he didn't have the same opportunity [as today's quarterbacks]. But most of all, I think, John should be known more for his leadership, for his attitude towards the game, and the hours that he put in studying during the week of the game."

Moore simply said that Unitas had it all, from a fabulous arm to leadership qualities to supreme confidence. "All of it. Of course it had to be a combination of a little bit of everything, and then improving on that." Teammates were well aware of the wordplay used concerning Unitas, believing Unitas truly could and did, "unite us."

One Colt teammate, running back Tom Matte, said Unitas was "the ultimate leader. You just looked at him and it was sort of like, some guy said, 'God's speaking here.' We had great, great trust and belief in what he could do. He was expected to produce and he just expected the best out of himself as he expected the best out of each of us, to give him the best effort that we could."

Clearly, Unitas did possess great leadership qualities and was a great handler of his men. His star tight end John Mackey often told the story about messing up a play when he dropped the football. As boos cascaded down, he feared going back to the huddle, fearing banishment to the sidelines. Unitas's daughter Paige picks up the story. "I think he was a rookie that year. He goes back and my dad called the same play, and he looked him right in the eyes and said, 'Silence the crowd.' And I think he scored, and Mackey later told me, 'That's the way your dad said, *I believe in you. It's OK that you messed up, but let's fix it.*'"

Marchetti recalled an incident from 1960 when the Colts traveled to Chicago. "It was probably the roughest game that I ever played in, and probably for John, too. He really took a beating and Jim Parker felt bad because Doug Atkins was giving Parker fits, and I can remember coming off the sideline and sitting next to John. God, he was bleeding, his nose, he looked terrible." Ewbank told Unitas he was going to pull him.

Marchetti continued, "John looked at him straight in the eye and said, 'Listen, you are not taking me out. If you take me out, I'll kill you.' John could have easily taken a couple of plays off and nobody would have said anything, but he didn't want to do that. He said a quarterback is the leader of the offense and he wanted to lead, and that's exactly what he did."

Unitas's receivers said he could throw with soft touch and finesse, or he could make his passes travel so quickly you almost expected jet vapors to trail behind the football. Defenders realized that fact early on, as Unitas led the NFL in TD passes from his first full season in the league, 1957, through 1960. No quarterback beside Unitas has ever accomplished that.

Safety Rick Volk, another teammate of Unitas, said, "When I first came to Baltimore John was the only person I really knew who played for the Colts because up there in my home state of Ohio and in Michigan [where Volk attended college], I was more of a Cleveland Browns and Detroit Lions fan, so I didn't know a lot about the Colts, but I did know about Johnny U, Raymond Berry, and Lenny Moore—guys like that, guys who had been on the team for quite a while.

"So when you line up against him in practice, you know it's Johnny U, but you just go ahead and try to do the best that you can—do your assignment and play within the team. You get a little bit intimidated at first because you're playing against these guys and you don't know what to expect—speed-wise and arm strength–wise, and them being savvy like they were, little things that they can do to throw you off a little bit. They might look you off and come back to the other player, the other receiver that they want to go to, and they can move you around with their eyes and things like that; but once the ball snapped, and the ball is in the air, it's like anything else—you've got a player, a receiver, and you try to become a receiver yourself when the ball's up in the air."

Marchetti added, "John wasn't afraid of hard work, and he wasn't afraid to take chances. If you check back on that championship game of 1958, we're down practically in the end zone and he throws a pass. How many quarterbacks would have enough guts to do that—to throw to Jim Mutscheller? But when they asked John about it, John just said, 'You're not taking a chance if you know what you're doing.'"

Fred Cox called Unitas the "prototype for all of them. You can say what you want, but it was a different type of game when he was playing. He just had a great arm and in a lot of ways he was totally different than the other quarterbacks [of recent years] because when he was playing the quarterback didn't move around. He was a drop back passer—and you stayed there in the pocket. It's quite obvious that his accuracy and his arm strength were just phenomenal."

Pottios added, "He was a smart quarterback, a cerebral type guy who would challenge you. He wanted to get you in a situation where he knew he could beat you. So he was always looking for that kind of a setup where your defense would be in a position that he could take advantage of."

Sticking with quarterbacks, the golden age produced a passel of Hall of Famers. Marchetti rattled off the names he felt were the best he ever went up against, and he began with Norm Van Brocklin. "He was good because—and John [Unitas] was this way—he knew where every receiver was, knew where to throw the ball, and he was the least-hit quarterback in the NFL. As far as I was concerned, I had a helluva time getting him because he was so quick with the ball, throwing the ball. You'd think you got him, and all of a sudden the arm would go forward, the ball would slip out of his hand and go to a receiver. He was phenomenal, in my opinion."

Van Brocklin, aka "The Dutchman," took two different teams to NFL titles, the 1951 Rams and, in his final season, an MVP year for him, the 1960 Eagles. He loved to throw long—his average of 15.2 yards gained per pass completion ranks fifth all-time. In one 1951 contest, he launched the football for five TDs and a glittering, unfathomable 554 yards, a total that to this day stands as the all-time high for a single game.

Some of the honors he earned include his selection to nine Pro Bowls, his MVP award in 1960, and his inclusion on the Pro Football Hall of Fame team for the 1950s. Only once in his career did he fail to finish in the top ten for touchdowns thrown, passer rating, and for the best pass completion rate. In addition, only twice did he fall short of top-ten status for pass completions and passing yardage.

Among his biggest statistical accomplishments are the four seasons in which he led the NFL in yards gained per attempted pass. Three of those seasons were in a row, from 1950, just his second year in the pros, through 1952, and in his best year for that stat, 1954, he established a personal high of 10.1 yards for every pass he threw. Plus, he also led the NFL that year by averaging exactly 19 yards for every one of his completions. Finally, through 2015, his stat of throwing a touchdown on 6 percent of all of his pass attempts stands at number ten in the annals of the NFL.

He even handled punting chores for his teams, once leading the league with his average of 44.6 yards per punt. Over his illustrious career, he even had three punts that traveled 70 or more yards.

Later, he became the head coach for the Minnesota Vikings, the first in the history of that franchise, and the Atlanta Falcons. However, he didn't fare as well with the coaching X's and O's as he did as a player. His overall coaching record stands at 66-100-7, and the best record he could muster was 9-5 with the Falcons in 1973, good for a second-place finish in the NFC West Division.

Another record-setting quarterback was Yelberton Abraham Tittle, whose unusual name and bald head may have led some people to think, "Here's a timid, unremarkable guy. Probably a businessman or insurance salesman." In truth, this man, better known, of course, as Y. A. Tittle, was calm under fire and stayed in the pocket with no trepidation at all. Before Unitas shattered records by the dozens, Tittle possessed almost every single one of the major passing marks—in fact, he established three of the biggest, most important records. He owned the lifetime record for the most touchdown passes with 212, and he held the top slot for the most career yards through the air at 28,339. His last major record to fall, like the other two, to Unitas, was his total of 2,118 pass completions.

The two-time league MVP also tied the record for the most touchdown passes in a game, seven, and in a season, thirty-six in 1963. Raymond Berry said it seemed as if Tittle, like precision pitcher Greg Maddux, threw nothing but strikes. Berry was correct—Tittle once led the NFL in completion percentage at 63.1 and another time he led the league with his passes being accurate 60.2 percent of the time. And *that* was in his next-to-last season when he was almost forty years old.

At the mention of Tittle's name, Joe Walton said, "Oh, Y. A. Tittle! He was one of my favorite people in the world. He was traded to the Giants the same year I was, 1961. When he set the record for throwing seven touchdowns in one game, I caught three that day including the last one to set the record.

"He was not only a very good pinpoint passer, he was a very tough guy. He would run bootlegs and he was one of the boys. He wasn't just a quarterback. Everybody liked him and the way he played. He was a great leader."

Myron Pottios said Tittle, a seventeen-year veteran, was a quarterback who "did everything right. He just did everything he had to do to win. He was up in age in the 1960s, but he was still good. He had no speed, he was old, but he won. He knew how to do the job and he knew how to win." At the age of thirty-seven he was still skilled enough to lead the NFL in TD passes with thirty-six. Plus, his league-leading quarterback rating of 104.8 that year, 1963, was a personal best and, at the time, the sixth-highest rating ever.

Marchetti said some of the best of his era were "Y. A. Tittle and Bobby Waterfield. They, along with Van Brocklin and Unitas, were probably the best in my league at that time. Tittle still has his recess pennies, though" joked Marchetti of Tittle's frugal ways.

Despite his achievements, naturally, there came a time when it was over for him. Sam Havrilak, like scads of people, has one image pop into his head, not unlike a word association game, when he hears Tittle's name. "I see the picture of him on his knees, bleeding from the face, when he was hit by one of the Steelers [John Baker]." The 1964 black-and-white photo also shows Tittle, thirty-eight, and in his final season, sans helmet, in his own end zone after throwing an interception that was returned by Chuck Hinton for a score.

Walton recalls the play vividly. "He really got beat up bad that day. He's on his knees with blood running down. I remember him getting back up and he still went on to play. I was always impressed with that one day in particular."

The year before that play, Tittle was the MVP, and the three previous seasons he had led his Giants to the championship game, but age caught up to him, and it was time for the battered Tittle to limp away from the game.

Another quarterback who gained fame in New York (before and after his days in the Minnesota Vikings jersey) was Fran Tarkenton. Like Tittle, his full name also sounded a bit flowery—Francis Asbury Tarkenton. Perhaps it actually sounded more regal. In any case, as if to dispel any conception that he was soft, his NFL debut quickly sent the message that there was a new gunslinger in town. He threw for four touchdowns that day back in 1961 and would later follow that up by winning three NFC titles for his Vikings.

Fred Cox said of his Minnesota teammate and close friend Tarkenton, "Francis was a great guy, but he was a typical quarterback. He was good, and he knew it, and that's OK—I never had a problem with that."

Cox said an NFL quarterback needs, and almost invariably has, a big ego and oodles of confidence—at least the great ones, that is. "You better be able to throw three interceptions in a game and know that your next pass is going to be a touchdown. That's just the way it is. If you don't have that kind of attitude in pro ball, you just can't play—and be worried about whether you're going to throw an interception. You're just not going to get it done. That's like a kicker worried about his last miss. If you worried about the last one you kicked. If you're even *thinking* about the last one, whether you made it or missed it, you're in trouble on your next kick."

Cox said he believed Tarkenton, the 1975 MVP, was "the first million-dollar quarterback" and marveled at his ability to succeed many times due to his scrambling skills. Most experts contend Tarkenton revolutionized the quarterback position when he defied the prevailing convention that quarterbacks had to stay in the pocket in order to succeed. He divested himself of tacklers with the same ease as he shooed flies away.

Cox reminisced further, "The amazing part of his scrambling is on Mondays, to loosen up, we would play kind of a touch football game, and it was absolutely astounding that people could not touch him. You'd go to tag him and he'd make some kind of little move and you'd never touch him. He just had amazing reflexes and, of course, we could go on and on about how many times he scrambled for first downs.

"I think he still holds the record for—what'd he scramble, well over a minute? Almost two minutes against the Bears. Try that sometime— go out and try to run around for two minutes with eleven guys chasing you."

Some hyperbole aside, Cox said there is no question in his mind that Tarkenton was more proficient at scrambling than Roger "The Dodger" Staubauch. "That's not taking anything away from Staubach—he was a great quarterback, but he wasn't even in Francis's league as far as being able to scramble."

Doug Crusan said that his Dolphins faced him many times and "when our defensive linemen were done playing the Vikings, they were thoroughly exhausted. He ran *all over the place*. You'd chase him and chase him. They'd go, 'You gotta be kidding,' because he would get back in the pocket, and then he's gone. He scrambled all the time, more than Staubach—he was always in motion." Many linemen who vainly pursued him grew to loathe him.

Tarkenton's total yards gained as a runner stands at 3,674, and he wound up with a rushing average of 5.4 yards per carry, more than men such as Gale Sayers, even though such a comparison certainly isn't a valid one. Tarkenton ran for thirty-two touchdowns, fifth-most for a quarterback, and you can bet a lot were not merely on sneaks.

Bob Hyland was a center/guard who, in his fifth season, became a Tarkenton teammate on the Giants, so he never had to give chase to Francis. "He was a fun guy to play against, and a much more fun guy to play with. He was a really gifted player. We didn't have a great offensive line. We had a couple of good pros, Doug Van Horn, Willie Young, Greg Larson, and myself, but we had a couple weaknesses. We did very well that year as far as sacks go, partially because of Fran—he understood his personnel around him very well. He knew what plays were going to be doable from a standpoint of the personnel. He had such a quick release and was such a terrific scrambler that we gave up very few sacks. We were under .500, but he made it interesting.

"Once he had all his offensive linemen up to a place he rented in Connecticut. He and Randy Johnson, the two quarterbacks, waited on us. We barbecued, and if we wanted a beer, he would go get it. It was a lot of fun. He was smart in letting his offensive linemen know he appreciated their efforts. He was a very interesting guy."

Many times Tarkenton's scrambles had another important by-product—it provided his receivers extra time to get open. Additionally, his pirouetting and his overall knuckleball-like elusiveness wore out hulking defenders who were soon spent and who became so frustrated they drooled at the prospect of getting payback by leveling the 190-pound jitterbug. It was a fruitless task, though, resulting in those defenders being able to relate to the frustration of a Tantalus.

How, perplexed coaches wondered, could they design a plan to defend against Tarkenton, a man who didn't even miss a game until his eleventh season? England may have had the original Sir Francis (Drake), but the Giants and the Vikings had the NFL's Sir Francis who, in a typical scramble, seemingly covered more ground than the famous explorer, Magellan, first sailor to circumnavigate the globe.

Pottios certainly knew the problems a great scrambler presented. "Here's Tarkenton—you've got him all boxed in. Next thing, he's scrambling all over and he breaks loose and hits a guy downfield for forty yards, and keeps a drive going. Those are the things that drive you nuts because there's nothing that you can do—you had the perfect defense called and everybody plays it perfectly, but because of his scrambling ability, he was able to disrupt it and make your perfect defense a no defense.

"He affected you mentally because you better get ready because you know you're going to be running all over the place, especially our defensive linemen. They said, 'Holy hell.' Psychologically, they knew what was going to happen. Once he started scrambling, they got to chase him all over, and that's when you get hit. When you're trying to chase him, you get a blind shot and those hurt.

"In my particular case as a linebacker, I cover my man. We have this defense and I'm responsible for this guy, right? So I have to watch him—say he goes ten yards down and goes out to the sideline. Now, here's Fran, he breaks loose and goes out toward my side. Now I've got to make a decision. I either have to let loose of my guy and come up and tackle Fran, or I have to stay with my guy and give Fran twenty yards to run down the field on my side.

"What can you do in that case? You can't come up until he crosses the line of scrimmage, so you have a dilemma there, saying, 'Wow, when do I come up?' Some guys get anxious and come up too fast, the receiver continues down the field, a lazy pass, touchdown."

Fred Cox continued, "The thing Francis had going for him that was really a great asset—he was extremely intelligent. He knew football inside and out. In fact, to the point where Bud Grant very rarely called a play for him.

"I can remember a number of times him telling [coach] Jerry Burns, when Jerry would be calling out plays for Bud to send in to Fran, 'Jerry, he's doing just fine without us.' Now that takes a lot of confidence."

Tarkenton deserved the confidence Grant had in him. Playing at the age of thirty-eight, he not only led the league in pass attempts, completions, and passing yardage at 3,468, but in doing so he also established career highs—all in his final season. Upon his retirement he, not Unitas or Tittle, now held almost every major passing record from his 47,003 yards (still number eight through 2015) to his 3,686 completions (number eleven) to his 342 touchdown passes (number six).

Tittle and Tarkenton were still playing at the age of thirty-eight, and Unitas was still hurling the football at the age of forty, commendable feats of longevity and by-products of talent. Then there's George Blanda. When Blanda, who seemingly could play for an eternity, finally quit, no man had ever played in more games or scored more points than this quarterback/placekicker. Incidentally, in each season from 1967 until he was forced into retirement in 1975 he was the oldest player in the league. Blanda outlasted Tittle and Tarkenton by *ten* years, and was still in uniform appearing in fourteen games at the age of forty-eight.

For Blanda's first ten seasons as a pro, he was with the Chicago Bears except for a virtually forgotten one-game appearance with the Colts. Team owner and head coach George "Papa Bear" Halas never seemed to trust Blanda as his quarterback. At first Blanda played behind legends Johnny Lujack and Sid Luckman, which makes sense. However, one season Halas had Blanda buried on his bench, listed fourth on the quarterback depth chart, behind men such as Ed Brown and Zeke Bratkowski.

In his first two seasons, 1949 and 1950, he had only thrown twenty-two passes, but he saw some action as a linebacker while also handling placekicking duties (he even returned two kickoffs). The Bears didn't award him the quarterback job until 1953, and he promptly led the league in completions and attempts.

However, his starting quarterback days were short-lived in Chicago and, aside from kicking, he mainly languished on the bench for the rest of his days as a Bear. From 1956 through 1958 he would toss just ninety-five passes. He quit after the 1958 season but joined the upstart American Football League, which began play in 1960. He joined the Houston Oilers that season, and one year later threw for a league high 3,330 yards and established a new pro record by cashing in on thirty-six touchdowns throws.

He thrived with Houston of the wide-open AFL—one day he chalked up 464 yards through the air. His 9.2 yards per pass attempt in 1961 was so lofty it still ranks fifteenth all-time for a single season, and his 17.8 yards per completion that year is now number twelve all-time. Perhaps the most notable feat from that golden season was his ability to hit pay dirt—9.9 percent of his passes resulted in touchdowns. To date that rate has been surpassed just five times.

Passes from his lethal arm and kicks off his booming leg riddled the air like bullets from a machine gun—or, better yet, given Blanda's age, like spray from a Gatling gun. Houston's ability to amass yardage and points was astounding. They piled up 6,288 yards, most coming on Blanda throws, when no other team had even sniffed the 6,000-yard level, and their 513 total points scored set a new pro football high. In addition to racking up points on his thirty-six passes, he chipped in even more points on kicks. One of his sixteen field goals soared 55 yards, which ranked as the second longest field goal ever.

In the 1961 title game, Houston defeated San Diego, 10–3, with Blanda accounting for all of the Oilers points, six on a pass and four more points on kicks. However, he did throw five interceptions in the game. At the age of thirty-four, he had engineered two championships over the league's first two seasons.

The following season, 1962, his record as a starting quarterback was 11-3, but he would never again top the .500 level as a full-time starting quarterback. Still, he guided Houston to a third straight championship game.

In 1963, 1964, and in 1965, he led the league in completions, but also in interceptions. Disenchanted, the Oilers put him on waivers and Oakland claimed him.

Gino Marchetti, perhaps factoring in all of the interceptions, didn't think Blanda was exactly a grade-A quarterback, certainly not of the same caliber of, say, Tittle or Johnny Unitas, saying, "He was a good second-string quarterback and he was a pretty good field-goal kicker. He lasted with the Bears for a few years then he went down to Houston and threw that wobbly pass of his—and he was very successful. The talent wasn't the same at that time [in the AFL versus the NFL]—eventually it got up there."

There's a good chance that few fans are aware of one not-so-glowing factoid about Blanda. His win-loss record for games as a starting quarterback is just a bit above the break-even mark. He won fifty-three of his regular season starts, tied one, and lost fifty of the games in which he started under center.

Mike Lucci, veteran NFL linebacker, expressed similar thoughts, saying that Unitas, for instance, was more precise in his passing than a Blanda or a Joe Kapp. However, Lucci also recognized greatness in Blanda, talented enough to kick in the pros "and do a helluva lot of things, but he just didn't look like he played pretty."

Blanda certainly got the job done in 1970, in his fourth *decade* in pro football. When he was forced to fill in for the Raiders' regular quarterback, Daryle Lamonica, Blanda's heroics left the world of football reeling. At the age of forty-three, Blanda, a Methuselah of a quarterback, came off the bench and, thanks to passes, kicks, and football savoir faire, led Oakland to dramatic wins in four games and a comeback to earn a tie in another contest.

Mike Ditka stated, "I knew George because he played with the Bears when I came in there as a rookie. The thing that made George good—now, not that he didn't have talent, he did have talent—[is that] he was the greatest competitor. He didn't like to lose in anything. And when you get people who have that initiative and drive, they find a way to make themselves better and to win."

Rich Erdelyi, who was Dan Marino's football coach in high school and also coached at Carnegie Mellon University, certainly knows his football. He once said of Blanda, "He always seemed like a tough, gritty guy, a competitor. He was, like thirty-seven, thirty-eight years old still playing quarterback—still running the ball! He would figure out a way to get it done." The fire inside Blanda was white hot, and age never cooled that off.

Tom Matte also praised Blanda, "He was the ultimate wisdom guy. I mean, he was always sitting in the background, ready to come in whenever you needed him, and he had the talent. If you take a look at what his talents were, there was another guy who was probably one of the most versatile players around the league because he was kicking and playing quarterback and doing everything. And he was a team leader, too."

Blanda's pro resume after his stunning comebacks was not over yet. He would not hang up his spikes for another five seasons, retiring one week before his forty-ninth birthday with twenty-seven seasons under his belt. That meant that well over half of his life had been spent in pro football.

By the end of his career, Blanda owned or shared thirty-seven professional football records, including the most passes thrown and passes completed in a single game, most TDs in a single season (thirty-six, tied back then with Y. A. Tittle), and the most touchdowns fired in a game (seven, tied with six others).

The bottom line is simple: Blanda is without doubt a deserving member of the Hall of Fame who carved out a permanent place for himself in the lore of the game. Kudos go out to Blanda, a man who tallied more points (2,002) and played in more professional football games than any player ever (340). Not only was he ageless, but he was also peerless.

Bart Starr was obviously another huge success. Matte said, "When you talk about the great quarterbacks that are around, you got Unitas and Bart Starr." Starr led his Packers to five NFL titles, more than such recent famous quarterbacks as Joe Montana and Terry Bradshaw. Not only that, Starr was able to go way beyond simply shining brightly in postseason play. He positively illuminated big games, putting up a record of 9-1. His quarterback rating in those playoff contests was a splendid 104.8, considerably higher than that of Montana, who checked in at 95.6. Of course Starr also gained fame by winning the first two Super Bowls ever played and by capturing the MVP Award for those contests.

The MVP of the regular season in 1966, Starr was named to the All-Decade Team of the 1960s, but what few remember is the start to his career was far from glistening. First of all, he was drafted in the seventeenth round as the 200th overall pick in 1956, almost an afterthought. In his third season, 1958, the Pack went 1-10-1 with his record as a starter being 0-6-1, and from 1956 to 1959 he guided Green Bay to just seven wins as opposed to sixteen defeats. In addition, over his first five years he threw almost twice as many interceptions as his meager twenty-three touchdowns.

However, true to his nature, he persevered. From 1960 through 1967, his dynastic Packers went 82-24-4 (73 wins came with Starr as the starting QB), went to the title game six times over those eight seasons, and won it five times, once with a 37–0 shellacking of the mighty New York Giants. In 1963, Starr's Packers went 11-2-1, yet did not make the playoffs in this talent-packed era.

Over one stretch, Starr threw 294 passes without throwing a single one to a player in the wrong jersey. His 7.8 yards-per-attempt lifetime ranks number eleven through 2015.

Starr was brilliant over a long (sixteen-year) NFL career—he's one of those relatively rare players whose career spanned three decades, as he played from 1956 through the 1971 season, all with the Packers. He was victorious in a shade over 60 percent of the 157 games he started.

It's difficult to choose which of the honors he won should be considered his greatest, but winning the MVP trophy of the Super Bowl has to be given a lot of weight—and, remember, he did that twice. In both the first and second Super Bowls Starr positively glowed. Back then, before the Jets' stunning win over the Colts, the NFL felt they were the superior league, and they felt pressure to prove that in the Super Bowl. Starr did just that, passing at a 62 percent success rate for 452 yards in those contests, good for a quarterback rating of 106.

Plus, who could ever forget the iconic picture (or video) of Starr plunging on a sneak in the waning seconds of the NFL title game against the Dallas Cowboys to ice the game that came to be known as the "Ice Bowl"? Starr and his Packers endured a day on which the windchill factor plummeted to the unfathomable depths of almost minus fifty degrees.

Bob Hyland was one of Starr's centers in Green Bay. "Bart is the first guy that any of us think of when we go back to our old days. He was pretty much the face of the franchise, and I had a lot of respect for him. I thought he was always very fair with me. He had confidence in me. He was the consummate gentleman. We had huge confidence in him in the huddle." Understandably so, as Starr was a leader and a winner.

Next up is Sonny Jurgensen, who threw for over three thousand yards five times, each time leading the NFL in that realm. He also put up over four hundred yards in a game four times and twice fired for thirty or more touchdowns to lead his league—in 1961 for the Eagles and six years later for the Redskins.

Pottios said, "To me, the best passing quarterback, the one who threw the most beautiful ball was Sonny Jurgensen." He was also, said Sam Havrilak, "A player's player. There are some guys that a team will play for—he's one of those guys."

One of Jurgensen's Washington teammates was Bill Malinchak, originally a third-round draft pick in 1966 by the Detroit Lions who, in his second season started only six games yet led his team in touchdowns and receiving yardage, and ended his career with an average of 14.5 yards per reception.

Malinchak said his quarterback "threw probably the finest passes. He had the nicest touch on a ball, firm, but the easiest pass to catch in football. I caught a lot of quarterbacks, and Sonny threw about as good a pass as anybody ever threw. There was nothing critical you could say about it. When Sonny threw the ball, say across the middle, he would never throw it high, always at your body.

"I remember when I first got there, when I got traded, I would do maybe a short post pattern, and I would give it a little fake or a wiggle. Sonny said to me, 'You don't have to do that here. Just go down, break, and get inside the guy [defender]. I'll get it into you. As long as you have a body between you and him, I'll get it into you.' Prior to that, you thought, 'Man, I got to get distance between my man.' Sonny didn't need that. He said, 'Cut it [the move] off. Body him up and just get inside him.'

"The one good thing is when you run across the middle, you want the ball into your body so you don't have to reach up and so you're getting kinda hung up to dry. You can't protect yourself. So Sonny would always throw the perfect pass.

"When Sonny threw, the only comment you could make was, 'Sonny, can you get the laces up when you throw it,' because he was that accurate. That made the point of how good he was." The laces reference, explained Malinchak, was a joke and a compliment. It was as if the receivers were saying his passes were so perfect, they had to tease him about *something*, so they'd chide him by growling that the laces on the ball weren't in the right position when they caught it. Of course, it's impossible to throw a football in such a way that the laces wind up exactly in one location.

Jurgensen's statistics made him a lock to win Hall of Fame status. Like Starr, Christian Adolph Jurgensen II enjoyed great longevity and played in three decades—eighteen seasons in all from 1957 to 1974. Over one decade, the 1960s, he had a stranglehold on one stat, ranking first in yards gained per game five times. His finest hour in that area came in 1967 when his arm accounted for 267.6 yards per contest.

One stat, seldom discussed and kept only from 1969 on, deals with times a quarterback took a sack. In the first year those numbers were kept, Jurgensen's line failed him, permitting opposing defenses to put him on his back a league-leading forty times for 322 yards lost, another NFL high that season. Despite all that, he amazingly still managed to lead the league with his average of 221.6 yards gained per game, his 3,102 yards on passes, and his 274 total completions. That year, quarterbacking for Vince Lombardi in his only season coaching a team other than Green Bay, Jurgensen was also able to lead his Redskins to a second-place finish in the then-named Capitol Division.

Yet another selection to the All-1960s squad as chosen by the Hall of Fame, Jurgensen and his 255 lifetime touchdown passes still place him in the top twenty quarterbacks of all time.

When Joe Namath threw a football, people took heed. Sam Havrilak said Namath's arm was so strong "he could wait until the receiver made the break and then rifle the ball in there," and he added that while a casual fan might think any NFL quarterback can throw that hard and that well, that's simply not the case.

He may have been injury prone, but even when he played on gimpy legs, he remained fearless. Dolphins defensive lineman Manny Fernandez said Namath and Unitas were probably the two toughest quarterbacks he ever faced. "You could just about break their ribs hitting them and they'd just get up, look at you, and say, 'Nice tackle.'"

Namath could dish out retribution when necessary, and do so cunningly. That apparently was a part of his toughness. Oakland's Ben Davidson blasted him with a cheap shot once. Instead of protesting to the refs or confronting Davidson, Namath calmly made his way back to the Jets huddle and instructed his linemen not to block Davidson. The 275-pounder barreled his way toward Namath who stopped him in his tracks, when he drilled the football right at Davidson. Arms raised high preparatory to blocking the pass, Davidson was exposed. The ball struck him right between his legs. Namath reportedly stared down at Davidson and wryly said, "See you next play."

Namath hails from Beaver Falls, Pennsylvania, and fellow native Steve Higgins, who, like Namath, played college ball at Alabama (and roomed with another future Jets quarterback, Richard Todd), painted a picture of Namath that would surprise some. He said Namath "is just nothing but nice and kind and humble. And when he comes into town, he doesn't like being in the spotlight. He likes sitting in the background supporting other guys. He's comfortable in that position."

Ken Thomas also grew up in Namath's hometown and said that the young Namath not only was an elusive and gifted runner, he also "had that cockiness, or maybe it was more self-assuredness." Despite that, "He didn't come across as, 'I'm the star.' He came across as a teammate."

Higgins disclosed another surprising fact. "He barely made the team in high school. His sophomore year he played one play. His junior year he got to play sparingly." It didn't take long for his prowess to direct the spotlight his way. In his senior season he led the team to the number one spot in Pennsylvania and number five nationally.

Later, Namath used that mighty arm so well he was the only quarterback during the era of the fourteen-game schedule to throw for over four thousand yards. Such displays led one Pittsburgh writer, Chuck Finder, to suggest Namath remains "probably the most famous of the great western Pennsylvania quarterbacks. You'd probably have to put him and Joe Montana as the most athletic of the western Pennsylvania quarterbacks. It shows you the power a handsome face, a good smile, New York, and some panty hose will do for a guy." He was alluding, of course, to a famous TV commercial that featured Namath's legs sporting panty hose.

Ironically, as good as Namath was, according to Pro Bowl linebacker Jim Houston, he was "not quite as good as the other five quarterbacks [from the Pittsburgh vicinity]." He was referring to Unitas, Blanda, Joe Montana, Jim Kelly, and Dan Marino. "But he was a good one." Houston continued, "I was a captain of the Browns defense, and we always had to consider what his tendencies were, but he always found a way to deliver."

It may be difficult to believe, but Namath, like Blanda, actually threw more lifetime interceptions than touchdowns. Fernandez said there were several reasons for this. "Well, he took chances, and he also played too long." Fred Cox saw Namath as "a riverboat gambler type of quarterback—he would throw into double coverage more than any guy I ever saw at that stage of the game."

Despite Namath's propensity for throwing interceptions, Fernandez has a truckload of respect for Namath, saying that, all things considered, he and Unitas were as accurate as they were courageous, and both "could throw the long ball, short ball, it didn't matter. They were great competitors."

Quarterbacks aside, many other greats of the Glory Years played Jim Brown's glamour position and were top-notch runners. Lenny Moore may not have had quite the ability or the stats of Brown (or the size), but he was not a light-year away. In fact, when Moore left the game, only Brown had scored more touchdowns than Moore's 113.

In one department he even outdid Brown, setting a record by scoring in eighteen consecutive games. He also had at least one touchdown of seventy yards or more in seven different seasons, and he was the first player to score at least forty-five TDs on catches and sixty on runs. In 1964, when his Colts made it to the title game, he led the NFL with sixteen touchdowns via the run. The Penn State star had talent galore.

In some ways, the longer Moore played, the better he got—certainly in ways other than just his physical prowess. Moore said he reached the point where he would return to the huddle and give useful information to Unitas such as, "John, this guy's twelve yards off me, man," and Unitas would respond, "There are a lot of slant patterns, and those kinds of things we can do in front of him then." Moore elaborated that if he took two quick steps, the defender, aware of Moore's speed, would give him room "because he didn't want me to get behind him. So we'd work things in front of him. Take what they give you. Take what is being offered by the other team and capitalize on it."

Asked about Moore, teammate Andy Nelson grinned. "Ah, Lenny. He was something. We had an intra-squad game we played every year at the stadium. I never will forget it. I went to tackle him and he wasn't there. I said to myself, 'I'm in a different league here.' I had never seen nothing like Lenny.

"He's got to be right up there with the best runners *and* receivers, too. He changed positions. He was a threat every time he got the ball, and the opposing teams knew that and sometimes double-teamed him."

Looking back over his career, Moore said he felt he was blessed by God. "Almost anything that I tackled, I could do; or anything I worked on, I could work it out. And that's nothing but God blessing your talent that he has given you, and you're taking that and working with it. If somebody asked me how do I do this or that, I can't tell them because I don't know. In other words, if I break a tackle or if I catch a certain pass, I can't explain it."

Moore still recalls a catch he made, one that he finds inexplicable to this day, that came against future Hall of Famer Dick "Night Train" Lane. "I dove for it, and I could see my arms outreached and that ball hit my hands and it stuck. And when it stuck, I pulled it into my stomach and I was in the end zone. I had beaten Lane, and John threw it. When I looked at that I said, 'Damn! I don't practice diving for the ball,' but that was a play that happened and God gave me the ability to be able to complete that."

Gino Marchetti had high praise for his former teammate who was a veteran of seven Pro Bowl games. "I think Lenny, God Almighty, if he was playing today he'd set records that they may never catch. He was so quick and he had those long legs with the chaps, the shoes taped on.

"I saw him run a touchdown backwards. We played the 49ers, and Pittsburgh was playing Chicago—if they win and we win, we win the 1958 West Division championship. We were losing, 27–7 at halftime. Lenny Moore took the game over, literally, with his running. On one particular play, he had cut over by the middle and somebody turned him around. And from the 20-yard line in, he was running backwards, and we scored. It was one of the greatest runs I ever saw him make. We ended up beating them, right there in Baltimore, because of Moore mostly.

"Pittsburgh won, so we did get the title—it was the most exciting thing I've ever done—and we sent Bobby Layne, who had a helluva good day [that day for the Steelers] a case of champagne—he probably drank it all."

Marchetti had further thoughts on his teammate. "During our day, Lenny Moore was the number one back. He was one of the few backs who played the out position, a flanker, that Weeb [Ewbank] made famous. He could catch the ball—he caught a ball once and I guarantee he must have flown ten yards horizontal to the ground to make the catch. It was a great, great, great catch—the crowd was going crazy."

Yet another Colt Hall of Famer, Raymond Berry, lauded Moore. "When someone asks me for my thoughts on Lenny, I ask, 'How much time have you got?' I've played in high school, junior college, college, the professional level for thirteen years, and I put in around twenty years coaching, and of all the talents I've seen on a football field, Lenny Moore has to be in the top three."

Statistics bear that out. Moore led the NFL four times with the highest yards gained per run average, topping 7.0 three times. In 1956 that average stood at 7.5, in 1958 it was 7.3, and three seasons later it hit 7.0 on the nose. Those three seasons still represent the tenth-, sixth-, and fourth-greatest single-season averages in the history of the NFL. Only Moore has ever cracked the top ten in this category more than twice. Moore also led the NFL in this department one other time, in 1957, this time at 5.0 yards per rush. In the Colts 1958 championship season he averaged 11.9 yards per touch.

Berry called Moore an elite player, comparing him to other do-it-all athletes of his era such as Elroy Hirsch, Hugh McElhenny, Frank Gifford, and Kyle Rote. "Lenny had speed, he had power, he could run the football inside, outside. He could run pass routes and catch well. I definitely think he was one of the best offensive weapons that I've ever seen on a football field, right there with Jim Brown and Unitas. He was a totally team-oriented player. Self-centeredness and selfishness were not a part of his makeup. He was not 'I, I, me, me,' *at all.*"

Tom Matte said he was delighted when he joined the Colts as a rookie in 1961 and became a teammate of Moore. "Let me tell you one thing, I walked into the penthouse from the shithouse with a guy that had so much talent. I played behind Lenny Moore, probably the best all-around running back who ever played the game. He could go inside and outside, as a receiver and as a runner. I mean there's nobody that could touch them. He had speed up the ying-yang. He was as fast as he wanted to be, and what a great player. And we had Jim Parker at that time, Gino Marchetti, and Raymond Berry—I mean, we had some tremendous Hall of Fame guys here that were fantastic."

Moore concluded his retrospective of his era and his playing days saying he was very proud of his career and "very proud of all my teammates that I had during the time I was there in Baltimore—it was quite a complete education: the coaching staff, the owners of the club, all the way down through. Not only was it an education, but it was a privilege, it really was, and a complete pleasure. All of that, yes, for twelve wonderful years of my life."

Even now, pondering what he has accomplished, Moore finds it difficult to realize what he has done. "Man, I didn't think I was doing all that," he mused. "It was God-given ability."

Simply put, Gale Sayers was a magnificent and electrifying running back. Playing for the University of Kansas, his ability to glide with unreal speed naturally led to his earning the nickname the Kansas Comet. Unfortunately, through no fault of his own, his career was meteoric.

Tackling Sayers—make that *touching* Sayers—in the open field was an almost impossible task. In his very first NFL exhibition game he had a ninety-three-yard kickoff return and a seventy-seven-yard punt return, and he completed a halfback option pass for a twenty-five-yard score. He continued to excel, recording a jaw-dropping lifetime 5.0 yards per lifetime carry, still seventh-best ever. Also, he averaged 30.6 yards per kickoff return for his career—no other player has ever topped that through 2015; and only two men ever put up more than his six touchdown returns on kickoffs.

Dick Butkus was biased, but he called his Chicago Bears teammate the best football player he ever saw. In fact, the two were teammates from day one. The Bears enjoyed a monumentally great draft, a genuine coup, in 1965 when they had the number three and number four overall picks and acquired Butkus, then Sayers, like a professional boxer suddenly coming up with a deadly one-two punch. The two men would forever be linked, the Sayers-Butkus duet *was* the Chicago Bears. Appropriately, they even had their uniforms retired on the same day.

The stark contrasts between the two are quite apparent—one represented chaos, the other grace; one epitomized smash-mouth contact, the other utter elusiveness, with hips more active than a hula dancer's.

Look deeper, though, and there are similarities between them. Before their college days, they both played running back and linebacker, even though it is difficult imagining Sayers leveling a quarterback. However, the main point of comparison is obvious—they symbolized the height of their profession. Unfortunately, they also shared a career nadir—they never appeared in a postseason contest.

Even though the shifty Sayers retired at the age of twenty-eight, his ticket to ride to the Hall of Fame had already been punched, and he was a cinch to be named to the All-Time NFL Team. He was, in fact, at thirty-four, the youngest man ever inducted into the Hall and he made First-Team All-Pro from his rookie season of 1965 through 1969 despite playing in just nine games in 1968. He made things look oh so easy at times.

Only one thing could stop Sayers: injuries. In fact, his shimmering statistics are even more remarkable considering he played in just sixty-eight NFL games. His first nasty knee injury came in 1968 when he was off to perhaps his best season ever before tearing a knee ligament in three places when tackled by Kermit Alexander who applied his shoulder to Sayers's right knee. Earlier Sayers had set a franchise record by rambling for 205 yards on twenty-four carries.

A determined Sayers somehow bounced back in the ensuing season and rushed for 1,032 yards to again lead the NFL, a veritable miracle considering the severity of his injury and the fact that he no longer broke off long runs—his longest run was just twenty-eight yards. However, another knee injury in 1970 reduced him to he's-only-human status, and in his final two seasons he was limited to playing in four games in all. Prior to that, though, he did things on a football field others could only imagine.

Even now, Sayers feels cheated, ruing the fact that sports medicine in his day was so primitive. Like a fan, he can only speculate what he could have achieved if he could have displayed his brilliance over a long career.

Teammate Bob Hyland said he remembers Sayers coming back from his first injury as being "very difficult, especially back then. They didn't have the methods that they have now—it has really advanced big time since back then. He just had recurring problems, which slowed him down, gradually, but at the end of his career he really had a tough time getting around the field."

Herb Adderley said, "He's the only guy I think could be running, stop on a dime, tell you whether it was heads or tails and not even break stride."[3]

Sayers was a bit like Jim Brown in that he was dangerous, but, said Dory Crusan, the difference was that while Sayers was quicker, he didn't quite have the fullback mentality that the bruising Brown possessed. "Sayers," said Crusan, "was a true halfback. Sort of like a scatback, a little, quick runner. Look at his hips and the way he ran. He was amazing."

Pottios added, "And if you played him on Astroturf, he had better traction. Wow. It amplified his speed so much greater. And, boy, you talk about being quick and being able to move, he was unbelievable. Regular grass will kind of slow you down some, but still, he had excellent speed and quickness, and he could accelerate."

One of the most dazzling displays ever witnessed in NFL play occurred in Wrigley Field on December 12, 1965, on a muddy field. How dangerous and explosively fast Sayers was, was never more evident than that day when he scored six touchdowns in a 61–20 drubbing of the 49ers. That scoring binge tied him with the only other men who ever crossed the goal line six times in a game, Ernie Nevers and Dub Jones. Sayers chalked up five touchdowns by the end of the third quarter. He was removed from the game around that point, but late in the fourth quarter he returned and ran back a punt eighty-five yards for a TD.

Teammates believe he could have easily scored a seventh touchdown that day. With Sayers in the lineup, Chicago moved the ball to the 2-yard line. He was pulled from the game once again, though, and Jon Arnett, finding a huge hole, scored effortlessly. Sayers who often said all he required to bust loose was eighteen inches of daylight, would have sailed into the end zone instead of Arnett. Incidentally, on that same day, Paul Hornung scored five touchdowns.

Sayers's 336 total yards in his historic contest came on a mere sixteen touches, with 113 yards produced on carries, 89 on catches, and 134 on punt runbacks. One touchdown came on a sensational 80-yard catch and run, one on a scintillating 85-yard punt return, and four TDs came on the ground. Astonishingly, he did all of that even though, with the Bears owning a comfortable lead, he sat out most of the fourth quarter. Plus, he achieved all of this in just his eleventh NFL start. For the '65 season, he led the NFL with a new record twenty-two touchdowns and 132 points produced—all as a twenty-two-year-old rookie! The twenty-two touchdowns by a rookie is still a record. Fourteen of his scores on the year came on runs, six on passes, and one each on a kickoff and punt return.

Hyland joined the Bears in 1970 and related another great feat by Sayers. "I never saw him when he was at his best when I was with Chicago, but I did see him at his absolute best when he came up to Lambeau Field about two years before when I was with Green Bay. I was out there snapping the punts and extra points before the game started. You take a look at the guys on the other team and Sayers was the one who everybody focused on. He was like a blur out there in the pregame warm-ups. I'm thinking, 'Boy, you gotta look out for this guy today.' And, sure enough, he had 205 yards rushing against a really, really good Green Bay defense. That was one of the greatest performances I've ever seen by a running back.

"If Sayers didn't have that series of knee injuries I think he probably would have been the greatest running back ever. The guy was amazing."

Of course, his performance in the 1968 season was also nothing short of spectacular. He played in only nine games, yet averaged a league leading 95.1 yards per game as he compiled 856 yards, which wound up being the fifth-highest NFL total for the entire season. Further, his average of 6.2 yards per rush also led the league, and he came in third for all-purpose yardage with 1,463.

In his first five seasons he finished second, first, third, fifth, and first for yards rushing. In 1966 he amassed a league-leading 1,678 yards from scrimmage and finished first in rushing with his career high of 1,231 yards. Clearly he could gather yards and score in so many ways. He once returned a kick 103 yards. Despite a short career played in an era of a plethora of stars, Sayers led the league in all-purpose yardage three times, rushing twice, and returns once in 1966 with his average of 31.2 yards per kick return.

Figuratively, his career paralleled a line from an old John Garfield movie: "Live fast, die young, and leave a good-looking corpse." For Sayers, the "corpse" was a superlative resume to which people still pay their everlasting respects.

Leroy Kelly was also a well-rounded offensive tool. His first two seasons saw him on the Browns bench pretty much when he wasn't returning punts and kicks. However, after teammate Jim Brown retired, Kelly stepped up big time in 1966, giving Cleveland another 1,000-yard rusher. The following two seasons the Browns kept their monopoly of league-leading rushers going with Kelly romping for 1,205 and 1,239 yards.

Kelly spent ten seasons in the NFL and managed to make them memorable ones. In 1967, he topped all runners by grinding out an average of 86.1 yards each game, and the following year he upped that average to 88.5, a personal high. However, that year he was overshadowed by another legend—Sayers averaged 95.1 yards per contest, pushing Kelly to second best in 1968. Still, Kelly remained a workhorse for Cleveland, the only NFL team he'd ever toil for. In 1967, he led the league for the most carries, and he duplicated that feat in 1968. Always reliable, his lifetime average was 4.2 yards per rush.

The Browns certainly knew who to go to, as Kelly also led the NFL those two years in touches. His seventy-four touchdowns on runs still holds down the number twenty-four slot on the all-time list through 2015. Athleticism ran in the family, as his brother Pat spent fifteen seasons in baseball's big leagues.

Sam Havrilak said Kelly was startlingly quick at hitting an open hole. "He just hit it faster than anybody of that era. He was through the hole when it was there and into the secondary." At that point, Kelly would then gallop for many a yard. Havrilak said that like Sayers, Kelly basically only needed about eighteen inches of daylight before it was off to the races.

Unfortunately, Kelly had the task of following Brown. Havrilak also readily recognized that Brown overshadowed Kelly. "How are you going to replace a legend? There's only one Jim Brown, just like there's only one Wilt Chamberlain—those guys come along once in a generation or so."

John Isenbarger, former San Francisco 49ers running back and wide receiver, said, "Kelly was in another league other than Brown. It's tough to follow a Jim Brown's footsteps and get accolades because you're not going to be as good as he was. And they were different type of runners."

Now, Larry Csonka's style was quite different from that of Kelly. Running straight ahead, he was more brute force than elusive grace. He fought for every extra yard he could get, as if the extra ground he gained was a precious piece of Park Avenue real estate. Born on Christmas Day, his gift to defenders was often an assault on them. It was almost as if tacklers were the running back and he was a linebacker, dishing out the pain.

When Miami got close to the goal line, Csonka, a true Mr. Inside power back, not only could smell pay dirt, he could taste, even sense another touchdown being added to his CV. Nearly salivating, he'd take a handoff and burst by, or through, anyone who tried to stop his progress. Put it another way, Csonka was to fullbacks what Dick Butkus was to linebackers.

In addition, he protected the football with his brawny muscles as if he had to deliver it to Fort Knox. Even though he was called upon to carry the ball again and again, he seldom coughed it up. Twice he went through an entire season without once fumbling—in one of those years he had over two hundred touches. On two other occasions he played out seasons with just one fumble and he averaged fewer than two fumbles per season over his eleven NFL seasons. To compare: Jim Brown averaged 6.3 fumbles each season.

Dolphins teammate Manny Fernandez said, "Everything you've seen and heard kind of tells the whole story. He'd rather run over you than miss you. And he *could* run over you. He was a truck. I mean, he brought it. He was one helluva powerful running back."

Havrilak observed, "Csonka was big, and they had a great offensive line and a great running back blocking for him in Jim Kiick. They always went with a two-back backfield and once Csonka got moving, up and down, north and south, it was very difficult to stop him [especially] if you tried to hit him high because he weighed so much. You know, in those days running backs didn't weigh more than 190, 195. When you have a 240-, 250-pound running back, that was very unusual. Today it's pretty common."

Miami's offensive tackle, the six-foot, five-inch, 250-pound Doug Crusan, said Csonka was more than just a bull, which he was. "He was a tremendous athlete. I don't think he ever lost a yard, ever—he was always going forward. He was a pleasure to block for. He was as big as I was. So you had a guy six foot three, 250 running the ball? Wow."

Crusan continued, "I don't know if Zonk ever outran anybody, but he'd look around for people to hit. He just was that powerful with those powerful legs."

Pottios went up against Csonka and said, "When guys like him start playing, and they get in a situation where they're blocking well and the team is all fired up, now they're playing downhill, and you've got this big load coming at you *every* play. And it's harder than hell—you can either get the hell beat out of you and they run over you, or you just got to step up and take them on. You're going to get the hell beat out of you one way or the other, so you might as well go out there and take them on. If you didn't, they were just going to come at you the next time harder and harder. Those are long afternoons when you have games like that and they've got momentum going their way."

Traveling back to earlier days, John Henry Johnson was once one of the NFL all-time leaders for career yards rushing, even though his 6,803 yards now ranks only sixty-sixth. Johnson was another workhorse—he still easily ranks in the top one hundred for career touches—who could be used as a halfback and fullback.

His services were always in demand, and he did a yeoman-like job for thirteen seasons from 1954 through 1966 for the San Francisco 49ers, the Detroit Lions, the Pittsburgh Steelers, and, in his final season, for the Houston Oilers. Over those years he finished among the league's top ten runners for rushing attempts, total ground yardage, and average yards gained on runs per game on seven occasions, and for touchdowns scored on the ground and average gain per rush five times. That all added up to his being selected to four Pro Bowls.

Pottios was a teammate of Johnson in Pittsburgh. "He was big and strong. For his size, he could do some juking—not like Gale Sayers, though. John Henry was more like Jim Brown; he had the strength and ability to juke and get away from you. Jon Arnett was like that, too, and Tommy Mason and Hugh McElhenny for juking."

Johnson played his college ball in the state of California (at St. Mary's). Marchetti called him one of the greats from his time period. "He was in the top three or four backs." Marchetti was correct. Upon his retirement only Jim Brown, Joe Perry, and Jim Taylor had more than Johnson's 6,803 yards rushing.

"We played each other a couple of times," Marchetti went on. "We were on semipro teams. He could run like a horse and he was as strong as a horse. One time he considered boxing. He was a *very* tough guy. I think he probably paid for it because the last time I saw him, he didn't recognize anything. I went up to him at the Hall of Fame and said, 'Hey, John, how you doing?' He didn't say anything."

Frank Gifford was versatility personified. He was a seven-time All-Pro at three positions for his New York Giants as a defensive back, halfback, and flanker. He also returned kicks and, at times, threw passes, and did some placekicking. He did so much for the team, he might as well have taken in the team's laundry to complete his resume.

In 1956 when he was so instrumental in his Giants winning the championship, he was named the league's MVP. It was the first NFL title for the Giants since 1938. His numbers included an average of 5.2 yards per carry and 11.8 yards per catch. His 1,422 total yards from scrimmage that year led the NFL and, surprisingly, marked the only time he would lead the league in a major offensive category. Still, over a twelve-year career, he excelled and was named to the Pro Bowl eight times. Not at all surprisingly, he was also named to Pro Football's All-1950s Team.

During his tenure in New York, the team won five conference titles. It's easy to see why this handsome, articulate man, the eleventh pick overall in the 1952 draft, became the face of the franchise. His 5,434 lifetime yards on catches stood as a team record from the day he walked away from the gridiron in 1964 until 2003.

Gifford did things so smoothly, his move to the TV booth was an easy transition (he had actually done some broadcasting while still active as a player). When he was teamed up with "Dandy" Don Meredith and Howard Cosell, television history was made. ABC launched its *Monday Night Football* telecasts in 1970, and they were an instant success, entertaining millions upon millions of viewers each week.

Much of the success stemmed from the chemistry and the personalities of the three broadcasters, who began working together in 1971 when Gifford replaced Keith Jackson. Gifford was the voice of reason and served as a mediator, a buffer between Meredith, who never took things too seriously, and the pontificating, pedantic, egocentric Cosell.

Gifford remained in his role for years, not leaving *Monday Night Football* until 1998. In 1977, the same year he was inducted into the Pro Football Hall of Fame, he won an Emmy for the "Outstanding Sports Personality" category.

Joe Walton, a Gifford teammate, stated, "I always felt like Frank was a little misunderstood. People thought he was an aloof kind of guy, but he wasn't. He had none of that typical football boisterous [attitude]. He was basically quiet, and that's why I was so surprised he had so much success in broadcasting. He kind of stayed to himself, but he was a great teammate. It really broke my heart when we lost him." Gifford passed away in 2015.

Charley Taylor was another multitalented player. He spent his entire career with the Washington Redskins from 1964 through 1977, first mainly as a halfback, then as a receiver. During the first two seasons, in which he was used extensively as a split end, he rewarded the coaching staff for putting him out there. The move paid off handsomely, as the six-foot-three, 210-pound Taylor led the NFL in receptions both years with seventy-two and seventy. In fact, in that first year in which he saw significant action as a receiver, 1966, he set a personal high with 1,119 yards on catches.

His greatness had been foreshadowed in his rookie season when he accumulated 755 yards on runs and 814 on receptions. That showing made him the first rookie in twenty years to wind up in the NFL's top ten in both rushing and receiving yards. He completed that season with fifty-three catches, which established a record for running backs. His rushing yardage was good enough to finish sixth in a league packed with talented runners. For instance, most of the running backs who had more yards were veterans who were also destined for enshrinement in Canton. That included Jim Brown, Jim Taylor, and John Henry Johnson. For all of his achievements, the third overall draft pick out of Arizona State simply strolled away with the Rookie of the Year Award.

Like so many of the all-time greats, Taylor was selected to an All-Decade Team, chosen for the 1960s squad by the Pro Football Hall of Fame. Over his thirteen seasons in the league he placed in the top ten nine times for receptions and six times for receiving yardage. In all, he accumulated 9,110 yards on catches for seventy-nine touchdowns. He even set a record when he caught fifty or more passes in seven seasons. One final statistic sums things up—when he retired, his 649 catches stood at number one all-time.

Bill Malinchak, a fellow Redskins player, recalled Taylor as being a quiet guy, but "he had really nice speed. He was six three, about 210, and he was a strong receiver. He was a running back at Arizona State, so when he got the ball, he was an excellent runner.

"He was probably the finest crackback blocker in football at that time. There was nobody like him. He was one of the guys who probably led to the change of rules because he would come back on guys and lay them out. He was unbelievable. I mean he was deadly on these safeties. It was always a safety he seemed to get.

"You could crackback high, low, head, legs, anywhere at that time—it didn't matter. He was laying guys out. He was a big, strong guy, and quick. He really used his legs when he blocked you. You'd get his whole body, it wasn't just his upper body hitting you. He would explode from the ground up. He had a certain way that he would block *through* you." Malinchak remembers some safeties being temporarily knocked out by Taylor's blows.

What he doesn't remember seeing is any opponents seeking revenge on Taylor. "No, it was pretty much accepted. It was legal." Safeties, though, did quickly learn to keep their head on a swivel when Taylor was around. "He had that reputation. You had to be careful. He made people pay attention."

Switching to Hall of Famers who were exclusively receivers, there's the balletic Lance Alworth, who was something special. A halfback in college, he was moved to the flanker position in the early 1960s, and went on to become the first player from the old AFL to make it to the Hall of Fame.

Alworth, like so many football greats, hails from Texas. Born in Houston, he switched allegiances a bit to play his college ball for Arkansas. While fans remember him mainly as a member of the San Diego

Chargers, he originally was drafted in 1962 by the San Francisco 49ers and by the Oakland Raiders. Both teams would go on to regret not signing him to a long-term contract. Ironically, the man who did sign Alworth was a man who would later gain fame with the Raiders organization—it was an assistant coach for the Chargers by the name of Al Davis.

Alworth made his pro debut in 1962, but played only four games and caught just four passes for San Diego. The next season began his stretch of sensational play. Two salient examples of the talent he flashed are the streak he once put together, a streak of catching one or more passes in 96 straight games (105 in all, counting All-Star games plus two AFL championship games), and the seven years in a row in which he almost routinely racked up over a thousand yards on catches.

During his prime he made frequent appearances on his league's statistical leaderboard. Start with 1964, when he was twenty-four years old. He led the way with his thirteen touchdowns on catches for the first of three consecutive seasons in which he managed that feat. The following year, he led the league in yards on catches with a remarkable 1,602 yards, which was good for two other league-leading stats, the best average per reception (23.2 yards) and the highest average of yards per catch per game played (114.4). In 1966, he was number one again for yards gained on catches and for the highest average of yards gained per game. Later, he added three more rankings at number one to his credit.

Furthermore, his career average of nearly nineteen yards per reception (18.9) still ranks number thirteen all-time and his touchdowns on catches, eighty-five, remains the fifteenth highest total ever. He even averaged almost exactly seventy-five yards on receptions per game over his eleven seasons, good for the number eleven spot all-time. Focusing only on his nine seasons with San Diego, excluding his final two years spent with the Cowboys, Alworth averaged more than fifty receptions a year and a thousand yards each and every season.

Alworth didn't do all this with his legs and hands, either. He said he constantly, sometimes even during a game, had to adjust to what defenses tried to do to him—and they did a lot to try to stop him. He said he rarely saw man-to-man defenses so he had to adjust his pass patterns quite a bit.

Sam Havrilak was both a runner and receiver who played five NFL seasons, four with the Colts. He is the answer to a trivia question as the first man ever to complete a pass (on an option play), catch a pass, and rush with the ball in a Super Bowl. Havrilak made it a point to study other players who manned the same positions he did, mainly receivers.

"Lance Alworth was pretty darn good and well respected," he said. "He played out there in San Diego—not very big [six feet, 184 pounds], but pretty fast, obviously—his nickname was 'Bambi,' so he ran [and leaped] pretty well, and he had great hands. He wasn't a route runner like Paul Warfield, but he got downfield in a hurry and [quarterback] John Hadl was able to deliver a lot of long passes to him."

Havrilak continued his analysis of receivers, calling Fred Biletnikoff "a very precise runner. You know, Oakland in those days liked to go deep all the time and he always made his bread-and-butter coming back for the pass, which a lot of receivers didn't do at that time, but that's the way they taught it at Oakland.

"He wasn't exceptionally fast, wasn't exceptionally big, but he had really good hands, and those were the days when everybody could wear Stickum on their hands, that real sticky stuff that was outlawed. Now the guys wear those gloves, and I don't see how they miss a pass with those gloves because they're so darn tacky that the ball just sticks right to them. He used more Stickum than any receiver in the league."

No question about it, Stickum or not (and it did seem as if his hands had been dipped in Superglue), Biletnikoff was as sure handed as a diamond cutter. He tied Raymond Berry's record for catching forty or more passes in ten straight seasons.

John Insenbarger echoed much of what Havrilak observed, calling Biletnikoff "the best receiver running routes, because he couldn't beat you in a foot race. Lots of people were faster than Fred, but he had quickness, and he ran really great routes. Plus, he used to put all the Stickum on his socks. That's why the wide receivers for the Raiders always stood up—they didn't get down in a three-point [stance], hell he had that stuff all over his hands. They had to change footballs out sometimes. They made it illegal, but, hell, now you got kids who wear gloves with these little nubs on them."

Havrilak also said Biletnikoff "perfected the technique of running the defender off and coming back for the ball. He was able to stop and change direction probably better than most receivers. He had great moves and the ability to turn guys' hips, turn them the other way to keep them off balance. And Lamonica and Ken Stabler got him the ball at the right time."

Sports fans tend to be obsessed with records and statistics, and Biletnikoff provided them with plenty of both. For fourteen seasons from 1965 through 1978, he was an Oakland mainstay, providing the Raiders with seventy-six touchdowns on 589 catches, which accounted for 8,984 yards.

When it came crunch time in postseason play, Biletnikoff always stood out. He established NFL playoff records with his grand total of seventy catches, ten touchdowns, and more than 1,000 yards (1,167). The topper came when he pulled down four passes for 79 yards, which put the Raiders in position to cash in on three scores during Super Bowl XI. He was presented with the MVP Award for those contributions. In all, he played in two Super Bowls and three AFL title contests and five AFC championship games.

An All-American at Florida State, he came to the pros off a four-touchdown day in a Gator Bowl win over Oklahoma. Continuing his excellence, in his first start, about halfway into the 1965 season, he snagged seven passes for 118 yards—he was off and running.

When Lenny Moore was asked to share his thoughts and opinions of John Mackey, he lavished praise on his old teammate. "Wow! God bless his soul. Whoo-wee. What a tight end! What a great blocker. Not only that, but after he caught the ball, unbelievable. Unbelievable guy to pull down. I remember there were two or three guys that were beading in on him, and I was on the flank, and I came back to try to put a block on somebody. John Mackey knocked me down before he knocked some of the other guys down. Knocked me down, too, because I was in his way. Wow! He was amazing. You have to watch the films when you talk about him. You have to see it. You say, 'Wow, look at this!'"

No wonder. Mackey could do it all from block to catch to bowl people over. Plus, for a tight end he ran quite well. "For a tight end, he was as fast as he needed to be," chuckled Moore. "He would just run you over, too. If you came to tackle him, boy, he'd be blasting guys. It's pretty hard to describe. He was just a real tough, *tough* end."

Indeed, Mackey tossed would-be tacklers from his back the way a bull sheds a rodeo rider, and it was no secret. "Mackey had it all," said Raymond Berry. "To have a tight end that could be a power punching blocker and to have the speed to beat people deep and with the hands to catch the ball is special. And he was a Bronko Nagurski after the catch. Trying to bring the guy down? Good luck. There's film after film of him catching the ball downfield, breaking one tackle, breaking another, running, breaking another one, and scoring after people were hitting him from every angle, but just not bringing him down. That was because of his strong legs, hips, and shoulders. He was explosive. When you watch John Mackey over a period of time, you just saw explosion—as a blocker, as a runner. And he had a heart like a lion even though, by today's standards, at six two, 225 pounds, he was far from being huge.

"He was physical and had good hands. Once he caught the ball, he was a load to bring down—the same as Mike Ditka, they had a lot in common, including the ability to run after they caught the ball."

Berry shared a side of Mackey only insiders were privy to. "As tough as he was, he was a walking time bomb because things would frighten him. It was a well-known fact that you had to be careful to not surprise him. People would play jokes on him to get him to react, and they never had any problem getting him to react. They'd put something like worms in his locker and watch him go to the locker and let out this yell, and everybody would laugh. That was John."

Sam Havrilak was another Baltimore teammate of Mackey. "I played with him for about four or five years—terrific tight end. I'll tell you a quick story about John. He hated anything that was like an insect or a worm or a bug or animal. So a couple of guys, when we were in preseason, shot either a muskrat or a squirrel or something and rigged his locker up so that when he opened his locker, it would jump out of it. The thing jumped out on his chest and he ran out of the locker room screaming.

"Once we were playing out in Kezar Stadium which was the 49ers' home before Candlestick Park. This was in 1969, I think, and John caught a pass and ran for about a ninety-yard touchdown and I think everybody on San Francisco's team hit him, but they couldn't bring him down—everybody said it was one of the greatest runs by a tight end in NFL history. But the reason John didn't go down on the ground was because it had rained and the dirt was so rich at Kezar Stadium they had a lot of worms there. When you look at the films of the game, he was the only one who had a white uniform—everybody else had mud all

THE BEST OFFENSIVE PLAYERS

over the uniform. He didn't want to go down on the ground where all the worms were."

Gino Marchetti, yet another Colt teammate of Mackey, tossed out random memories of the great tight end. "In college he was a fullback. Big John dressed next to me. He had tremendous speed and strength. If he had a weakness, it was his hands weren't as good as they liked. He had a tendency to drop one once in a while, but he was still good enough to make the Hall of Fame."

When Mike Ditka became the first tight end inducted into the Hall, he asked a very logical question, "Why wasn't John in first?"[4] Assuming Mackey was the first was only natural. He was so talented he changed the way coaches used their tight ends—employing them as bona fide offensive toosl, and not merely as blockers who would on rare occasions catch a pass. In 1966, for instance, six of Mackey's touchdowns went for fifty yards or more, hardly the accomplishment of the normal tight end of the era. Likewise, his 15.8 average yards gained per reception for his entire career was proof of his value. Evidence, too, that a new era had been born.

Mackey not only was selected for the All-Sixties team, he was so respected and he symbolized the tight end position so perfectly that today the best tight end in college football each year is presented with an award named after Mackey.

Pottios tossed in the name of another tough tight end. "Jackie Smith was physical, like Pete Retzlaff. He was big, about the size of Ditka and Mackey, and when he caught the ball, you better hit him and get your arms around him because you weren't [otherwise] going to bring him down."

Smith went six feet, four inches and 235 pounds, and he was so durable he spent sixteen seasons at his position. The first fifteen were spent with the St. Louis Cardinals where he established his Hall of Fame credentials. Actually, he never led the NFL in any major category and he only broke into the top ten for seasonal accomplishment such as total receptions a few times. However, he was steady and kept putting up solid numbers. For example, he posted a lifetime average of 16.5 yards per catch and ran for almost 8,000 yards on receptions for his career, helping him make it to five Pro Bowls. He even ranked in the top ten for the longest punt of a given season twice.

Unfortunately, and unfairly, many people today remember Smith for one play that took place in the one year he didn't spend in a St. Louis uniform, and in the one game that matters the most each season. Playing for Dallas against the Pittsburgh Steelers in Super Bowl XIII, Smith had been acquired for his experience, blocking ability, and dependability. This, he knew, was to be his final game of his career.

A veteran of 215 games, he had compiled more yards on catches than any other tight end ever had. He was also, at thirty-eight years of age, the oldest player in the game. While he didn't get any passes thrown his way (he had no receptions during the regular season), and while he had, in fact, only been used to block on a handful of running plays against Pittsburgh, he was about to be the target of a Roger Staubach throw to the end zone. He was also about to have a date with infamy.

Smith lined up on the Pittsburgh 10-yard line in a third down and three situation. The Orange Bowl clock showed 2:46 to go in the third quarter and the Cowboys trailed by a touchdown, 21–14. Smith ran his route, wound up in the middle of the end zone, unguarded. Staubach spotted the wide open target and threw. Inexplicably, the usually surehanded Smith dropped the football, but to be fair, the ball had been low and somewhat behind Smith. The drop, though, is what most fans remember. Nothing else. The Cowboys settled for a field goal and the Steelers went on to win the game, 35–31.

While Smith was troubled for a long time by the dropped pass, he could find solace by remembering that Dallas would not even have been in Super Bowl XIII if he hadn't made a game-tying touchdown catch in a 27–20 win over the Atlanta Falcons in the first round of the playoffs. He can also find comfort any time he chooses to simply by glancing down at his Hall of Fame ring.

For quite some time the answer to who is the greatest wide receiver of all time was simple—Raymond Berry. Many of his records have since fallen, but he still stands as a legend and one of the greatest players the game has ever seen. As a matter of fact, Marchetti still believes his former teammate to be the best receiver of all time.

Marchetti knew Berry to be fully focused on anything he undertook, especially on all of the facets of football. "He was the kind of guy who washed his own uniform, made sure it was clean." In short, Berry was a perfectionist and no detail was ever too small for him. Football for Berry was an around-the-year and almost an around-the-clock proposition and he worked tirelessly to perfect his craft.

One time Berry complained to Marchetti about his rather low salary. Marchetti related, "He told me that general manager Don Kellett wasn't going to give him a raise." Kellett insisted Berry "was almost maxed out," causing Berry to explain his cause to Marchetti, "Listen, I play football twelve months a year. I work at football twelve months a year. Half of these guys will go home and not touch a football until next July. So I should get more money."

James Brown may have been the hardest working man in show business, but he had nothing on Raymond Berry. Marchetti said, "He made it because he worked hard, he ran hard, he did calisthenics, he was in bed at 9:00. He did everything right—everything you should do as a professional athlete. A lot of us probably should have done more after watching him."

Andy Nelson, a Colts defensive back, said, "Raymond Berry was really something. He had all these handicaps like a bad back and he was slow, but he was one of the greatest receivers of all time. He had the moves. He had a net he'd put up between the goal posts, and I'd throw passes to him sometimes after practice. He'd stand by the net and say, 'Now don't throw the ball right to me. I want you to throw it behind me, six inches off the ground,' and so on.

"He worked on the tough catch, and every day he'd do that. He put that to work in the '58 game in the two-minute drill—John Unitas and Raymond Berry. All you had to say was, 'Two-minute drill,' and they went right to it. The other team would say, 'Here they come again!'"

Marchetti continued, "Berry was fantastic. In my first year after I retired, I went to see a game in Baltimore and the Colts were playing Green Bay. It was late in the game and the Colts were losing. Raymond went on a fifteen-yard pattern and cut to the right in the middle of the end zone. John threw him the ball. Raymond missed it, dropped that ball. And you could just hear the people sigh. You could hear the fans saying, 'Oooooo,' when Raymond Berry dropped a pass because it just never happened. The fans were in shock. All the guys on the sideline: 'I can't believe it. Did you see that?' People didn't boo. Rare? That's the only time I ever saw him drop a ball.

"And he had the work habits that made John what he was, too. He wanted to catch a hundred or hundred and fifty passes every day after practice. Guys were tired and wanted to go home, but he wouldn't do that. He'd stay out there and catch passes. I can't remember when he ever fumbled, either." In reality, Berry handled the ball hundreds and hundreds of time, more than six hundred, and fumbled just once in his thirteen-year career.

"He gave a lot and he made catches you won't believe," Marchetti marveled. "Plays you wouldn't believe like one in Detroit where he overran the ball, threw his body up, horizontal [parallel] to the ground and made a catch with his chest, pinning it to his chest. It may not sound like much, but, believe me, if you had seen it you'd have said, 'Wow.'"

Lenny Moore vividly remembers a game the Colts played against the San Francisco 49ers. "We came from behind, they had us down something like, twenty or thirty-something to seven at halftime, and we came back and beat them. We beat them simply because of what Raymond put out there about working with John.

"What Raymond did was look at all the positions, and he would go to the guys and just say, 'Do you think you can handle him or handle that [particular play or duty],' just like he came to me and said we need more of you in our offense one time. He took charge, helped others, and often came back to the huddle to tell Unitas when he was sure he could beat his man on the next play."

Pottios also respected Berry, "a possession-type receiver. You knew if there was a situation where the Colts wanted to pick up a first down, or they wanted to keep possession of the ball, throwing a certain type of pass where they knew they were going to make a completion, he was the guy, the go-to guy, the guy they could count on."

Barry recently verified a famous story, which some felt was apocryphal, that has been repeatedly told about his uncanny knowledge of the dimensions of a football field. After running precise patterns for years, he knew a football field better than virtually everyone but a groundskeeper.

Once, while working as an assistant coach for the Cowboys under Tom Landry during training camp, Berry was sharing his knowledge with a Dallas quarterback and a number one draft pick, receiver Dennis Homan. After the regular practice at Thousand Oaks, California, had concluded, Berry had Homan run sideline patterns, and Berry just sensed something was amiss. He later approached Landry, telling him the field's dimensions were a bit off. Trusting Berry, Landry had the field measured and it was, in fact, too narrow.

Berry recalled, "Yeah, it's true. From the hash mark to the sideline was a yard, maybe yard-and-a-half off. You get such a feel for the fine points so I was aware of it."

The litany of Berry's records stretches almost as long as his arms extended to haul in a pass over his helmet. A slightly abridged list includes the record he once set by stringing together six games in a row with 100 or more yards on catches as well as his record ten consecutive seasons with forty or more receptions. He finished first or second in the NFL every season for five consecutive years for the most receptions, and in eight of his thirteen seasons he was in the top ten in that department. His personal apex came in 1961 when he snagged seventy-five passes in twelve games. Three seasons he led the league in yards gained on receptions, once with 1,298 yards in just twelve games.

The six-time Pro Bowl honoree also caught fourteen touchdown passes (seventh-best ever at that time), again during a twelve-game season, in 1959 when he scored eighty-four points, more than any other player aside from those who did some or all of their scoring on kicks. The ensuing season his average of 108.2 yards per game on catches was also the seventh-best all-time output.

In the 1958 NFL championship game, Berry went berserk, setting new records for the most catches, twelve, and the most yards on catches, 178.

When he retired after the 1967 season, he held the record for the most lifetime catches (631), most career yards on receptions (9,275), and only Don Hutson, Tommy McDonald, and Art Powell owned more touchdowns on catches than Berry's sixty-eight. In fact, his sixty-eight TDs were surpassed by only eleven men, regardless of position played, at that time.

The first-ballot Hall of Famer was selected to the NFL's all-time squad for its first seventy-five years along with fellow wide receivers Jerry Rice, Lance Alworth, and Don Hutson.

Don Maynard was a contemporary of Berry and wound up breaking one of Berry's most glorious, cherished records. Maynard became Joe Namath's favorite target and would go on to enjoy fifty games in which he amassed over one hundred yards on catches, an NFL first. However, this fleet receiver's pro beginnings were far from auspicious.

Like Berry, Maynard played in the Greatest Game Ever Played, the 1958 NFL title game, but with the losing New York Giants, not the Colts. Back then Maynard, a rookie, mainly ran punts back, but he was also listed as Frank Gifford's backup as a New York runner. He sat out the next year because the Giants cut him loose and, apparently, no other NFL team felt he was good enough to acquire. Once he became a member of the New York Jets, though, his career took off like Olympian gold medalist sprinter Usain Bolt shooting off his starter's block.

Ten years after the 1958 championship game, Maynard, who actually became a New York *Titan* in 1960 (after spending a year in the Canadian Football League), would help his team, by then known as the Jets, win the Super Bowl over the Colts.

As for the record that Maynard broke of fellow Texan Berry, it was the one he eclipsed in 1968, one year after Berry's retirement—for the most yards ever via receptions. Maynard would go on to become the first receiver to reach the ten-thousand-yard plateau.

Maynard is still number thirteen for career touchdowns scored on catches (eighty-eight) even though he never played in a sixteen-game season. He also still ranks high, sixteenth, with his lifetime average of 18.7 yards per reception.

Chuck Mercein called him "a very interesting character, quirky, a real deep southern Texan." A true Texan indeed, Maynard played golf wearing snakeskin cowboy boots with spikes. Mercein said, "He's known to be very frugal. I think he was one of the first guys ever to have a car that, instead of using gasoline, I think used propane gas. Thank God nobody ever hit that car."

Manny Fernandez and his Dolphins remembered Maynard well. "I wish he had never been born," he laughed. "He made our lives miserable. He could get deep now. He pretty much embarrassed the DB's we had in the '60s." Fernandez felt Maynard had the speed of guys like Cliff Branch, Bob Hayes, and Lance Alworth. "Don had tremendous speed—he got by people, outran everybody to the ball."

When it comes to Olympic-caliber speed, the Glory Years had one receiver who actually was a gold-medal winner, Bob Hayes of the Cowboys, also known as "Bullet Bob." Berry called Hayes one of the most talented natural athletes he ever encountered. "You just can't find a guy with Olympic speed that can catch the football—this guy could. Not many sprinters can convert to professional football, but Hayes was one of the rare exceptions. He brought speed to the game that nobody in the NFL had."

This man, whose career ran from 1965 through 1975, seemed to be a streak shooting across the field. In four of his eleven seasons, his longest touchdown catch and run went for eighty or more yards. His longest score on a reception ever came during his second season in the league when he dashed ninety-five yards into the end zone. It's almost unimaginable, but that distance wasn't enough to lead the NFL that season. Detroit's Pat Studstill scored on a ninety-nine-yard pass and Homer Jones of the New York Giants hauled in a ninety-eight-yard touchdown catch.

In Hayes's first two seasons he stood atop the NFL for touchdown catches with twelve and thirteen respectively. In both of those seasons he also wound up with more than 1,000 yards on catches, with 1,003 and then 1,232 yards. Then, during the next two seasons, he went over 900 yards on pass receptions.

In addition, he averaged a lustrous 20.0 yards per catch lifetime, and in 1970 and 1971 he led the NFL with averages of 26.1 and 24.0 yards per reception. On one occasion, 1967, his blistering speed helped him lead the NFL in punt return yardage, and in the following season he led for yards per punt return, 20.8, helped largely by a 90-yard journey into the end zone.

Once when Dallas head coach Tom Landry was timing his players over the distance of forty yards in training camp, Berry was impressed as he observed Hayes loping down the field. Landry, unimpressed, just laughed, explaining to Berry that Hayes wasn't, and never did run all out in such circumstances. He had no records to set or anything to prove to anyone. Berry estimated that Hayes could have run the forty at just a bit over four seconds or so.

Who knows, that may have been an underestimation, because in the Olympic finals back in 1960 for the 100-meter dash in Tokyo, he turned in a record time of 10.06. That earned him one of two gold medals, with the other one earned as a member of the 100-meter relay team. Hayes also became the first man to run a 100-yard dash in 9.1 seconds.

Berry said that it was as if the moment the ball was snapped Hayes was within a split second of being open. Slight exaggeration, but the defensive backs who attempted to guard him knew they had to give him lots of room, fearful that he would get by them for a long pass. In effect, for him to get an easy completion, according to Berry, all he had to do was "run down the field and break out or in or hook, and he's open on the short routes."

Pottios remembered when Hayes broke into the league. "He was the number one guy you wanted to stop because, as a defensive player, you didn't want his team to score an easy touchdown against you—like on a sixty, seventy-yard pass—so he was always a concern. Any time you have a lot of speed as a receiver, you had be concerned."

Before Berry and Maynard, and long before fellow speedster Hayes broke in, one of the first receivers to establish impressive records and cause eyes to pop was Elroy "Crazy Legs" Hirsch. Both quick *and* fast, he loved to go deep, and his evasiveness earned him his colorful moniker. His 1952 average of 23.6 yards per catch is number twelve all-time. However, what he accomplished in 1951 went even further in insuring he would secure a spot on the All-Decade Team. He won the receivers' version of the Triple Crown, leading the league in receptions (sixty-six), yards on catches (1,495), and receiving touchdowns (seventeen). On top of that, he led the NFL with a 91-yard romp for a score. His seventeen touchdowns matched an existing record, and ten of his receptions went for 40+ yards. In addition, he put up the most points scored that year (102), and led the NFL with the highest average of yards per catch (22.7—and he'd up that to 23.6 the next season), and his average of 124.6 yards per game on receptions was an NFL best. That's not all, in his clean sweep of honors, he also led the league in total yards from scrimmage and all-purpose yards (1,501). No one-year wonder, his lifetime average of 18.2 yards per catch still ranks number twenty-five all-time.

Berry looked up to Hirsch, who, in 1951, during a twelve-game schedule, caught passes for a new record 1,495 yards. "He was making these catches over the shoulder, directly over the head, with outstretched fingers, on the dead run. He'd catch it and run another 40 yards. He was spectacular."

Hirsch was versatile, too—he kicked a handful of extra points, threw twenty-two passes, completing twelve, returned punts and kicks in three seasons, and once returned a kick eighty-eight yards with his crazy legs pumping away. He even had three interceptions in 1946 in the old AAFC.

Gino Marchetti firmly believed that one of the greatest receivers of his time was Hirsch. "He was something. He taught me a lesson. We played the Rams in Baltimore and he was playing in tight so they could get an angle on me on end runs and whatever. That's what good coaches do—they moved him maybe three or four yards to my left, I guess, and they would run this sweep toss, and I probably had my eye on the ball too much. Anyway, he was sitting out there and every time I'd go to hit him, he'd come from the side and just whack me.

"All through the game he kept saying, 'Nice going, Gino. Nice going.' and 'God, Almighty, you really hit hard.' Here I am walking back to my huddle feeling like a giant. There's a big man, a big name in the NFL at that time. I felt really great. They beat us 42–6, or whatever.

"Next day at the meeting the first thing out of Weeb's mouth—he's upset because we didn't show very well—was, 'You know what? If anybody in this room would've told me that Crazy Legs Hirsch could block Marchetti, I would have *never* believed it, particularly because he blocked him all afternoon.'

"So there's old Hirsch complimenting me, and I'm eating it all up, but all the time he was knocking me on my butt and I never realized it. I thought I was blocking him out, but he was blocking me. The films embarrassed me and the coaches kept rewinding the plays, 'Watch this,' Weeb or the line coach would say. 'What were you doing there, Marchetti, huh? Sleeping?' So, big lesson learned."

Paul Warfield was as fluid as quicksilver. Over his career he averaged one touchdown for every five receptions. His eighty-five career touchdowns on catches placed him number three all-time when he retired.

Chuck Bryant was an Ohio State teammate of Warfield when they won the national title in 1961 (as selected by the Football Writers Association of America). Bryant said, "He was probably the best athlete that I've ever known. We were playing in Ann Arbor and Paul, our left halfback, hadn't had a great year—he was still kind of tentative. We ran '18 Sweep,' which was a sweep to the right. He ran around the end and made a move on the defensive back to the inside, then went outside, and the defensive back just fell flat on his back, and P. W. went for, I think sixty yards for a touchdown. In that same game he also caught a swing pass and went for around fifty, but that's just the type athlete he was. He could break it open at any time.

"He could do everything. He was a great track star. He long-jumped against the Russians in the USA versus USSR dual meet in 1962 and came in third place." Warfield is now honored in the Ohio State Hall of Fame as both a football and track star.

Sam Havrilak was a student of the game. "As a receiver, you look at other receivers in the league, and I thought that Paul Warfield was probably one of the best route runners of any receiver of that era—not very big, but a very precise route runner and he had a real good set of hands, very smart. Even when he played for Cleveland he was like that, but then he got with Bob Griese down in Miami and he just had tremendous seasons down there."

Pottios said receivers often fit into a category, such as the tight ends, who often are the possession-type men who can be counted on to get open for short passes to keep drives alive; and then there are the speedsters, who are capable of cashing in on long scores. He called Warfield the rare type of pass receiver who was a combination, a possession type, but "with speed to beat you." In fact, his 20.1 average yards per catch ranks tied for the number four spot all-time, one-tenth of a yard per reception ahead of Bob Hayes.

As a rookie in 1964, Warfield caught a career high fifty-two passes and helped his Browns win the NFL championship. Later, he continued to shine with Miami as an integral part of their back-to-back titles and their undefeated season.

A teammate there, Doug Crusan, called Warfield "a gazelle. A perfectionist—the way he ran his routes, his body type. If I'm a defender watching films, watching him run his routes, I know I'm going to get beat. You'd say, 'Doggone, what a move that was.' He had a real fluid stride and he could just change it, and he could catch a ball in a hundred different ways, I think." Even though old records and standards for excellence have changed, Crusan still says Warfield is in his top ten receivers of all time.

2

HALL OF FAME
DEFENDERS . . . AND MORE

Naturally, Hall of Famers were also in abundance at positions other than the ones covered in chapter 1. The focus here is on the defensive side of the football (with a few other greats such as some offensive linemen sprinkled in). Many of the brightest stars of the era, especially the linebackers, will be profiled in the chapter on the game's toughest men.

As great a defensive end as Gino Marchetti was, he said there were a few opponents who gave him a difficult time. "We really had a battle—one was Bob St. Clair for the San Francisco 49ers. He was a teammate of mine at USF. When we played the 49ers, he was one of the toughest."

At just three inches shy of the towering seven-foot mark and checking in at 265 pounds, the team captain of his 49ers for three seasons certainly was tough and, experts say, quite intelligent. St. Clair was so imposing and talented that San Francisco even used him on defense at times in goal-line situations. In addition to that, he was a valuable member of special teams. His height surely was a factor when, in 1956, he blocked ten field goal attempts.

Nevertheless, St. Clair felt that, as an offensive lineman, just about the only personal satisfaction he got from playing the game at that position was blasting an opponent, driving him to the ground. He was equally skilled at pass and run blocking, but it was on run plays that he could really tee off on the opposition.

Coincidentally, after playing high school football in his native city for San Francisco Polytechnic, the 1990 inductee into the Hall of Fame continued playing his entire post–high school career, save for one season at Tulsa, in a San Francisco uniform, as a Don in college, and as a 49er from 1953 to 1963. He only left the University of San Francisco because they stopped their football program after the 1951 season. St. Clair was one of nine players from the Dons' 1951 team to make it to the pros.

Raymond Berry also remembered the ongoing titanic mano-a-mano duels between Marchetti and the hulking offensive tackle. "St. Clair would fit in with the modern-day linemen without any problem. Gino had to play him twice a year even though he only went six foot four and around 245 pounds, and it was always a battle. When those two went up against each other, you were looking at a classic match."

St. Clair was almost impervious to pain. He broke two bones in his lower back once and didn't miss his next game, and, in a 1957 contest, he broke his shoulder and continued to play for eight more minutes before leaving the game.

A member of the All-Decade Team of the 1950s, St. Clair never shied away from contact. On the contrary, he thrived on it with animal-like ferocity. The animal metaphor is, in one way, apt. St. Clair used to eat raw steak and raw chicken, and blood would run down his chin at times. Those eating habits, developed when he was a child and his grandmother, a Yaqui Indian woman from Mexico, fed him raw meat, earned him the cringe-inducing nickname "The Geek."

Art Donovan played alongside Marchetti as the Colts left defensive tackle. When Donovan's name came up, Marchetti mulled, "Fatso. God Almighty. He couldn't run, but I tell you one thing, he could play the position of defensive tackle. They used to run Art Donovan in the forty and he's taking about, almost six seconds. But it's hard for me to understand why it's so important for a lineman to run sprints in a five-and-a-half- to six-second mark. Why, hell, like Art, the farthest they had to run was maybe five yards or six yards, and he was quick as a cat. He was as fast at five yards as anybody on our team. After that, he'd get lost."

Marchetti stressed that some of the keys to the Colts success were not merely the big names such as Unitas. "You take a guy like Donovan. He deserves, and should have gotten, a lot more push [publicity] than he did. If you looked at him, here's a 280-, 300-pound defensive tackle [he was officially listed at 263], around six two, fat, but when you watched him play—and he played next to me, so I used to watch him a lot—you'd learn from him. He was probably the best pass-rushing tackle in the league at that time."

Some coaches liked to have one of their defensive linemen occasionally crisscross with the defender next to him, what Marchetti referred to as "crossing the line to get a better pass rush." However, the Colts didn't employ that scheme much. "I didn't like that. Art didn't like it— I'd have to go in front of him or he'd have to go in front of me, and he was too slow. And he was too fat, a helluva lot to run around—I didn't like *that*, but I loved him."

Donovan usually was positioned in the middle of the line in the Baltimore 4-3 defense, but would sometimes be stationed at nose tackle. Berry commented, "What Art brought to the job was he weighed about 265, but he had this great quickness and tremendous upper-body strength. He was built in a kind of squat way. The scouting report on him was always, 'You just can't trap him.' Teams like to run traps against tackles to create a crease up the middle, a hole. But they gave up trying to trap him because he had the instincts and such outstanding quickness that a pulling guard trying to trap him would run into a concrete wall. On the pass rush he was quick and put pressure on the quarterback up the middle."

On top of his talent, Donovan was charming, endearing, self-deprecating, and hilarious. Another Baltimore teammate, Andy Nelson, said that, "Artie was a comedian who kept us laughing, but on the field he was a very serious guy. He was a good friend to all of us."

Fred Cox was in awe of his Minnesota Viking teammate Carl Eller. "He had the most unbelievable physique of anybody I've ever seen. He looked like he was chiseled out of stone. You could see every muscle in his body. I don't imagine his body fat was more than six or seven percent. For a guy who was as big as he was, and weighed as much as he did, to have that little body fat was unbelievable."

In the speech he gave at the Hall of Fame induction ceremony in 2004, Eller spoke of his upbringing in Winston-Salem, North Carolina, saying his parents, though poor, instilled values in him. In addition, unlike many of his peers who did not dare to aspire to great things, Eller strove for greatness. His drive began when his father passed away when Eller was young and he turned his negative, bitter feelings into a burning energy he expended on the football field.

That impetus was all it took. Football then provided him with a scholarship to attend Minnesota and play for the Golden Gophers and later gave him a livelihood and great status as an NFL superstar.

At six feet, six inches, 247 pounds, and with obvious, early-on recognizable Hall of Fame–caliber talent, he was truly unbelievable. He not only was named to six Pro Bowls, he was First Team All-Pro in five of those Pro Bowl seasons. Already a star in the 1960s, he continued to shine into the next decade—so much that he was chosen as a member of the First Team All-1970s.

Over one three-year period of time he was responsible for forty-four sacks, quite a feat given there were three other members of the Purple People Eaters unit also vying for sacks. When he finally ended his career, he had the third-highest total of opponents' fumbles recovered in the annals of the league, twenty-three.

The defensive end gave offensive linemen, running backs, and vulnerable quarterbacks nervous tics over sixteen seasons from 1964 through 1979. Eller was one of those players who spent his entire career with one team, something that becomes a rarer and rarer feat as years roll by.

The excellent website Pro Football Reference lists the best players ever based upon their "Career Approximate Value," a statistic meant to measure just how important the men were to their team's success. Atop the list is Peyton Manning, and the highest-rated defensive player is Reggie White (number five all-time). Eller is number twenty-three on the list.

Eller had great company on the Vikings defensive line. Alan Page is a great example of that. On the "Career Approximate Value" chart, Page, in fact, stands seven spots ahead of Eller.

A defensive player has to be pretty darn good to win the NFL MVP Award. Alan Page achieved this in 1971, one of the four seasons he was tabbed as the top defensive player in the NFC. As a matter of fact, Page was the very first defensive player ever to walk off with the MVP trophy. Born in Canton, Ohio, in 1945, he was destined to return there to be inducted into the Hall of Fame forty-three years later.

Page could do almost anything on the defensive side of the football. He blocked twenty-eight kicks and is unofficially credited with a stunning 170 career sacks, just 30 shy of the all-time record.

Cox said Page was a man you "didn't want to make mad. We were playing a championship game against Los Angeles in Minnesota and Page kept complaining to the official that they were holding him, which was true. As far as I knew, that was the only way you could block him.

"Finally, he got so upset he took his helmet off, threw it on the ground, and it must have bounced twenty feet in the air. And, of course, they gave him a fifteen-yard penalty. He put his helmet back on and the next three times they snapped the ball, they lost twenty-five yards—Page either tackled the quarterback or the running back for [those] losses. He was just an amazing player. I have never seen somebody with the quickness that he had, and it wasn't like he was that big—he was about 260 [listed at 245 pounds]."

Doug Crusan's voice reflected his distaste for having to battle Page in the trenches. "Oooh, yeah! I played against him. He was one of those quick Notre Dame guys, excellent. Long arms and very, very mobile."

Cox knew Page was so overpowering and skilled he didn't need much time to hit mid-season form. "Alan became a state Supreme Court judge in Minnesota. He went to law school while he was playing, and Bud [Grant, Vikings head coach] encouraged him to go to school during training camp because when we practiced, if Alan was there, you could never get anything done because every time the offense tried to run the ball, he would be in the backfield somewhere. He actually, for five years, went to law school while we were in training camp and he would come back and play the last exhibition game then play the rest of the year."

Gino Marchetti admired players such as the Dallas Cowboys great defensive tackle Bob Lilly. "I think he was the best lineman in the league during our period. Oh, Jesus Christ, I used to like to watch him, the moves he had, the quickness he had, the strength he had. He had everything you would want as a defensive lineman.

"At first they didn't find a spot for him—they put him at defensive end, tackle, right side, left. They moved him all over. Then they finally put him at right defensive tackle and I want to tell you he was the best. I complimented him one time at the Pro Bowl and he complimented me. He said, 'You know, Gino, I used to watch you all the time.' I told him the same—and I did. You didn't catch him with both feet in mud."

Offensive lineman Crusan didn't exactly shudder when facing Lilly, but it was not something to look forward to. "Lilly was tall, rangy, with long arms—you read about that all the time how they look for pass rushers with long arms. He was difficult to block. He was a quick, intense player with raw strength. Just a big guy—long, probably close to six foot six, well put together. He was a heckuva player."

Lilly was one of those players who made Texas his home for almost his entire football career. He attended high school in Texas and Oregon and then was based exclusively in the Lone Star State, with the Cowboys and earlier with TCU.

Lilly's great instincts meant he was often on the ball, and once he even led the NFL in return yardage of fumbles. He failed to make it to the Pro Bowl in just three of his fourteen seasons. As for being strong, dependable, and resilient, he started every game during that long career. From his rookie season of 1961 through his last game in 1974, he came to play, and play well at that. He not only started, he excelled, making eleven Pro Bowl squads over his fourteen seasons. Teams frequently double- and triple-teamed him—not to do so was sheer folly—and he still dominated.

Sam Havrilak succinctly summed up Lilly. "He is considered one of the greatest defensive linemen to play in the league." That's almost another understatement as Lilly, quite the package, listed officially at six feet, five inches and 260 pounds, made all-decade teams for both the 1960s and 1970s, a rare feat. Further, he is also on the NFL All-Time Team.

One can utter the name of Merlin Olsen in the same breath as Lilly, one of his contemporaries, because they both easily stand among the greatest linemen ever. Olsen, a six-foot-five, 270-pound defensive tackle, played from 1962 to 1976.

As with Alex Karras, an acting and broadcasting career followed his NFL days. One Rams teammate, Myron Pottios, said, "I think Merlin would have been successful no matter what he tried to do. He was just that kind of person."

Not everyone believed he was headed for success, though. Unbelievably, his ninth-grade basketball coach cut him, saying he would never be an athlete. That prompted Olsen to become even more determined to follow his dream and to strive for greatness.

An All-American and Outland Trophy winner out of Utah State, it was quite revealing also to note that he was a Phi Beta Kappa. During the off-season he, unlike so many athletes, returned to college, not to finally get his bachelor's degree, but to earn a master's in economics. Many writers credit the cerebral, steady Olsen as being the anchor that was so instrumental in making the Los Angeles Fearsome Foursome so great.

A member of the Rams' All-Time Team, naturally, Olsen, the overall third draft pick in 1962, could always be counted on. He did the dirty work in the trenches for 208 contests with the last 198 of those games played consecutively. Just the fact that he played in fifteen seasons and was named to fourteen straight Pro Bowls from his rookie season of 1962 through 1975 says a lot. Upon his retirement, he held several records including one for the most times being tabbed for the Pro Bowl, and the Rams franchise record for the most lifetime games played and for the most consecutive games played.

Olsen was so good for so long he was named to two All-Decade teams, for the 1960s and 1970s, and when it came time to select the NFL's 75th Anniversary All-Time Team, there was no doubt he would be a member of that illustrious unit.

Olsen was so dominant he was one of those defensive players who accomplished the near-impossible task of winning the Bert Bell Award, which is given to the top player of the year. Olsen did this in 1974, making him just the second defender to win the award. Andy Robustelli won it a dozen seasons earlier, and the next defensive player to cop the honor didn't come along for another dozen years after Olsen, when Lawrence Taylor won his award in 1986.

"Olsen," said Chuck Bryant, who played on several college all-star teams with him, "was very subtle. He didn't go out and party with the players. He was kind of conservative and reserved. He didn't yell and scream and do things like that on the field."

Although he played a violent sport, he became known as a gentle giant, a man with wonderful values to go along with his talent.

Pottios observed, "Merlin was just a solid, good guy, an All-American guy. He was a smart guy, a Phi Beta Kappa who was well versed in speaking, and a super ballplayer and great family guy. He knew how to handle situations and people. He never got out of line. I never saw Merlin lose his cool or get out of line, or show anger whether it be on or off the field."

Besides the men who hunkered down on the line of scrimmage, several defensive backs of the era stood out, such as Mel Renfro. He came out of the University of Oregon, the same college that produced quarterback Norm Van Brocklin. Renfro's job, however, was to bat down, tip away, or pick off passes, not complete them.

With Renfro's help, his Cowboys, the only team he ever suited up for, played in eight NFL or NFC championship games and four Super Bowls. During the Renfro reign, Dallas had a veritable monopoly on division crowns, winning nine of them. As a rookie in 1964, the Cowboys second-round draft pick led the NFL in kickoff and punt return yardage. He also led his team that season with his seven interceptions—veteran receivers weren't picking on *this* rookie. He even earned an invitation to play in the Pro Bowl in his initial pro season—he had to sit that one out, though, due to an injury.

Renfro wound up with 2,246 kickoff return yards over his career, which ran through the 1977 season—that was good for an average of 26.4 yards per return. Another 842 of his lifetime yards gained came on punt returns. Very versatile, over his career he scored at least one touchdown on an interception, punt return, and kickoff return. A pure athlete, he played both free safety and cornerback, making the switch to cornerback in his fifth season. It was at that position where he experienced his biggest glory and success.

Renfro made the Pro Bowl a grand total of ten times, doing so consecutively from his rookie year on. He was an All-Pro five times. He once said that it took speed—he ran the forty-yard dash in 4.6 seconds, a very good time in his era—to do his job at the level at which he played, but there was much more to it. He also cited quickness and his agility, but pointed out that beyond all that, it also took an intense analysis of opponents to be an all-around defensive back.

As a former All-American at halfback and a collegiate track and field great, he had all the tools a defensive back could ever want. Not only could he intercept passes, he could shut receivers down. Sam Havrilak, a receiver and running back, remembered, "I had a difficult time getting open against him. He was a smart player."

In 1969 his ten "picks" topped the league, but in his final eight seasons he intercepted just twenty-one more passes. Why? Well, other teams weren't oblivious. Renfro was one of those defensive backs who prompt opposing coaches to say, "He's so good, we just won't pass the ball his way." Still, his fifty-two lifetime interceptions mean only twenty-five other men have ever surpassed him in that department. Once he picked off a pass, he could run with the ball, accounting for 626 yards on such returns.

Cornerback Herb Adderley was another winner, and certainly no dummy on the gridiron, either. Teams who were fortunate enough to have him defending receivers and coming up to stop the run became quite chummy with success.

Over his twelve-year career from 1961 through 1972, his teams—the Packers, for his first nine seasons, and the Cowboys—went to the title game seven times and won the championship on six occasions. Imagine that—he went to the championship contest in more than half of his seasons and won it all in exactly half of his years in the NFL.

As a matter of fact, Adderley is tied with two other men, both fellow Packers, tackle Forrest Gregg and guard Fuzzy Thurston, for being on the most championship teams in NFL history. Adderley's teams played in a total of seventeen postseasons games and only wound up on the losing end twice.

Adderley, a converted running back, was like the NFL's version of Forrest Gump, popping up at so many historic moments. For instance, he was a Super Bowl fixture, playing in four of the first six of those contests. He also recorded one of the first interceptions in Super Bowl history, and the first Super Bowl interception to be run back for a score. In Super Bowl II, he plucked down a Daryle Lamonica pass and returned it sixty yards for a touchdown. That ran up the score to 33–7, and Green Bay coasted to a 33–14 annihilation of the Raiders.

Through the 2015 season, only eight men have run back interceptions for more yardage than Adderley's 1,046. In addition, only ten players have had more touchdowns scored on interception returns than his seven. Overall, the Packers' first-round draft selection out of Michigan State in 1961 came up with forty-eight interceptions.

He provided further value to his teams as a kick-return artist. Over the course of his 120 career kickoff runbacks, he piled up 3,080 yards. All of his achievements led to his being named to the Pro Football Hall of Fame All-1960s Team.

At one point in his days with Green Bay, Coach Lombardi told him that he was the finest cornerback he had ever seen, and that, of course, covered a lot of ground.

Another defensive back who displayed his prowess early on was Lem Barney. He came to the NFL via Jackson State where he was a three-time All-Southwestern Conference great. Over three collegiate seasons he intercepted twenty-six passes, an omen of greater things to follow soon thereafter. Actually, though, coming from that school there were not too many experts who knew much about him, but he did become a second-round draft pick by the Detroit Lions.

The Lions considered using him as a wide receiver, but they wisely shifted him to the cornerback position. As a rookie in 1967 his speed and instincts helped him lead the league in interceptions with ten (tied with Dave Whitsell of the New Orleans Saints). To that point, only twenty-one men ever had more interceptions in a season than Barney, and, remember, he got his ten "picks" as a mere rookie.

Barney's 232 yards on interception runbacks and his three touchdowns on interceptions also topped the entire NFL. In fact, those three scores fell just one shy of what was then the NFL season record. He was an easy selection for Defensive Rookie of the Year accolades.

Over his eleven-season career, he averaged exactly one touchdown scored per year, spending that time exclusively for Detroit. He earned seven trips to play in the Pro Bowl.

Sam Havrilak stated, "I remember we were watching film and were going to play Detroit, and we were watching Lem Barney who was, obviously, a Hall of Fame cornerback. His feet, when he went into a backpedal, moved so fast you could hardly even see them move—he had a lot of speed, a real good ballplayer."

Understatement aside, Barney was so valuable to the Lions because he could score in so many ways. He once scored on a 71-yard interception, another time on a 74-yard punt return, and he threw in a 98-yard kickoff return. Lifetime, he averaged 25.5 yards per kickoff return for 1,274 yards, and his career punt return yardage stands at 1,312.

Barney went on to register fifty-six total picks, prowling the secondary with grace and skill. He totaled 1,077 yards on interception returns, and that still places him number eight all-time.

One great defensive back played in parts of three decades. Dick Le-Beau, born in London (Ohio, that is), began his NFL days in 1959 and didn't call it a career until after the 1972 season. Raymond Berry, as talented as he was, didn't exactly look forward to going up against Le-Beau, but he had to do just that twice each season because LeBeau's Lions were in the same conference as the Colts.

Berry saw LeBeau as one of the smartest cornerbacks he ever played against. "He was bound and determined you weren't going to get a touchdown on him, and he pretty well carried that out."

LeBeau was a part of the Ohio State University championship squad of 1957, where he was utilized as a running back who, over twenty-eight games, ran for just 526 yards, averaging a rather uninspiring 3.8 yards per rush.

Scouts must not have been overly impressed with LeBeau, as he wasn't drafted in 1959 until the fifth round (number fifty-eight over-all)—of course, back then, as difficult as it is now to conceive, there were thirty rounds in the draft and 360 players were drafted in all. The Cleveland Browns gave him a look, but they cut him during rookie training camp prior to the start of the regular season.

Detroit picked him up and he cracked their starting lineup for the final six games of the 1959 season. One year later, he began a stretch of twelve consecutive seasons with at least three interceptions. He was still plying his trade well in 1970 when he arguably enjoyed his best NFL season. His nine interceptions led the NFC (Johnny Robinson of the AFC Chiefs had ten to top the overall NFL).

Among LeBeau's highlights are his sixty-two career interceptions, third-best ever when he retired and still number ten, his 762 yards on returns on interceptions (number thirty-five), and his being named to the Second Team of the Pro Football Reference's All-1960s team. He also set a record for cornerbacks by playing in 171 straight games.

Bill Malinchak said LeBeau, a former teammate of his who became a highly sought-after coach when his playing days ended, was "a very professional, organized football player that was dedicated to football. He studied the Civil War—I think a lot of coaches read books about different generals and how they attack. I don't know if that was Dick's motivation, but he was very interested in warfare. He was just totally football, always. He was always a coach on the field almost, and he turned out to be one of the great coaches in professional football."

Malinchak is correct. The first year after LeBeau retired as a player, the Philadelphia Eagles came knocking, asking him to be their special teams coach. He accepted the job and has never been out of the coaching ranks since then, always in demand and working for forty-four straight seasons, spending the 2015 and 2016 seasons with the Tennessee Titans.

In between, he also held such titles as head coach, assistant head coach, defensive coordinator, and defensive backs coach for the Packers, Bengals, Steelers, and the Bills. Counting his playing days, this football "lifer" has spent an unfathomable fifty-eight years in the NFL—that may not exactly put, say, George Halas to shame, but imagine what LeBeau's pension check must look like!

Moving on to the offensive line, one of the greatest players ever to toil there was Baltimore's Jim Parker, equally effective as a guard and tackle. In fact, he was the first man who played exclusively on the offensive line to make it to the Hall of Fame, and he was First-Team All-NFL as a guard or tackle in every season from his first, 1957, through 1965—every one of his seasons except his last two.

Lenny Moore said he owed a great deal of his success to Parker. "He was something else. I laid right dead on his hips when I was running because I didn't have to worry about somebody knocking the hell out of me because they had to go through Parker to get to me."

Berry, who was inducted into the Hall of Fame in the same class as Parker, recalled, "Parker and I played side-by-side for eleven seasons. He was one of the best offensive tackles that ever came into professional football. His ability to pass protect John Unitas's blind side was without comparison. He was such a force there on pass protection, and on run blocking, too. He was able to move people out of the way and create holes. Any coach would've been happy with just the way Parker protected and gave time to a guy like Unitas, but he did it all."

The quick, six-foot, three-inch, 273-pound Parker provided protection so often for Johnny U, he was aptly nicknamed "Unitas's Bodyguard." Everyone knew he protected his quarterback like a mother hen tending to her newborn chicks, but they also knew he did that with a dose or two of brutality thrown in as needed.

In fact, Parker was the kind of offensive lineman who, rather than absorb punishment (as offensive linemen who are often called upon to pass block often do), handed out the punishment. A Hall of Famer, the Ohio State alumnus Parker almost effortlessly took care of snarling defensive linemen. He also dealt with vicious opposing linebackers, men who just about glowed with excitement when anticipating a blitz so they could administer bruising tackles.

As effective as middle linebacker Ray Nitschke was, just as Superman had a kryptonite problem, Parker was Nitschke's nemesis, a lethal weapon who gave him fits. Moore tells the story of how Parker frustrated Nitschke. "I remember Ray well. I was out at the Pro Bowl and Vince Lombardi was the coach at the time. Ray came to me and said, 'Lenny, I had a bead on you as a middle linebacker once and I was going to knock the hell out of you. Every chance I had, I tried to get you to have fear, but that damn Jim Parker. Every time I thought I was going to knock the hell out of you, there was Jim Parker. He was pulling from the guard position, and he got to me before I got to you.'"

Moore said Nitschke continued to seek every opportunity he could to drill him in an effort to intimidate, to put Moore on the defensive. If he achieved that goal, Moore would have been concentrating more on the Packers' star defender than on doing his job carrying the football. Of course, Nitschke could never totally attain that goal because, aside from Parker, Moore, a tough Hall of Famer himself, would never let that happen.

The year Parker concluded his career, 1967, was the rookie season for a great guard, Larry Chatmon Little. This was a man who often led Miami runners on sweeps as a vital part of the Dolphins' run of three straight Super Bowl appearances. Miami would not only win two of those Super Bowls, they would ring up their unmatched undefeated, championship season in 1972 when they went 17-0.

Little is the only Hall of Fame player ever to come out of Bethune-Cookman, but the Miami front office wouldn't have cared if he had come from Jupiter. Actually, Little began his playing days with the Chargers as an obscure free agent—undrafted by all of the NFL teams. While he had been the team captain and an All-Conference player in college, his school, while producing many NFL players, was, as mentioned, far from being a funnel that led to Canton.

San Diego gave up on Little after two uneventful seasons—in his second season he started just twice for them. The Chargers swapped him to the Dolphins shortly before the start of the 1969 season. After starting ten of twelve Miami games that year he seldom sat on the bench again.

The right guard was a part of a unit that allowed Miami to run for two thousand or more yards yearly for an entire decade. Playing on that same illustrious line was Doug Crusan who said of Little, "When we got him from San Diego, boy, did he turn into a heckuva player, a pulling guard who was big. He was a character, an enjoyable guy. When you see him now, it's like you just saw him ten minutes ago."

It's not like the Miami runners, such as Larry Csonka, needed too much help up front, but having Little made things a lot easier for the ground game. Crusan said, "Coach Shula was big on weight and our linemen were all around 250 pounds, except Little [at 265]. He carried it well and had good speed."

During the unblemished 17-0 season, the Dolphins set a record (since broken) by rambling with the swift Mercury Morris and rumbling with Csonka (with Jim Kiick assisting) for 2,960 yards, all with Little usually in the middle of things.

Little used all of his tools to win honors such as being named the NFL Players Association AFC Lineman of the Year in 1970, 1971, and 1972. The latter two years the Dolphins ended up playing in the Super Bowl. Clearly, having him on the line was huge.

Gino Marchetti was once asked which offensive lineman was the toughest one for him to go against. He quickly selected the six-foot, four-inch, 249-pound Forrest Gregg, a star mainly with the Packers. Marchetti critiqued, "I came into the league I was kind of small, light, but he was probably the lightest guy I played in front of that gave me a helluva lot of trouble; but I gave him a little, too.

"I don't think he was the strongest guy I played against either, but my greatest asset was speed and quickness and those were his assets, and that made him hard to play against. He was tall, hard to see over, and tough—he had it all. When we went against each other it was pretty good competition."

Gregg realized he could get out-powered by burly defensive line-men, so he devised ways to beat his bigger, stronger foes. He studied them and found weaknesses in their game. Armed with such intelli-gence it was then simply a matter of execution on his part.

Some experts go so far as to label Gregg the best pro offensive tackle of all time. It was no coincidence that he played for winners so often—he was what helped his teams win on so many occasions. He was a member of three Super Bowl winning teams, one with Dallas, and, overall, owns six NFL championship rings over a fifteen-year career. Over that span, the former SMU teammate of Raymond Berry was a First-Team All-Pro seven times.

Plus, he never called it in or took a day off. He set a record, since broken, that even an ironman like major league baseball's Cal Ripken Jr. would admire—Gregg played in the trenches for 188 consecutive contests stretching from 1956 until his final season (1971) spent with the champion Cowboys under Tom Landry.

Going from being coached in Green Bay by Vince Lombardi, who once called Gregg the finest player that he ever coached, to Tom Land-ry, another legend, also helped Gregg's post-playing career. He soaked up a great deal of football wisdom and strategy from the two Hall of Fame coaches.

It was only logical, then, that the highly intelligent Gregg became a head coach. Four years after his final day as a player, he was hired by the Cleveland Browns, but the team lacked the talent to go very far. Two seasons went by before Cincinnati hired him as their head coach and he guided the Bengals to their first Super Bowl in just his second year on the job. That season, 1981, he also won Coach of the Year honors. He wound up his coaching days back with his original team, leading the Packers for four seasons from 1984 through 1987.

Too often NFL centers don't get a whole lot of recognition, but Viking kicker Fred Cox said Mick Tingelhoff was deserving of lavish praise,

"He snapped every snap for every kick that I ever made. He was like Jim Marshall—Mick played seventeen years without missing a game."

Actually, with Marshall and Tingelhoff they not only didn't miss a game, they established streaks of consecutive *starts* that were admirable. They were football's answer to Cal Ripken Jr. and Lou Gehrig. Marshall started 270 consecutive games, 289 counting playoff games, and Mick Tingelhoff was in the lineup from the opening whistle in 240 straight games, 259 with postseason games added in.

Those streaks still are the second and third longest ever—only Brett Favre, a quarterback, ever rang up a longer stretch of starts. Tingelhoff added another staggering accomplishment to his durability streak—he didn't even miss a single *practice* over his seventeen-season career.

Cox went on, "Mick was so good at snapping that when we went out to warm up, he would snap a few balls to Paul Krause, and Krause would tell him where the strings were. Mick would then move the ball before he snapped it, and then snapped it so at least 98 percent of the time when Krause caught the ball the strings were forward. It was just uncanny how good he was. Today when I think about the guys they have who snap for punts and guys who snap for extra points and field goals, I think of Mick who did all of that and was phenomenal at it."

Tingelhoff and Krause were so good, other kickers would comment on how fortunate Cox was to have such a kicking crew. "It's kind of a closed [fraternity]," concluded Cox, "and you get to know most of the guys [other kickers] and you talk to them. It doesn't take them long to know who's got the great holders and who's got great centers."

Speaking of Krause, he was much more than simply a great holder on kicks. Playing into the 1970s, and just one season short of playing in a third decade, he established a record for career interceptions with eighty-one, a total that, remarkably, still stands as the NFL benchmark. That feat, accomplished over 226 games, was foreshadowed by the output of his rookie season (1964) when he picked off a dozen passes to top the NFL.

Cox continued his praise for Krause, who held for Cox on kicks for ten years, calling him "the best holder that ever played the game. He had the greatest hands. He was a phenomenal basketball player when he was in college [at Iowa]. He was an offensive receiver [and runner in college] who could have played receiver in the NFL.

"That's what made him such a great defensive back—for a guy to intercept eighty-one passes, that's unheard of. But he did it because he played like a basketball player. When they would throw a pass down the field, Paul always caught the ball at the very height of his jump." And he did it often enough to be inducted into the Hall of Fame just five years after he retired, a true no brainer decision for those who cast ballots.

3

FUNNIEST QUOTES AND TALES

Players of the Glory Years were tough, but even they had their light moments; and many of the men from the era were, either by nature or by accident, very funny men. The obvious comedians are players like Alex Karras, Art Donovan, and Don Meredith, but there were many others who made the time period one of wit, satire, and hilarity.[1]

Don Meredith enjoyed a fine career as the quarterback at Southern Methodist University. He had been recruited by a slew of colleges, coming out of Mount Vernon High School in Texas, but finally decided to attend SMU. He explained his decision to attend that university, tongue in cheek, by saying, "It was close to home and easy to spell." Meredith wound up playing his entire high school, college, and pro career based in his home state.

Meredith went on to star in the NFL with the Dallas Cowboys, and he still holds the franchise record for the longest touchdown pass ever, a ninety-five-yarder to the man once billed as the fastest human being alive, Bob Hayes. However, it was Dandy Don's *Monday Night Football* gig that gave him a stage on which to display his sharp wit and earned him enduring fame.

During the program's first-ever broadcast back in 1970, he provided the color commentary for the New York Jets versus the Cleveland Browns clash. After Fair Hooker, a Cleveland receiver snagged a pass, Meredith commented, "Isn't Fair Hooker a great name?" Then, pushing the envelope, he added, "I haven't met one yet."[2]

Meredith's mind truly did work quickly and in a most uninhibited manner. One sportswriter said proof of Meredith's nimble ways came when a wide receiver who had just come back to play after suffering from a bout with the flu ran a long pass route. Apparently he was not fully recovered from his illness and, right there on live television, he threw up. Meredith deadpanned, "Now there's something you don't see on TV every day."

Another time he opened a telecast of a game from Denver by saying, "Welcome to the Mile High City—and I really am."[3]

Perhaps his best impromptu bit occurred during an Oakland Raiders blowout of the Houston Oilers from the Astrodome in which the camera panned the audience, searching for a crowd shot of interest. They got more than they expected, though, when a bored spectator they had focused on, suddenly realizing that he was on television, shot his middle finger at the camera. Just prior to that angry display, commentator Howard Cosell had been pontificating about how the fan's appearance portrayed how tiresome the game itself was. However, when he noticed the obscene gesture, Cosell, unaccustomedly, was at a loss for words.

Meredith, though, unfazed by the awkward moment, commented, "I guess we'll have some more shots of the crowd for you in a little while, folks." Later he reportedly (there are many versions of his exact quote) added a spin on what the fan's intentions had been. "Howard, he just wants to let us know he thinks we're Number One."

The Pittsburgh Steelers enjoyed success with a pair of fine running backs who complemented each other: Rocky Bleier and Franco Harris.

A reporter once asked Bleier, who happened to be bald, if he could somehow possess several ideal attributes, what would he come up with to change himself. He mulled it over and decided he'd like to have "the body of Jim Brown, the moves of Gale Sayers, the strength of Earl Campbell, and the acceleration of O. J. Simpson." Then, wrapping up the wish list, he tossed in, "And just once I would like to run and feel the wind in my hair."[4]

Many fans know Steve Spurrier for his college coaching exploits, but he was an NFL quarterback for ten seasons. Once he was telling fans of his Florida Seminoles team about a fire at Auburn's football dormitory, one that had destroyed twenty books. "But the real tragedy," he quipped, "was that fifteen hadn't been colored yet."

When John Brodie was a star quarterback for the San Francisco 49ers, he was used as the holder on extra point and field goal attempts. When asked by a reporter why such a highly paid, valuable quarterback had to hold the football on kicks, Brodie deadpanned, "Well, if I didn't, it would fall over."

Dallas Cowboys guard Blaine Nye came up with a good line that holds true in the NFL as well as in, say, the world of business, politics, or the military. "It's not whether you win or lose," he commented, "but who gets the blame." Another time he spoke of the anonymity of those who toil on the line of scrimmage, "Offensive linemen are like salt. Nobody ever remembers the brand they buy."

When the Green Bay Packers took on the Dallas Cowboys on New Year's Eve in 1967 in Lambeau Field for the right to move on to the Super Bowl, the weather conditions were absolutely horrid. At one point during the game the windchill factor registered an unfathomable minus forty-eight degrees.

The year before, in their defeat of the Cowboys in Dallas, Green Bay had five different players score a touchdown to win the conference title and advance to Super Bowl I. At game time that day, the thermometer read forty degrees.

Legendary Packer coach Vince Lombardi actually hoped for a bit of bad weather in Green Bay for the 1967 title game because he believed his team was better acclimated to inclement weather conditions than the Cowboys of Texas clime.

He got what he wanted and more. One Packer, defensive tackle Henry Jordan, commented, "I figure Lombardi got on his knees to pray for bad weather," he grinned before adding, "and stayed down too long."[5]

Split end Max McGee was one of Lombardi's key weapons from 1954 through 1967. The fifth-round draft pick led the NFL in yards gained per reception in 1959 at 23.2, but came up even bigger for his coach in the very first Super Bowl, a 35–10 drubbing of the Kansas City Chiefs.

In that contest McGee snared seven passes for 138 yards, more than half of the yards Bart Starr would throw for in all, and two of the Packers' five TDs. Subbing for the injured Boyd Dowler, McGee's seven receptions were three more than he had recorded during the entire regular season.

Lombardi, however, played no favorites. As a strong disciplinarian, he felt free to dish out stiff fines and hit McGee with a then-stinging fine of $250 for breaking curfew. The next time he caught McGee breaking his curfew rule, he upped it to $500 and admonished him, "And the next time it'll be $1,000. And if you find anything worth $1,000, let me know and I may go with you."[6]

Strict, but clearly able to flash his sense of humor at times, Lombardi responded to being named the Italian of the Year by asking, "Where does that leave Pope John?"[7]

When Mike Ditka became a coach in the NFL, he had more than one run-in with the press. He felt the members of the media that he had to deal with had little understanding of the game, and he resented their attitude at times. He once joked, "What's the difference between a three-week-old puppy and a sportswriter?" He promptly answered his own question, "In six weeks, the puppy stops whining."

Joe Namath could toss around one-liners as well as he could the old pigskin. He used one classic line for his autobiography, *I Can't Wait until Tomorrow . . . 'Cause I Get Better Looking Every Day.*

Once a writer teased Namath by asking him if his major at Alabama was basket weaving. Namath's retort was, "Naw, man, journalism—it was easier."

Living up to his playboy reputation, Namath stated, "If a doctor told me I had to give up women, I'm sure I'd give up doctors."

Jim Brown, as mentioned earlier, led his league in rushing every season he played except one. He may, in fact, be the greatest running back in NFL history. He hung up his #32 jersey for the final time after the 1965 season, still at the peak of his game, coming off a season in which he riddled opposing defenses for 1,544 yards. Brown appeared in the movie *The Dirty Dozen* with veteran actor Lee Marvin. When Marvin was asked to comment on Brown's theatrical skills, he said that Brown was "a better actor than Olivier would have been a fullback."[8]

Art Donovan came from an interesting background. His grandfather had been a middleweight boxing champ, and his father was a boxing referee who officiated fourteen heavyweight title fights and twenty Joe Louis bouts, including both of his fights against Max Schmeling.

Donovan is said to be the first true defensive lineman to make it to the Hall of Fame, and that happened despite having his pro football career curtailed until he was twenty-six years old because he had enlisted in the US Marines. A veteran of action in the South Pacific, he was also the first pro football player to be inducted into the Marine Corps Sports Hall of Fame.

In a way, after the service, he led two lives: one as a superlative defensive lineman and another as a television celebrity in the same vein as baseball's Bob Uecker. Donovan became a popular guest on television shows such as Johnny Carson's *The Tonight Show*. He became famous for his sense of humor, which was often aimed directly at himself.

Some say he weighed as much as 310 pounds, but he wasn't too concerned about it. He claimed that in his thirteen years of football training camps he did a total of thirteen push-ups. For most of his career his helmet had no face mask, and once star quarterback Norm Van Brocklin, in retaliation, fired a pass right into Donovan's face. Donovan later quipped, "I couldn't believe he'd just wasted a play like that. I guess he was mad. You have to respect a guy like that."[9]

He often joked about his weight, and once even stated that he was a light eater. He quickly added, "As soon as it's light, I start to eat."

Sam Havrilak recalled NFL meetings being held in Baltimore. "We ate dinner during the meetings and Art, being a prodigious eater, would order three *triple* hamburgers, three on one bun. He would eat two and have the waitress wrap the other one up in tin foil and he would leave. Jim Mutscheller told me, 'He'll go home, jump in bed, watch TV, and put the hamburger on top of the television to keep the hamburger warm. He'll turn the sound down and face it to the wall so it wouldn't keep him awake, and when he woke up in the morning he'd eat it.'"

Johnny Lujack had an unusual career. A bona fide star at Notre Dame, where he won the Heisman Trophy in 1947, his pro career was, sadly, all too short and, for many fans, therefore quite forgettable (or unknown). That is, except, by and large, for several sterling accomplishments.

For example, one season he led the NFL in pass completions and attempts; yards thrown (2,658); touchdowns through the air (twenty-three); and yards gained per completion, per attempt, and per game played (221.5). In addition, Lujack once launched six touchdown passes in a single game and ran for another that day in a total, 52–21, annihilation of the old Chicago Cardinals by Lujack's Chicago Bears. In that game, due to his passing, running, and kicking extra points, he was responsible for forty-three points—only a George Blanda field goal and a two-yard plunge by George Gulyanics put up other points on the scoreboard for the Bears. On the afternoon, he established a new NFL record with his 468 yards through the air, a record which stood until Norm Van Brocklin broke it in 1951.

Lujack also earned First-Team All-Pro honors in 1950, when he led the NFL with eleven rushing touchdowns, then a record for a quarterback. But he was through after the 1951 season, playing only four seasons in all and in just forty-five games, including some in which his main functions were kicking and/or playing defensive back (in his rookie season he picked off eight passes to set a franchise record). After retiring in 1952, he spent two seasons as a backfield coach for the Fighting Irish.

At any rate, during his quarterback days with Notre Dame, he had one dreary day in which he threw three interceptions to Army defender Arnold Tucker. Asked by Irish head coach Frank Leahy why he had thrown those passes to Tucker, Lujack responded, "Coach, he was the only man open."[10]

Paul Hornung was another Notre Dame standout. Like Lujack, Hornung played under Frank Leahy. On one occasion Leahy caught his star runner smoking. Just as Leahy spotted Hornung, he was crushing a cigarette into the floor with his foot. Leahy reportedly said, "Do you see what I see near your shoe, Paul?" Hornung came back quickly with, "Yeah, Coach, I see it, but you take it. You saw it first."[11]

Norm Van Brocklin was not only a Hall of Fame quarterback for the Los Angeles Rams and the Philadelphia Eagles, lasting in the NFL from 1949 to 1960, but "The Dutchman" also coached in the league from 1961 through 1974.

As a player, he accounted for 173 career touchdown passes, threw for 23,611 yards, and completed 53.66 percent of his passes. His record as a starting quarterback was 61-36-4 (back when games sometimes ended in a tie). He led the NFL in various categories numerous times, including several punting departments such as his booming seventy-two-yard punt in 1956. Van Brocklin made it to the postseason from 1949 to 1952 and again in 1960 when he was voted the league's MVP and Player of the Year. In fact, in 1951 his Rams won the NFL championship and, after being traded to the Eagles, he led them to the title in 1960.

Playing days over, he handled the head coaching duties for the Minnesota Vikings from their first year of existence, 1961, then became the head man for the Atlanta Falcons in 1968. One of the big changes he saw take place in the game over his long involvement in the NFL occurred with the huge influx of foreign players who were skilled at soccer-style placekicking.

Chuck Mercein was with the Giants in 1966 when Hungarian-born Pete Gogolak joined the team after spending two years with Buffalo. "He revolutionized the game because you get a level of power out of your hip, your glutes, your body by kicking [his way]. Forward, you're just really kicking with your quadriceps."

Many of the soccer-style specialists were long-distance booters, men such as Garo Yepremian, who once celebrated a field goal by exclaiming, "I kick a touchdown!" Now, the accurate soccer kickers consistently give their teams booming but boring three-pointers. Meanwhile, spectators yearned for more excitement, clamoring for more touchdowns on sparkling runs and breathtaking bombs.

Van Brocklin was asked for his thoughts on how the NFL could cope with the problem of so many field goals being kicked. His solution? "Tighten the immigration laws."

Jim Finks had a long distinguished career at various levels of the game. He played for the Pittsburgh Steelers from 1949 through 1955, coached Notre Dame one season, and served in an administrative capacity for several NFL teams, earning Ring of Honor distinction for his work with Minnesota. For example, his work there as the Vikings' general manager produced the team's first NFL Central Division title, which triggered a long run of success. The Vikings would win their division championship eleven times over the next fourteen seasons and make it to the Super Bowl on four occasions.

Finks was the man who was mainly responsible for putting together the Purple People Eaters defense, which featured Jim Marshall, Carl Eller, Alan Page, and Gary Larsen. That formidable front four is still the only quartet of defensive linemen to go to the Pro Bowl together, with all of them being selected to the squad in 1969. Half of them are also Hall of Famers, Eller and Page.

Finks clearly had a lot on the ball. Once he even slyly managed to criticize the refereeing crew after a game in which he felt they had cost his team a win. When asked what he had thought of the officials that day, he avoided a fine for criticism by saying, "I'm not allowed to comment on lousy officiating."

Alex Karras became a celebrity in television and movies after he ended his pro football career. He was quick with the quip, and his sense of humor helped lead him to his acting career. He almost stole the show in his role as the immensely strong but not too bright cowboy in the movie *Blazing Saddles*, and he later had his own sitcom, *Webster*.

When it came to keeping his team loose, former Lion Bill Malinchak said, "Nothing could beat Alex Karras. I played with him for almost five years and he was the most entertaining football player ever. I mean, when we were at training camp I remember we would be waiting for the coaches on benches right outside the dressing room. Alex would hold court. He'd mimic the coaches and everything the guys could relate to. It wasn't surprising to us that he went on to a great career in television and movies because he was a talented, talented guy."

Of course, in real life he was far from stupid, but that didn't stop him from joking, "I never graduated college, but I was only there for two terms—Truman's and Eisenhower's."[12]

Jim Marshall was great, but he suffered through one moment of ignominy. Once, in a 1964 contest, after he had scooped up a fumble by San Francisco's Billy Kilmer, Marshall got disoriented and rumbled sixty-six yards—in the wrong direction! He had run into his own end zone. Later, he was asked what he was thinking during his run back. "I saw my teammates running down the sidelines. I thought they were cheering for me." One San Francisco player who *was* cheering for him—a safety who had pursued Marshall down the field—came over to him and patted him on the back as a sort of, "Congratulations, and thanks for the score."

A Viking teammate, kicker Fred Cox, said his reaction to Marshall's running the wrong way was simple. Cox deadpanned, " I was thinking, 'Jim, you're running the wrong way.' The greatest part of that whole situation was he was running the wrong way and he was so fast our defensive backs were chasing him and couldn't catch him, and Fran Tarkenton is off the field running as hard as he can down the sidelines yelling at him, 'You're going the wrong way.' It was a comedy act.

"The only positive thing I can say is we were playing San Francisco and we ended up beating them. The two-point safety didn't enter into the game's outcome, but it provided a moment of levity never to be forgotten—and the play *could have* been a deciding one.

"The only reason it was two points was he was so excited when he got into the end zone, he threw the ball out of the end zone. If he had just dropped it on the ground they would have fallen on it for a touchdown. It was just a crazy event."

New York Jets quarterback Joe Namath was doing an interview once with the egotistical Howard Cosell. The abrasive journalist asked "Broadway Joe" how many great sportscasters he felt there were. Namath smiled and replied, "One less than you think, Howard."

Tom Landry was a coaching legend, leading his Dallas Cowboys from their first year of existence, 1960, all the way through the 1988 season, racking up 250 wins. His winning percentage was .605 even though his early teams were weak expansion-quality clubs that dragged his percentage way down.

One of Landry's most dependable running backs was fullback Walt Garrison. No doubt part of the reason he was so tough was the fact that he had been a rodeo rider since he reached the age of twelve. This is one Dallas player who truly was a cowboy—in fact, the title he chose for his autobiography was *Once a Cowboy*. Plus, his contract with Dallas once included a signing bonus of a new horse trailer, not cash. Garrison wound up playing for Landry from 1966 through 1974, and never played for any other NFL team or coach. He played in both Super Bowl V, a 16–13 loss to the Baltimore Colts, and Super Bowl VI, an easy, 24–3 win over the Miami Dolphins.

After his career with the Cowboys was over, Garrison was asked if he had ever seen Landry smile. He grinned and replied, "I don't know. I only played there for nine years."

Garrison was the type of runner the following quote (attributed to many, and used to describe many runners), fits perfectly. "With Walt, if you need a yard, he'll get you a yard. If you need five yards, he'll get you a yard." Meredith put it a bit differently, and somewhat more positively. "If it was third down and ya' needed four yards, if you'd get the ball to Walt Garrison, he'd get ya five. And if it was third down and ya needed twenty yards, if you'd get the ball to Walt Garrison, by God, he'd get you five." [13]

Garrison's brand of humor was sometimes self-deprecating. Long after he had become a pro, he ran into Texas Longhorns coach Darrell Royal and asked him why he hadn't recruited him. After all, Garrison was a Texas-born player, and he played his high school football in Lewisville, just a bit over two hundred miles from the University of Texas campus. Garrison reported that Royal's reply was, "Well, Walt, we took a look at you and you weren't any good." [14]

E. J. Holub played back in the day when people speaking to the media weren't as politically correct as they are nowadays. Holub, a Kansas City linebacker, broke into the AFL in 1961 with the old Dallas Texans and went to the Pro Bowl five times over his ten-year career. However, playing pro football came at a high cost. Lamenting the fact that his chosen profession had caused his knees to get torn up and operated on, he said, "My knees look like I lost a knife fight with a midget."

Pete Gent played for the Dallas Cowboys in the 1960s and was a teammate of Don Meredith. In one game Ross Fichtner of the Browns intercepted three Meredith passes. The following week Meredith tossed four touchdowns to several Cowboys. Gent approached Meredith after that game and said, "Don, you sure as hell made a terrific adjustment this week, not having Fichtner to throw to. It really surprises the hell out of me how you get your timing down, working with different receivers every week."[15]

Dan Pastorini could also be wild with his passes. Once he put on a demonstration of his passing in front of the media by standing in the parking lot outside of his hotel in Baltimore. He heaved a football up to a balcony perched on the sixth floor. Later, reporters told John Unitas of the display and he quipped, "Yeah, but his receivers were on the second floor."[16]

Slinging Sammy Baugh whose great career stretched into the 1950s, had a great quote about the 1940 championship game between his Redskins and the Bears. The game ended up in a monumentally lopsided shutout with Chicago winning 73–0.

The Redskins nearly tied the game early on at 7–7, but a pass to Washington end Charley Malone that seemed to be on target for a score was not caught. Asked if things might have been different if Washington had scored, Baugh replied, "Hell, yes, the score would have been 73–6."[17]

When Oakland's Fred Biletnikoff was presented with the MVP trophy for his play in Super Bowl XI, he took observers off guard when he said, "A stick of gum would have been enough."[18]

Jack Kemp (1957–1969 in the pros) was a seven-time Pro-Bowler who made First-Team All-Pro twice, starring primarily for the Buffalo Bills. Both on the field and off, he was a winner.

As a starting quarterback he won sixty-five games, lost just thirty-seven times, and played in three ties. Kemp saw postseason action with his Buffalo team in three of the first four seasons he was with them, and his Bills won the championship of the old AFL in 1964 and again the following season. Earlier he had made it to the AFL playoffs in 1960 and 1961 when he was with the Chargers—they were located in Los Angeles in 1960, then became the San Diego Chargers the following season.

After he retired as a player, he went on to enjoy a career in the world of politics as a New York congressman. He felt that his days in the NFL helped him later on. "Pro football gave me a good sense of perspective to enter politics. I'd already been booed, cheered, cut, sold, traded, and hung in effigy."[19]

Joe Don Looney, whose father, Don, once led the NFL in receptions and yards via catches, was a halfback for five seasons, spending time with, get this, five different teams. He was also, in the words of television's Deputy Barney Fife, "A nut." The fact that he played for five teams and only lasted forty-two games in the NFL partially tells his tale. He had talent—at Oklahoma he led his team in rushing with 852 yards in 1962, helping take the Sooners to the Orange Bowl—but his prowess didn't translate well in the pros.

For one thing, he had an utter disregard for authority figures. He said he refused to toss his used socks into a locker room bin put there for that purpose because he resented being told what to do, even if it was a sign that was doing the telling. That applied to his coaches, too. He frequently refused to show up for practices. He is also said to have once run in one direction, his own, rather than in the direction the play had called for. He explained his "logic" by saying, "Anybody can run where the blockers are. A good football player makes his own holes."[20] In college he punched a student assistant coach.

Bill Malinchak was a close friend of Looney when they were teammates with the Lions for part of the 1966 season. "He was an All-American out of Oklahoma. He was a gifted athlete. He had size. He had speed. He had good running skills, but Joe Don was one of those guys who was dancing to a different drummer.

"I remember one incident where we were playing Atlanta, and Joe Don was alternating at running back. He had a really good first half [twenty-eight yards and a TD on four carries] and they took him out, alternating him. He was getting upset. We were sitting on the bench, and he said, 'I figured it out.' I said, 'What'd you figure out, Joe Don?' And he said, 'I'm going to punch Harry Gilmer.' Harry was our head coach. I said, 'What!?' He said something like, 'He's messing with me.' He was having a great first half and they were pulling him out, so he didn't understand it. He was so upset. I said, 'Please. That's not going to solve anything.'

"So we went in at halftime and he didn't do anything that drastic, but he did quit at halftime—he didn't come out for the second half. We traded him, but that was Joe Don's personality. He was different."

The New York Giants had drafted him in the first round as the twelfth overall pick in 1964, but they had seen enough of him before he had time to lace up for an actual game to decide to trade him, doing so after just twenty-five days. Baltimore kept him just one year and Detroit had him for 1965 and three games into the 1966 season when Washington acquired him. He played for the Redskins one full year, didn't play at all in 1968 due to serving in Vietnam, and ended his NFL days with a meager offensive output in three games for New Orleans. Over those contests he ran the ball three times for negative 5 yards. He ran for 724 yards over his entire career, less than what he had chalked up in one year at Oklahoma.

He had actually begun his college career at the University of Texas where he reportedly had four F's and a D in his classes. He dropped out, transferred to Texas Christian University, where he later was kicked out of school. Finally, he found success at Oklahoma where, in 1962, he was an All-American halfback. The next year, however, head coach Bud Wilkinson kicked him off the team after he punched a coach.

Most of his fame came from his flaky and wild ways. There's a story about the time his Lions coach wanted to have Looney shuttle plays in to the quarterback. Looney refused to do the chore and shot back, "If you want a messenger, call Western Union." The trade to the Redskins ensued shortly thereafter.

Steve Sabol, who ran NFL Films, believed Looney was the most uncoachable player in the history of the league, and reported he often ran the wrong way in practices on purpose. At best he'd go through the motions. Clearly not fond of practicing, Looney once muttered, "If practice makes perfect and perfection is impossible, why practice?"

His coach for the Colts, Don Shula, was reluctant to use Looney's punting skills. In fact, Shula went so far as to say, "I was afraid to put Looney in the game to punt because I didn't know if he would punt. He might do anything."[21]

After Looney's days on the gridiron, he became interested in things such as mysticism. He even went to India to study meditation under a Swami. Later he finally settled down in Alpine, Texas, in a solar-heated home that had no electricity or telephone. The eccentric Looney died in 1988 at the age of forty-five when his motorcycle didn't handle a curve on a Texas highway and he crashed. An opposing player once said of Looney, "Never was a man more aptly named."

Perhaps the closest anyone came to the antics of Looney was Tim Rossovich, a first-round draft pick by the Philadelphia Eagles (fourteenth overall pick) in 1968. He played in just two years of the 1950s–1960s golden age, but he made his mark on the league and lasted through the 1976 season. He even made it to the 1969 Pro Bowl. However, the six-foot-four, 240-pound defensive end and middle linebacker out of the University of Southern California (where he roomed with future actor Tom Selleck), was a bit of a wild man—some said a hippie in search of a padded cell. To borrow a line from Alex Karras to describe Otis Sistrunk, Rossovich also must have come to the NFL by way of the University of Mars.

Actually, that may be understating things. Rossovich was good friends with Steve Sabol, who shared a story about the time he was hosting a party and he heard a knock at his door. Opening it, he saw Rossovich standing there with his clothes on fire. Rossovich was unruffled, but Sabol and a friend placed him on the floor and put out the fire. At that point, Rossovich calmly stood up and said, "Sorry, I must have the wrong apartment," and walked away. Another routine day in the life of Tim Rossovich. He would light himself on fire again and again, on purpose, of course. Once he set his hair, teased into an Afro, on fire for a photo shoot for *Sports Illustrated.*[22]

Sam Havrilak remembered the time his Colts faced Rossovich. "He was the middle linebacker and I was going across the field, caught a pass, and he tackled me but wouldn't let me up. He was holding my head down to the ground and yelling at the same time."

His odd eating habits also drew attention. He was known to eat pages of his playbook, cigarettes, insects, and even glass—and would often open his beer bottle by biting off its top. One time, borrowing a stunt from baseball's Casey Stengel, right after Rossovich got the attention of his friends, he opened his mouth as if to speak, and a bird flew out.

What did such crazy antics lead to after his football days were through? An acting career. Hollywood or Bust. After all, he seemed to crave attention—once, not too long after being in a coma, he banged his head on his locker over and over again to prove to his coach that he had recovered. What was he thinking? Perhaps a Johnnie Cochran-like, "If my head doesn't split, you must acquit."

4

THE TOUGHEST PLAYERS

When asked if the players of his era were tougher than those of later eras, Lenny Moore's answer was unequivocal, "Oh, without question. They'd knock the hell out of you. They could hit you any way, and their whole thing was to hit you hard enough to take it out of you so that you couldn't be who you were supposed to really be.

"And we would look at every team and watch every situation, and we would say, 'Hey, that's who we're going after'—take the steam out of him by knocking the hell out of him. If he's on the kickoff team, we're going to have somebody take a shot at him. That's the way it was, all the way through."

Some of the hard hits were cheap shots, and there certainly were some dirty players around. Johnny Sample even titled his autobiography *Confessions of a Dirty Ballplayer.* However, George Belu said that there have always been a few players who, say, at the bottom of a pile of players do something dirty, "but as a whole it was, and still is good, hard-nosed, legal football. There were a few guys who were real 'jaws,' guys who kept talking all the time through the whole game, but I don't think the game has ever been nasty or dirty.

"I think it has always been played really, really hard. There were a few corners in the NFL who were really physical, but they were not dirty—they played with intimidation. If you caught the ball, they were going to go ahead and smack you pretty good.

"But when guys like Butkus tackled you, they tackled viciously. They wanted to tackle you, not to maim or hurt you, but to let you know,

'Hey, I'm over here, and you're going to have to deal with me the whole game.' They try to soften you up by hitting you hard, but it wasn't a dirty game."

In theory a pro should be impervious to intimidation, but in reality, a hit from a Butkus could, in fact, make some players become cautious, even fearful.

Some players, not all. Moore said he was blessed that he could not be intimidated and it was simply because, "You were in a game where you were going to get hit, be knocked down, be jumped on."

It was quite common for opponents to taunt, even worse, try to intimidate, but Moore was immune to it all. "In a game where you know you're going to be intimidated by what they say, you make sure that you close your mind and not listen to some of the things that they say over the line or whatever. If you let that get to you, that would take from you."

It can certainly be argued that things were quite rough during the golden age of the NFL, if for no other reason than because of today's rules versus rules that existed earlier. A lot of new rules came into being in an effort to protect players from injury. More aware of health issues such as concussions, the NFL cooked up rules like those legislating against leading with the helmet, which make football in the twenty-first century less violent—at least in theory.

Even as far back as the days of Pittsburgh's prototypical rough-and-tumble linebacker Jack Lambert (1974–1984), there were players who argued that new rules designed to protect players from injury, especially the highly paid, highly skilled quarterback position, were, in fact, making the pro game soft, much softer than conditions of the 1950s and 1960s. In 1978, Lambert clobbered Cleveland quarterback Brian Sipe and was penalized for hitting him late. Lambert, disagreeing with the call and what he felt was a much too liberal rule protecting passers, famously stated that quarterbacks should wear (or start wearing) dresses. Advocates of the manly style of play in the good old days feel that nowadays the game has deteriorated to the point where laying a player out with a clean, but explosive hit is taboo.

Myron Pottios said, "Well, the game *is* softer to protect the quarterback, but you can't get them hurt because, number one, you're paying them big money, and, number two, people want to see points on the board, they want to see that long pass. They don't want to see 3–0 or

6–3 games. That's why all the changes in the defense came about—so the offense can score more."

He said the league does that because, over the years, the defense catches up with the offense. "They find a way so they slap them down, saying, 'We can't have this because you're taking away from the fans.'"

In the 1950s and 1960s, nobody figuratively donned a dress, not even the quarterbacks—John Unitas, for one, is featured in this chapter. However, any discussion of toughness begins with one position. Former St. Louis Cardinal Chuck Bryant put it tersely, "Linebackers were the toughest guys on the football field. They had to be tough. The rules have changed, but when you used to run across the middle in the old days, they didn't have that five-yard rule. Those linebackers used to knock you on your butt all the time. Those guys were nasty, mean inside."

Gino Marchetti also put it concisely, "Middle linebackers? You almost have to be nuts to play that position. They were tough—you couldn't get them out of the game with a little tweak. They'd just come back at you."

He added that his Baltimore coach, Weeb Ewbank, "used to say, 'The most dangerous person on the field is the linebacker.' He'd point out during his meetings that linebackers were the enemy of our offense more so than anyone else. I think most coaches would agree."

Sam Havrilak commented, "If you look back in the forties through the sixties, there were a lot more players who, I won't say they tried to put people out of the game, but there were a lot more hits [they made] that were legal then that are not now.

"I'll give you an example. Bill Pellington, who was a Colt linebacker, broke his arm and he was allowed to play with it—he put it under a foam arm pad, but with kind of a metal plate in there. And he would use that to club players during the game.

"Players got away with a lot more things because the referees let them do it back in those days, and that's the way it was. That was the tone of the NFL. It wasn't as refined a league as it is now. It was a little more gritty, let's say."

Havrilak phrased it another interesting way, "Let's just say there were players who tried to get away with things that weren't exactly in the rule book."

Ten-year NFL veteran Bill Malinchak fully agrees with Havrilak, his former childhood neighbor and high school teammate. "The thing that comes to mind—certainly being a wide receiver—you would come in contact with the linebackers. When I played, there was a group of them that were outstanding players like Ray Nitschke, Butkus, and Tommy Nobis of Atlanta.

"You couldn't run across the middle without getting clotheslined—that was their territory. They would give you a wake-up call. Nobis got me. I had to look back for a pass, and if you do that, and not pay attention to that middle linebacker, you were going to get clotheslined. The middle linebackers back then would dominate teams. Tough guys, real tough guys. Guys who had a great 'motor' like Butkus. He gave it everything he had from the time the ball was snapped until the end of the play. The guy never stopped. There are certain guys who have it programmed—somehow they never take off a down, never. Never rest."

Any discussion of toughness should begin with Bears middle linebacker Richard Marvin Butkus. In a blue chip era of linebackers, he was a solid gold commodity. Born in the City with Broad Shoulders, he was pure Chicago through and through. He was also ursine in many ways, from his massive paws to an enormous torso to a head that seemed positively squished into his helmet. Likewise, on his twelve career kickoff returns and twenty-two interception returns he often lumbered like a mad bear determined to scratch out extra yardage.

The youngest of nine children, he fought and toiled for everything he got. To paraphrase a line from a poet, Carl Sandburg, who is closely associated with Chicago, Butkus was the type of player who rolled up his sleeves, spit on his hands, and got to work. He played the game like a sadistic bounty hunter who excelled at bringing in, or *bringing down*, his target.

Back then linebackers typically went about 210 pounds. Butkus, who always stood out from the crowd, went six-feet-four and 245 pounds. He was a Pro Bowl player eight times, missing out just once, in his final season (1972). Like Jim Brown, the career of Butkus was relatively short. Still, one television show labeled him the most feared tackler ever.

In the book *ESPN Sports Century*, a section on Butkus stated that a survey of NFL quarterbacks picked him as "the second-most-feared defender in the league." Were the quarterbacks comatose not to pick him first? Well, no. The poll was conducted twenty-one years after Butkus had retired! The book also stated Butkus "challenged whole sidelines to fight,"[1] and during a meaningless exhibition contest he was slapped with four personal foul penalties. This was one mean, tough SOB.

Surprisingly fast, Butkus may have been a middle linebacker, but he covered the field, sideline to sideline with elan. His nose for the football helped him set a record for the most fumble recoveries in a career, twenty-seven. How many of those loose balls he caused in the first place is unknown. Jim Marshall topped the record with thirty recoveries, but he played in 163 more games than Butkus, well beyond double Butkus's 119 games.

In his final two-and-a-half seasons, his knees were so shot he couldn't even practice with his teammates. Doctors had advised him to call it quits, but, even though he continued to answer the bell under such a handicap, he still earned Pro Bowl honors twice.

Although he didn't need confirmation of his greatness, the NFL stamped their imprimatur on him when he was named to the Hall of Fame All-Decade team for the 1960s *and* the 1970s even though he played only fifty-one games in the '70s. He also made the 75th Anniversary All-Time Team in 1994, and, of course, he was inducted into the Pro Football Hall of Fame. In 1969, his Bears reeked at 1-13, yet one poll named him their Defensive Player of the Year. Butkus personifies his position so much, an award, bearing his name, is now presented annually to the nation's best college linebacker.

Still, honors aside, the best testimonials come from his peers. Havrilak was playing the Bears in just his second NFL season. Chicago took a 17–0 lead in the opening quarter, and still led, 20–14, in the fourth quarter before a Unitas to John Mackey scoring pass put the Colts on top. "We were running out the clock at the end of the game and I was a running back that year. Right at the end of the game Unitas called a play, 'Right 34' where the fullback is to lead me up into the '4' hole which is kind of between the right guard and right tackle. And Butkus, who was a maniac, had been scouting us, of course, and he was a little P-O'ed because they were losing. So he read the play and blitzed between the guard and tackle, beat the center, went right by the fullback, and, just as I got the ball in the backfield, he hit me and knocked me backwards, right on my back.

"Then he's laying there on me, with his face mask right against mine, and the saliva is running down his face. I didn't know what to say. All I could finally say was, 'Nice hit, Dick.' He didn't say anything." He didn't have to.

Everyone has a favorite Butkus tale. John Isenbarger prefaced his with a chuckle and some background. "I played on a lot of special teams, so I'd rush the punter and play end on a punt or kickoff return. I've got a picture of me rushing the punter against the Bears. I was going to make an effort to try to block the punt. Unfortunately, Butkus was the up back, and he blocked me. Butkus hits me. I'm elevated. Unfortunately, I thought I'd leave my feet and I'd get a better hit on him, right? Well, I was wrong. He even put me up in the air higher."

Then there's the film footage of the time a runner, who had built up some steam, was hurtling full speed through the line. A split second later, Butkus has him off the ground, the runner's legs still churning and flailing in mid-air, but going nowhere, looking like a rag doll being shaken by a German shepherd.

Chuck Mercein's Butkus story begins, "When I went to high school, I went to New Trier, a suburban school in Illinois. Dick went to Chicago Vocational School, or CVS. We graduated in 1961. When the *Chicago Tribune* printed the All-State football team, I found out that the two key players whose pictures were not just head shots, but full shots, were myself and Butkus. I was very impressed with his statistics. He was much bigger than me, like six three and 235, I think, in high school. He was not only a tremendous linebacker, but a fullback, too. So I met him the first time at the University of Illinois at Urbana-Champaign, where they had the All-State banquet. What a formidable, mature individual he was already. I was like a kid compared to this guy.

"He was being recruited heavily, as a lot of us were, to go to Illinois. The coach, Pete Elliot, had Dick right on his right side at the dais. I talked to a guy next to me, 'Look up there. I bet you that's Ray Nitschke,' because he's an Illinois boy, too. He said, 'No, that's Dick Butkus.'

"He was that impressive. He was probably the guy that hit me the hardest of any guy I played against. He was the only one who hurt me when he hit me. On one play in particular in Milwaukee County Stadium he crushed me on my left knee, causing me to tear some ligaments. My knee and foot were on the ground, and I was still standing up—that gives you an idea of the right angle he put my leg at. I thought he broke it for sure. He would hit right through you. He didn't hit you and sort of cease to hit when he made contact. It was like he was trying to drive his shoulders right through your body. Like if Mike Tyson were a football player—he hit right through you. He wasn't kidding around. His ferociousness was incredible.

"My first experience playing with him was four years after graduating from high school. We went to the College All-Star Game in Chicago. It was no fun scrimmaging against him, that's for sure. The real proof of the pudding was when we played the NFL champions, the Browns, in the game.

"I had always been a tremendous admirer of the great Jim Brown. I scored ten points and thought I might get some votes for the MVP, but Butkus actually shut Brown down. The first time they played each other—and he wasn't intimidated by Brown a bit—he tackled the shit out of him. He held him to, like, fifty yards when Jim would average a hundred yards waking up in the middle of the night."

Offensive tackle Doug Crusan's college team, Indiana, faced Butkus when he was in college at Illinois. He didn't so much tackle as maul people. "That's a good way to put it," said Crusan. "He was almost like a grizzly bear. That's the only term I can use for him. When he hit you, you were going down—it just depended on how hard and which way.

"The doggone guy was *big*. He even went down on kickoffs. To get him off the field was unbelievable." Unbelievably, almost impossibly, difficult to do, as he craved action.

Bob Hyland, a former NFL center, said he played a few games against Butkus. "We really went at it pretty good. When I was traded to Chicago, I remember being at training camp and the way the Bears used to do it was to line your lockers up in numerical order. Butkus was 51 and I always liked to wear number 50. So the Bears gave me 50 and my locker was right next to Butkus's. The first day we were at practice, I reached my hand out to shake with him and he wouldn't shake my hand.

"It took me about six weeks to earn his respect, and we finally shook hands and we had a pretty good relationship, but he was a tough son of a gun. I thought he was the greatest linebacker ever, and what a great leader and example for the rest of the players. He was a really, really positive example of how you should play the game. I mean, he hated to get off the field—he liked being on the kickoff return team, liked being on the punt return team.

"His favorite thing, of course, was to absolutely try to kill the center snapping the long punts. Back then, there were no restrictions. Now, I think, you can't hit the long snapper until after the ball is released for a second or two. Back in the old days, he used to try to hit you as you were releasing the ball and put you right on your backside, hoping that the next snap would be bad because you're thinking about him. He was brutal, but a good teammate."

Perhaps the most dramatic of all the tales from the Butkus saga is the one Malinchak related. His memorable rendezvous with Butkus occurred when he was playing on special teams, too. "I was a wedge buster my rookie season for Detroit. Just like everybody else, you play on special teams your first year. I was R2, the second player from the end on the right. Wally Hilgenberg was the second one from the left.

"My job was to try to take two guys down on the wedge—you had four guys on the wedge that would lead the returning back on kickoffs. So I was supposed to go down and come in from the side and take those two guys on the end down, and Wally [was to do the same on the other side]. We were fairly successful doing that, and the key was getting down there fast enough—and you were coming in from an angle, from the outside. These were the big guys, they had these guys who were six three, six five, 260 pounds, or whatever, leading the wedge up.

"I was doing it for the year and I thought, 'This is not too bad.' Then we played Chicago. Butkus was one of the four wedge guys, and he was on my side. When I started coming down the field, running, Butkus didn't run straight up, or he didn't turn around and look to see if the guy caught the kickoff or anything. He just looked straight at me. He had watched the films, obviously. He knew I was coming, and I looked at him and he was running straight at me instead of [being in his wedge]. I'm flying down there, and I said, 'Oh, my goodness. This does not look good.' He's still coming straight at me. I went down lower and he went down lower, and I went down lower—just tried to get lower than him.

"We kinda met, I don't know, a couple feet off the ground. We just had this collision. I don't remember anything—I saw on the film what happened—when we hit, we kind of exploded in the middle. We went up, and then I went back, and my helmet literally exploded off my head. It was totally cracked open and the face mask was hanging off. That was my first concussion. I had three that year. I just remember hitting him head-on.

"Then I was wobbling off, trying to figure out where I am and what I'm doing. You kind of look at your jersey. By that time a couple of guys had my arms and they took me off the field. That's my Butkus experience. It was quite a collision and, obviously, I got the worst of it." Most people did against Butkus.

Butkus, well aware of his reputation as a monomaniacal defender who just about frothed at the mouth over the prospect of laying out an opposing ball carrier, joked about his bruising ways and single-minded determination to inflict pain and fear. "I wouldn't ever set out to hurt anybody deliberately unless it was, you know, important—like a league game or something."

Butkus often tackled up high, sometimes twisting a runner's head or body as if he were opening a screw top plastic water bottle. He summed up his philosophy of defense and intimidation succinctly. "I want to just let them know that they've been hit, and when they get up, they don't have to look to see who it was that hit them."[2] Miami's Larry Little once claimed that in the midst of a scrum Butkus, long before the ear-biting episode of Mike Tyson, tried to bite him. Butkus denied this.

Running back MacArthur Lane sadly muttered, "If I had a choice, I'd rather go one-on-one with a grizzly bear." Another opponent observed, "Dick was Moby Dick in a goldfish bowl." In the meantime, Butkus explained why he was so gung ho on making his bone-jarring tackles. "The idea of hitting someone hard isn't for your ego. It's to make them forget about the ball."[3] Judging from his myriad hits it's safe to say he was the root of more severe cases of amnesia in the NFL than anyone else.

Pottios, a linebacker himself, said Butkus simply "destroyed people. He was the best. He was awesome. I loved his style, his attitude on the field, and the way he played. Butkus stood out above all of them." Butkus was head and shoulder pads above others, a bona fide Babe Ruth of the NFL, a true Sultan of Swat.

Green Bay's Ray Nitschke was yet another rough customer. In 1999, *Sports Illustrated* called him the third-greatest linebacker ever, behind only Butkus and Lawrence Taylor. He belongs. Like Butkus, even the name Nitschke sounds rugged, and he was.

John Isenbarger mused, "Dick Butkus and Ray Nitschke during Green Bay's heyday—if they don't have concussions, I don't know who would because they hit you with everything they had."

A Packer teammate of Nitschke, Chuck Mercein, paid his respects to Butkus, then added, "You didn't want to have to go against Ray Nitschke, either. He was such a tough hitter, too. Like Sam Huff."

Hyland played for the Bears one year after spending three years as a Packer. Being a former teammate of Nitschke, said Hyland, really didn't give him an edge. "No. You know what you have. You know the guy is extremely strong. He's a big-time hitter, and by that I mean sometimes a guy wants to punish you so much it can take away from his ability to get to the ball. Well, he had a little bit of that in him where he really wanted to pound you. If you could just stay with him for a second or two, it could be a pretty complete block, but he played it pretty straight.

"But I'll tell you, he was a scary guy. He loved playing the role of being the intimidator—not only on the field, but off the field. Inside he was a good guy with a good family life, but he really liked having the reputation as a really brutal, tough guy on the field, and he lived up to it pretty well. He was a tough kid from outside of Chicago who liked being tough."

An integral part of the Packers dynasty—Nitschke was named the MVP of the 1962 championship game—when he hit someone, he had about as much sympathy for his targets as a branding iron. George Belu said, "He epitomized a middle linebacker. You loved his intensity. The thing you admired so much about him was how he'd fill from tackle to tackle. He was a real force against the run, and even when he ran outside the box he got up with you—he came there to smack you. He wasn't just going to go ahead and sort of roll you down. Years ago, we always used the term "he really hits with a load" about linebackers and defensive ends that really bring it, and he came there *with a load*."

There really was no shortage of tough linebackers in the Glory Years, and the fact that Nitschke made it to the Pro Bowl only once attests to that.

Overshadowed by Butkus? Hyland said, "I would say so. They're both in the Hall of Fame so that's as far as you can go. They are two comparable players. You'd be thrilled to have either one of them on your team, but I think Butkus might have been a little more effective. But Ray was right there with him. It's a close call between those two."

Another tough act was Bill George, widely believed to be the first man to play a pure middle linebacker position, and easily the first man to become a star at that position. He did so as a Chicago Bear, a precursor to the admittedly tougher Butkus, but a Hall of Fame caliber player to be sure.

George came to the Bears out of Wake Forest as their second round (future) draft pick in 1951. The Bears first used him as a middle guard in a 5-2 defense which was the norm of the day, but when he came out of his stance, stood erect, and took a stride off the line, he became a middle linebacker in what became the 4-3 defense. That simple change is said to have altered the defensive complex of the NFL.

It 's also been stated that the first time he transformed himself into a middle linebacker took place in a game against the Philadelphia Eagles in 1954—and the game of football has never been quite the same since. George, always skilled at sniffing out opponents' plays, apparently noticed the Eagles were dumping short passes just over his head and that by not making a move to engage the Philadelphia center, but instead dropping back a bit at the moment of the snap, he could take away those passes. On just the third time he employed his new tactics he made the first of his eighteen lifetime interceptions. Always around the football, he also recovered nineteen opponents' fumbles.

George played defense fiercely, but with intelligence and an extremely high level of skill for fifteen seasons. He was a First Team All-Pro selection eight times, including seven straight selections, and, much in demand, he played in eight consecutive Pro Bowl contests. He was even used to kick a few times, and once scored twenty-five points in a season, including a dozen points on field goals.

Marchetti said if a player such as George wasn't in the crazy mode "when you get [to the NFL as a linebacker], by the time you're finished, you're in that mode. I was lucky I played defense and so did he."

Joe Walton recalled the time his Giants were preparing to play the Bears for the NFL title in 1963. "We had a running back named Phil

King. He was a little bit of a nervous type, got very hyper before the game. I wasn't a part of it, but some guys on the team wrote a letter to Phil saying, 'I can't wait. You're the first guy I'm coming after. Don't try to block me because I'll tear your head off.' And they signed it Bill George, Chicago Bears; and Phil shit his pants."

His nickname, "Mad Dog," says it all about Mike Curtis, who was so awe inspiring even his peers sounded like star-struck fans, mouths agape, when discussing him. Lenny Moore, who took many a hit from some tough linebackers in his playing days, fit the doting fan description in a 2014 interview when asked about Curtis. He simply chuckled and said, "He was an all-around great linebacker, man. Mike was something else, man."

Curtis proved that in a 1971 contest versus Miami in Baltimore. A fan ran onto the field, picked up the football as the Dolphins were just breaking from their huddle, and began to run away with his souvenir. It was a souvenir he would not hold on to for long.

Curtis ran from his position and leveled him with a shot to the fan's upper body. Colt teammate Sam Havrilak stated, "Mike just hit him and knocked him right on his ass. The guy wanted to take Mike to court to sue him for damages. When the court date came, the guy never showed up. I guess he got cold feet."

The fan's ultimate memento from the incident was a trip to a hospital—that, and a night in jail. After the game Curtis was presented with the football by the Colts equipment manager. That incident led to the Curtis autobiography being titled *Keep Off My Turf*.

Curtis had been trained to search and destroy ball carriers, to bring down anybody carrying a football, so that day he had turned himself into a heat-seeking missile and leveled the fan. That tackle made observers grimace as if they had just felt the blow.

Crusan, there that day with his Dolphins, was one such observer. "There was a timeout and the offense was in a huddle. The next thing I know, there's a pair of glasses that came flying through the huddle." Curtis later said basically that he was telling the fan that he didn't have a seat out there, so he certainly didn't belong there. He then made it his job to remove the interloper. Crusan went on, "Oh, boy. Curtis was very quick and fast. That poor guy. That was the last time he ever did anything like that."

Havrilak remembered that Curtis "came here in 1965 from Duke. He got hurt and was out for a year [most of 1967]—he had knee surgery. Then he came back and they tried him as a running back, but that didn't work out, so they put him at outside linebacker at first. Mike was kind of a different guy in the sense that once he got on the field he kind of went into a trance and became another person. He wouldn't tolerate anybody not giving 110 percent.

"He was a pretty tough guy. Even in practices, he was going 110 percent, so if you were a receiver or a running back, you had to protect yourself all the time when you were in his area because he might just reach out and hit you."

Curtis, not especially big for his position at 232 pounds, became the first NFL player ever to earn All-Pro honors at both the outside and middle linebacker positions. Primarily remembered for his bruising tackles when he was with the Colts, he administered pain around the league from 1965 through 1978. One season he made fifty-nine solo tackles and chalked up twenty-one assists, yet played in only seven games.

People called Curtis the Dick Butkus of his day, and opposing quarterbacks readily confessed they were intimidated by him; and some even said he was more fear inducing than Butkus. Incidentally, in 1966 Curtis even averaged 21.3 yards per kickoff return for the three times he performed that duty.

Miami benefited greatly from having Nick Buoniconti as their middle linebacker. In the Dolphins' undefeated season it was Buoniconti who anchored that spot. Smart and savvy, he became a Hall of Famer (Class of 2001), and he was named to the AFL's All-Time Team in 1970, but initially virtually nobody even wanted him.

Buoniconti was drafted almost as an afterthought by the AFL Boston Patriots, way down in the thirteenth round, and not one NFL team bothered to select him at all. Perhaps it was due to his size. Everyone from scouts to his own college coaches were firmly convinced that he was way too small to play in the NFL. He stood just five feet, eleven inches and, compared to many future defensive stars, barely nudged the needle on the scales, weighing in at 220 pounds.

Yet this determined man ignored the critics, proving them all wrong when he endured the rigors of playing amid all of the ferocious action that takes place at the middle linebacker position for fourteen seasons. He lasted, and starred, all the way from 1962 through 1976 with the exception of his missing the entire 1975 season.

He ended his days with thirty-two interceptions, countless tackles, numerous honors, and endless bumps, bruises, and pains. The rugged Buoniconti's awards included being named to the first team of the All-1960s squad by two polls and his selection to eight Pro Bowls. Perhaps even more impressive is the fact that in the evaluation of the statistical tool known as Career Approximate Value, Buoniconti still ranks number ninety-four, tied with several players such as Mean Joe Greene and fellow linebacker Clay Mathews (through the 2015 season), and behind just a few other linebackers.

Miami teammate Doug Crusan said his team was glad to get Buoniconti from Boston in 1969 after he had been with the Patriots for seven seasons. "He was very intelligent. He knew the game. In practice when you had to block him, which I did in multiple plays that we had, I mean to tell you, your feet had to move so fast to even think about getting to him. He was probably the quickest linebacker that I ever played against, and he was on my own team. He was so quick he'd go under you, cut around you, and he was a great leader for that defense that we had."

Plus, Buoniconti had already done well in the NFL. He helped his Bills win the AFL Eastern Division championship in 1963. The following season he set a personal high with five interceptions, and in one game during his final season with Buffalo, 1968, he picked off three passes. In fact, he played in five of his eight All-Pro games as a member of the Patriots.

With the Dolphins he impressed everyone and was even named the team's MVP in his first season there and two additional times—in 1970 and 1973, the season he set a Dolphins single season record with 162 tackles. That total, which included 91 unassisted tackles, worked out to an average of twelve and a half tackles per game over his thirteen contests played that season. He was yet another great who obviously possessed an uncanny nose for the football.

In college, Buoniconti had played three ways—he was a guard on the offensive line, a linebacker, and a tiger all around. Myron Pottios said, "He was my old teammate at Notre Dame. I think he wasn't any more than 210 or 215. It's just amazing for him to play all the years he played and he still hung in there and did a great job. To play in the middle and take the beating and dish out all those hits and blows—it's mind boggling, hard to believe. He was a very smart guy and very successful after football, too. That tells you his I.Q."

Sam Huff loved leveling opponents, and he did it quite often. He gained so much notoriety for plying his craft, CBS produced a 1960 show entitled *The Violent World of Sam Huff*, assigning the venerable Walter Cronkite to host the homage.

Huff's head-to-head battles with *the* two Jims, Brown and Taylor, soon became legendary. Onetime Huff teammate Joe Walton stated that the Huff vs. Brown heavyweight matches constituted a bigger rivalry than Huff vs. Taylor. "He had great games against the Cleveland Browns every time we played them, and the team *was* Jim Brown, you gotta understand that, but it was hard to keep Brown from getting his yards. Sam probably had big games against them because he was quick to the ball. He had unusual speed and quickness. That was a great move the Giants made, moving him to linebacker."

Walton, a Pitt grad, noted, "Sam played offensive and defensive tackle for West Virginia, so I played against him in college in the Backyard Brawl, one of our big rivals. When he was with the Giants, he became my teammate. I always loved Sam. He was not only a great player, but another thing about Sam is he could run so well. He had good speed for a man his size [six foot one and 230]."

Walton said that despite Huff's image for violence, he didn't have that "don't even look at me" game face prior to taking the field on Sundays, not like another Giant, defensive end/linebacker Tom Scott. However, "He did get fired up for games, I know that. He was so tough, though, you didn't want to mess with him. Very similar to Nitschke and Butkus—in that category. You [opponents] didn't want to end up being around him on the field. You went the other way."

George Belu called Huff "a linebacker that played with a lot of *effort and tenacity*. He played the game so hard and he was another one of those players that you really watched. You love to see him make a hit, get back to the huddle, then go, 'Come on. Bring on the next play.'"

In all, Huff spent eight seasons with the Giants and helped them reach postseason play six times, copping the championship in 1956.

When Huff was traded to Washington, he felt betrayed. Mercein said, "Sam was very volatile. At the end of his career he was very, very upset that he got traded. He thought he'd be a Giant forever. He really hated [Coach] Allie Sherman for trading him.

"I, unfortunately, was part of one of the two teams that set the record for overall [combined single game] scoring, still a record. We [the Giants] were playing the Redskins down in D.C. in 1966 and Sam had been traded, so he's playing middle linebacker for them. We were losing this game, 69–41, and the game was almost over. We had the ball and I was telling the quarterback, 'Just give me the damn ball. Don't throw it anymore. We don't want to get another interception.' We just wanted to run the clock out.

"But somehow the Redskins got the ball back with very little time left, and Sam Huff, on the sidelines, talked Otto Graham, the Redskins coach, into sending in Charlie Gogolak to kick a field goal at the end of the game to make it 72–41. And he did it just because he was so pissed off at Sherman for letting him go. So he actually sent the play in, and they scored 72, the most points ever scored in a National Football League game. To this day you can't mention Sherman to him without him going nuts."

Mercein also remembered how, "When he tackled you, he would let you know it. He was pretty rough. He would say unprintable stuff to you. He was old school, but a heckuva football player."

Another middle linebacker who dwelt in a violent world was number 66, Chuck Bednarik. Belu called him "one of the last throwback players to [old time] football. You just loved to watch him play because he played so hard and viciously. He ran the football field. He never took a play off."

Bednarik must have loved to be in the middle of things, as he also played the center position in some seasons. Fearless, he had gone directly from his high school graduation to the US Army where he flew thirty bombing missions as a gunner in World War II. Soon after the war, he continued to gun down the enemy, this time wearing NFL uniforms.

Born in Bethlehem, Pennsylvania, perhaps the greatest gift "Concrete Charlie" ever gave to his Eagles was the game-saving tackle he put on Jim Taylor in the 1960 NFL title game versus the Packers. On the last play of the contest Taylor was headed for an apparent score when he ran into a human concrete wall. Bednarik brought him down on the

9-yard line and pinned him down until the clock ran out. The defeat was Vince Lombardi's first and only postseason loss—after that he posted a perfect record at 9-0, winning five NFL championships.

In the Eagles' win over Green Bay, the thirty-five-year-old Bednarik, who had switched from being a linebacker to become the team's center in 1958, was on the field for fifty-eight and a half of the game's sixty minutes (sitting only during kickoffs), but for about half of the season that was pretty much the norm. In Philadelphia's fifth game an injury to a linebacker forced Bednarik into doing double duty. To this day, many consider him to be the last true sixty-minute man. He was an Iron Man year in and year out, missing just three games over his fourteen-year career.

When asked his opinion of more recent two-way players such as Troy Brown and Deion Sanders, Bednarik scoffed, pointing out the dual action they saw didn't entail nearly the type of rough contact he dealt with.

Bednarik earned All-Pro kudos as both a center and linebacker. Like Butkus, he never hid his emotions. Even decades after he last hung up his cleats, when he spoke of his intensity on the football field he snarled and seemed to spew spit with each sentence he muttered.

George Belu commented, "With Bednarik, you always saw the effort and the intensity that he played with. It wasn't like it is nowadays with the close-ups on television, but you still saw the intensity even though you never could see that face up close like you did with Bill Cowher."

Meanwhile, Marchetti said his teammate Colt middle linebacker Bill Pellington "was probably the meanest guy that ever wore a uniform, the meanest guy I ever played with, and he was my best friend. Ask any-body that played during that period against him. If they ran a crossing pattern, they'd go five yards out of the way *not* to go near him because he had the sharp elbows and he'd lay them out.

"And what made him a little meaner, he'd do it in practice. The guys would complain about it and he'd say, 'Listen, they're going to do that to you in a game, so don't worry about it.' I'm just glad I wasn't the guy running across the middle.

"He used to have his game face on in the locker room. I remember one time we were playing Detroit and on a certain defense he was supposed to go out and slow the tight end from going down the field. And he was beating the hell out of him.

"The tight end went to the referee, complaining and complaining, and he finally said, 'Goddamnit, why the hell don't you just give him a gun?' The referee checked Bill, and he had a little extra strength there, taped up underneath his jersey. He had something that would give people a reason to worry. In other words, Pellington often hid an object such as a metal plate in a hidden place such as under his jersey and/or under his padding. The referees always checked him, but somehow he hid it.

"He would play with a cast and tape it. The referees checked it, but during halftime he'd take the tape off so that the cast was harder on the head—without that tape that they made him wear on his broken arm."

A twelve-year man, Pellington was solid. Marchetti noted at times they played on the same side of the field. "He'd talk to me all the time. If I got blocked, he was there, which made it easier for me to rush the passer or do something out of character [some unexpected tactic or move] because of his ability."

Then there was Joe Schmidt. Marchetti said, "I think he was the only linebacker who had good sense. They're crazy, no doubt about it." The middle linebacker out of Pitt was equally adept at covering the pass and the run. He made nine Pro Bowls over his thirteen-year stint in the NFL, he helped his Lions win two championships, and he is yet another linebacker from the 1950 All-Decade Team.

Chuck Mercein nailed it, "He was cut from that cloth of the great middle linebackers of that era. All of those linebackers from that era were tremendous hitters. He was a tremendous football player. He became quite a good coach, too."

Schmidt was the Lions' head coach from 1967 through 1972, his only head coaching stint. He won 56 percent of his games, excluding seven ties. In 1969 his team went 9-4-1 and a year later he led them to the postseason. However, a defensive struggle in the Division Championship game versus Dallas ended in a 5–0 victory for the Cowboys. Detroit held Dallas to a first quarter field goal until a safety in the final stanza ended the scoring. Schmidt did a fine job that year, taking a team with just a few Pro Bowl caliber players to contention.

Schmidt and his Lions did an even better job in 1957 when they won the NFL championship in a 59–14 mauling of the Cleveland Browns. Schmidt was in his fourth of six straight seasons in which he earned First Team All-Pro recognition. He would miss out on that honor in 1960, but made First Team again in 1961 and 1962.

In that championship win over Cleveland, the Lions put two touchdowns on the scoreboard in each quarter with a first-quarter field goal thrown in. Their quarterback, Tobin Rote, passed for four touchdowns and ran for one, while Schmidt carried his load, picking off a pass.

One week earlier, Schmidt had also intercepted a pass to help Detroit top the 49ers of Y. A. Tittle and Hugh McElhenny, 31–27. Down by six points entering the final quarter, the Lions rallied for a touchdown and a field goal to advance to the title game. While they did win it all in 1957, Detroit has never again won the NFL championship. Only the Cardinals franchise has a longer active dry spell in league history, as their last title came in 1947.

One championship ring and one from the Hall of Fame will have to do for Schmidt; it's a lot more than a bundle of other players have to boast of. He also was hailed by the Pro Football Hall of Fame as a First Team selection to their All-1950s squad.

Hardy Brown may be an obscure name from the past for many fans, but his opponents knew his name, his reputation, and, if they were smart, knew his location on the field at all times. An NFL-produced television show featuring the most feared tacklers ever placed Brown at number five. He proudly wore the title as the Dirtiest Man in Pro Football, literally knocking opponents out from 1948, when he began his pro days with the Brooklyn Dodgers of the old AAFC, through 1960.

He stood at just six feet and weighed 190 pounds, tops, but he knew how to hit, and hit hard, often using his shoulders like a prize fighter's jolting uppercut blow. Many of those shots went to the head area, and he doled out bruises, concussions, and broken bones—he specialized in jaws and cheekbones, and bruises.

When asked if he recalled Brown, Gino Marchetti concisely stated, "Oh, sure. He was that guy who hit with his shoulders." Then, when asked if he ever played against Brown, Marchetti laughed, "No. No, thank God. I know a back who used to tell me he was scared of Brown because of his toughness and the special way he had of hitting you with his shoulder and arm, and said, 'You *felt* it.' When he ran the ball, he tried to avoid him. He wasn't worried about a long run, he was worried more about Brown."

Brown once reportedly belted a player so hard an eyeball popped out and dangled down to his cheek on a tendon. Whether the story is lore or reality, it was a typical tale of Brown.

One theory to explain his violent ways relates to his upbringing. His father was murdered, and Hardy wound up being raised in a rough environment in an orphanage.

Norm Van Brocklin said Hardy was like an Old West gunslinger who puts a notch on his gun for every person he has killed. Brown figuratively put his notch "on his belt for all the jock straps he got."[4] Brown himself knew he was considered to be the dirtiest man in the game, but seemed unfazed by that charge. Instead, he seemed to relish that image and once estimated he knocked out as many as eighty players, adding that he felt no sympathy for those he leveled. Hardy deserved the nickname the Assassin long before Jack Tatum.

Brown said a member of the Rams once told him that the team had posted a $500 bounty on his head, and many players tried to knock him out of action to claim that prize. Upon learning of the reward on his head, instead of becoming furious and seeking revenge, Brown instructed the Rams player to hit him so he could fake an injury and leave the game. Then, said the crafty Brown, the two of them would split the bounty.

Ask any expert circa the 1950s who the greatest defensive end in the history of the NFL was, and the answer that would quickly be shot back would be Gino Marchetti. He was named to the Pro Bowl every season from 1954 to 1964. He didn't make it in his first two seasons, but did in every other one of his full seasons in the league, a stupendous run of eleven years in a row.

Plus, he was First-Team All-Pro every season from 1957 through 1962, and again in his final season of 1964. Naturally, he was selected for the Pro Football Hall of Fame's All-1950s team and the 75th Anniversary All-Time Team. In fact, in 1972, as if to reaffirm his prowess and legendary status, he was voted as the greatest player at his position of all time.

Marchetti went six feet, four inches and 244 pounds, not exactly huge, but he was so very quick—and tough. They say he once played about two quarters of a game with a separated shoulder. On another occasion, he returned to action just two weeks after he had undergone surgery for appendicitis.

When he was eighteen years old, he fought in the Battle of the Bulge. After seeing heavy action in World War II, Marchetti, like other battle veterans, never again experienced raw fear or even a modicum of self-doubt. They knew there was nothing in the NFL that could make them tremble.

Late in the 1958 championship game between his Colts and the Giants, Marchetti broke two bones and was taken by stretcher to a safe spot behind the end zone so he could watch the game. Doctors wanted to rush him directly to a hospital. Marchetti refused, he would watch the rest of the game before getting attended to, he said.

The injury took place on a play in which his tackle was responsible for the Colts forcing the Giants to punt late in the fourth quarter, ahead by three points, but unable to run the clock out. "There was a minute and thirty-some seconds to score," Marchetti said in a 2016 interview. "I wanted to see it, to be a part of it, and I did see it." What he got to see was a field goal to tie things up.

However, when the game went into overtime there was a very real fear that he might be trampled by exuberant fans when the game finally came to an end. He continued, "When the word came down that we were going into sudden death, that's when they decided to 'Get Marchetti out of here.'"

Only then did they carry him off the field. He still refused to be taken to the hospital, though, insisting they take him to the Colts locker room so he could greet, and hopefully celebrate with his teammates when the game finally finished. His leg could wait.

Getting him to the locker room wasn't all that easy. Marchetti remembered, "They carried me, but I decided to be a smart ass and I said, 'Hey, wait a minute. Let me down right here.' They did. So I was lying there ready to watch the [overtime] kickoff. The first thing you know, there were policemen coming out and they forced me off the field. They carried me into the locker room, and that was hell because I was lying there not knowing who was going to win the game." Despite the large crowd, Marchetti said the locker room "was very quiet—I couldn't hear anything and I had no radio. It was hard to take."

After what had to seem an endless wait, Bill Pellington came in and roared, "We're the world's champs." "Then," joked Marchetti, "we had our Coke."

Marchetti said his insistence on watching the end of the game was simple. "After playing many years and getting the hell beat out of us—we were a very poor team when we first went to Baltimore—to play in the championship game was a big thrill and honor."

Lenny Moore said of Marchetti, "He had some unbelievable talent, talent that normally you could only give to him from a basic point, but he's one of the guys that could take it past that given point to where only an outstanding individual could do. Evidently, God gave them that extra instinctive [ability]."

Moore said Marchetti was typical of many of the Colts. "Sure, you could teach about a block, teach them how to tackle, the basic routine, but some of the plays that they made are so outstanding you say, 'Wow, how did he do that?' but even he doesn't know how he did it."

Raymond Berry observed, "Gino was just a rare combination of tremendous competitive spirit and great ability. He was so athletic, quick, and strong. His intensity as a competitor was probably more than any other defensive player that I've ever seen. He was the whole package. When you think about the Baltimore Colt defense from those days, you start with Gino Marchetti because he provided the pass rush that limited the opposing quarterbacks' time in the pocket."

Against the run, said Berry, forget it. Other teams had difficulty running sweeps and off-tackle plays largely due to Marchetti. "He was just a dominant, outstanding player, our number one defensive force during our championship years.

"If I had to highlight one thing, what with his quickness, it was a case of, 'Woe to the right tackle that had to try to block him because when the ball was snapped, he was lightning fast.' Trying to keep him off the quarterback was impossible.

"Gino was a combination of great competitive spirit and tremendous football instincts along with great strength for his 245 pounds. He had such great foot quickness and balance, two things to behold. I don't know if Gino ever got knocked off his feet. He had the ability to use his hands that was amazing. An offensive tackle trying to fool around with Gino Marchetti was in for a long day at the office.

"I remember watching him many a time when the ball was snapped. His first move was to grab the tackle's shoulder pad on the right side, and he would slip opponents with his quickness. He was practically unblockable."

Marchetti's path to the NFL and eventual fame was mentally torturous at first, but he endured, mainly due to his love for and devotion to football. "Well, I went out for football in high school, and I never got a uniform. There were only thirty-six players on my whole high school team—it was a small town. They only had twenty-four football uniforms and the coach didn't give me one—I didn't make the team as a freshman.

"So I talked to the coach and said, 'I would like to practice with you.' He said, 'OK, but stay out of our way.' So I practiced with them for a whole season, not playing or being able to dress up for the game or any of that stuff. That was my love for the game of football—I practiced every day with those guys and never got an opportunity to play. I could have easily walked away and done something else like play basketball, but it was just built into me—I don't know why I had such a love for the game.

"Then from there I joined the army and that put the body on me, that put me in shape and brought me up to 225 [pounds], and built up my muscles and strength. Then I went to Modesto [junior college], from Modesto to USF [the University of San Francisco], then to Baltimore." His path to the NFL was finally complete.

However, there was still the learning curve to cope with. Marchetti went into details about the tactics he became aware of and then enjoyed using as a defensive end. "I was a boxing fan so I used to watch boxers and how quick their hands were, how they used their hands and how to secure a victory. So I started using my hands more and I strengthened them so that I could grab a guy by the shoulder pads and kind of throw him around a little bit to clear a path for me to get through.

"And I'll tell you who taught me those moves. Don Joyce. He was a Colt, but when I played against him, he was with the Cardinals and they were trying to make an offensive tackle out of me. We played the Cardinals down in Houston and what happened was he turned me every way but loose. I mean, he beat me and beat me. I had a headache.

I walked off the field and Joe Campanella came up to me and he said, 'You had a bad day, huh?' I said, 'I don't think I'm going to make it. They told me this guy wasn't the best.' But I did make it. I learned from that year that they put me at offensive tackle. I learned from the guys that made it tough on me to block, from the moves that they would put on me and the quickness."

His love of the game was still strong late in his career. He reflected on a decision he made when he said he believed it was time to quit playing for the Colts, a belief he soon recanted. "One thing I was glad that never happened was when I was going to retire. I told [the front office], 'I don't want to play in Baltimore any more. I want to go home and play close to my family.' And I held out, but the only trouble was the second day of training camp I called back and said, 'I'm on my way.' My holdout wasn't very long."

Marchetti shared another seldom-told story, confessing there was a trick he employed to help his effectiveness. "I probably played 90 percent of my time on the field offsides [sic]. I took as much ball as they would let me. The referee would say, 'Hey, Marchetti, you're getting a little close.' And I said, 'Thank you. Thank you.' And I trained myself to watch two or three guys on the line of scrimmage. You'll hear them say, 'Why doesn't he watch the ball? You'll never be offsides.' Well, that's bullshit. What I used to try to do was watch the tackle, the guard, and the center, so that if the guard went first, I would get an advantage over the tackle. If the center went first, I would be able to protect myself.

"So by watching them, I was able to get off the ball. I was reading the keys. That was Weeb's big thing when he came to Baltimore, 'Read the key.' He taught us the keys. If you get off the ball before the offensive tackle, he ain't got a chance. But if he gets off the ball, then you ain't got a chance."

Myron Pottios knew of other Marchetti attributes, calling him "just a real smart player. He wasn't overbearing power-wise. He didn't come and destroy people, but he was real good."

No dummy (or pauper), Marchetti wound up owning restaurants with teammate Alan Ameche. "We ended up with approximately five hundred stores. We had them all over the joint—125 were Rustlers Steakhouses, and we had, I think, a hundred KFC take-homes. "

Once, when asked what he was most proud of, he replied, "It is something that you would *never* guess what it is. The thing I'm most proud of is I never got a fifteen-yard penalty in fourteen years of playing in the NFL." That feat is akin to Wilt Chamberlain's having played his entire 1,045-game career without once having fouled out.

Marchetti resumed, "I thought that was something—I never bragged about it or told anybody about it. I'm telling *you* about it because who gives a damn today. And that's what gets me today in games when these guys make those stupid penalties, like hitting a guy when he's been down for three minutes and all of that stuff. It's stupid. You hurt your team."

Actually, Marchetti wasn't even aware of his fifteen-yard-penalty-free streak until Ohio State coach Woody Hayes informed him. "I went in to talk to him one day and he told me, 'Listen, I want to congratulate you.' I said, 'Why?' Hayes said, 'You played without getting a fifteen-yard penalty on your team. Don't worry how I knew—I know. I just want to congratulate you on that, not many people do that.' That made me feel pretty damn good."

When complimented on never having lost his temper to draw a major penalty or done "anything stupid," Marchetti quipped, "Well, I might have done things *stupid*. I never got caught."

With a menacing expression on his face and seething brutality in his heart, another great defensive end, Deacon Jones, was a sight to behold. The looming figure of Jones, six foot five and 272 pounds, caused trepidation around the NFL. He was a fourteen-year veteran who mainly played for the Rams. He was a "Bring 'em back dead or alive" type of player who was a two-time Defensive Player of the Year (1967 and 1968).

He was part of a defensive line so great it earned the nickname "the Fearsome Foursome." Now, that nickname had been used to describe the front four of several other teams, such as the Lions, but this one was the crème de la crème, mainly because of Merlin Olsen and Jones. Dick Butkus believes—and he should know about defense—the Rams front four was the best ever.

NFL scout George Belu said while Olsen and Jones gained the most notice, the entire Rams defense was cohesive and just about unparalleled. "The great thing about them is they played as a unit. You love to see that, to see that Fearsome Foursome. Everyone made plays. They were not, 'Hey, look at me.'" Belu mentioned one exception to their normal businesslike attitude took place every now and then when Deacon got to the quarterback and uttered something like, "Hey, I'm coming to get you," for the purpose of intimidation.

Jones, as mobile and fast as he was imposing, once assessed his own awesome talents, boasting that he was the best defensive end in the game and that he wouldn't like to play against himself. Asked about Jones, Tom Matte said, "Deacon? Christ, he could run faster than I could."

Both Matte and Jones were correct. Opposing quarterbacks who went down under his fierce pass rush cowered, absolutely loathing the prospect of playing against him. And he never phoned it in, nor did he sit out much—over his fourteen seasons he missed just three games. He was so respected he sometimes drew not just double, but triple teaming. *Not* employing such tactics was tantamount to taking a toothpick to a knife fight.

Interestingly, Jones coined the term "sack," even though technically speaking he never recorded one because that wasn't an official statistic until 1984, ten years after he retired. Jones, who saw himself as a quarterback killer, believes that he, and not Bruce Smith (with two hundred), would own the all-time record for sacks if the NFL had kept track of them during his playing days. Some researchers, though, estimate his sack total to be 173.5. In 1967 and 1968, Jones had (an unofficial) total of twenty-six and twenty-eight sacks during fourteen-game seasons. In 1984, in a sixteen-game season, Mark Gastineau set the initial official record for the most sacks in a year with six fewer than Jones's twenty-eight. Even now, the season record stands at just 22.5 (set by Michael Strahan in 2001). In any case, like the bell that stimulated Pavlov's dogs, the snap of the football set Jones to salivating, anticipating his payoff, yet another QB sack.

Marchetti, who was once unofficially credited with a dazzling total of forty-three sacks, had a great deal of respect for Jones, who employed the head slap better than anyone. "And you could do it then," said Marchetti. "There was nothing crazy about it—you'd do anything you could to get at that passer, whether it was head slap, knee slap, whatever, it was in your [repertoire]. When you weren't having a good day, you'd look to see what you could come up with to pull you up to being the type of player you want to be."

For the uninformed, the head-slap tactic involves a defensive line-man clubbing an opponent, usually right after the ball was snapped, on the helmet. The ideal target was the helmet's ear hole, and the result of the slap was often a ringing in the player's ear and sometimes enough disorientation to give the pass rusher an edge.

In 1977 the NFL banned the use of the head slap due mainly to Jones and the sheer destruction he wrought with that quick, punishing move. Neither that, nor the fact that Jones had retired three years earlier stopped him from using it one last time. After he gave his accep-tance speech when inducted into the Hall of Fame, Jones strode over to the bust of himself which was displayed on stage in his honor and head-slapped it. For the record, teammate Rosey Grier taught the move to Jones.

Despite his on-field persona, Pottios, a Ram teammate of Jones, called him, "A super, super ballplayer. Deac was a good guy—loved to hang around with him. He was funny and always wanted to be the person who was on stage. No matter where we were or what we were doing, he was the guy."

Jones, who was nicknamed the Secretary of Defense, was also on the NFL's 75th Anniversary All-Time Team and, in 1994, was selected as the "Best Defensive End of the Century" by *Sports Illustrated*.

As noted, Jones did not invent the head slap. Rosey Grier taught it to him, although it's safe to say Jones perfected that move and employed it more (and probably better) than anyone else. But the truth is another defensive end, Doug Atkins, actually came up with the strategy in the first place.

Atkins was born in Knoxville, Tennessee, and stayed in state to play his college ball at the University of Tennessee, actually going there on a basketball scholarship. A huge and agile player, the All-American drew the attention and rapt interest of scouts, and was quickly gobbled up by the Browns as the eleventh overall pick in the 1953 NFL draft.

Seventeen years after leaving college he was still active in the NFL at the age of thirty-nine. He spent two seasons with Cleveland before moving on to play for Chicago, the venue for most of his success. At the tail end of his career he was with the expansion New Orleans Saints for three seasons. Saddled with a very poor team, Atkins would play in twenty-nine losing contests versus only twelve winning efforts as a Saint.

Still, as George Belu said, "Atkins was a force to deal with. He had great size, athletic ability, and tenacity. He was a snap-to-whistle effort player." He seemingly was on a constant quest for the ball carrier.

As strong as Atkins was, he once admitted that while he didn't really feel the pain after being hit until the day following a game, he found the fatigue of wrestling with and trying to shed huge opposing linemen to be absolutely draining. No one ever claimed that making a living in the NFL was easy, not even for Hall of Famers like Atkins.

Atkins, who once won the Southeastern Conference high-jump championship in college, used an unusual tactic: he often reached quarterbacks to sack, harass, and hurry them by leapfrogging over blockers.

His Chicago coach, the legendary George "Papa Bear" Halas, once called Atkins the best defensive end he had ever seen. Halas was especially thankful to have Atkins on his side when the standout helped Chicago win the NFL championship in 1963.

Gino Marchetti said the thing an opponent had to do when opposing Atkins was something Baltimore's Jim Parker did very well—he would not get the six-foot-eight, 275-pound behemoth angry. "If you treated him nice, Doug would go along with the program, wouldn't have a real good game, but if you got him upset for some reason, he'd throw you at the quarterback." No exaggeration—Atkins literally would shove or throw an offensive lineman backward and into the quarterback. Parker called the surprisingly quick Atkins the meanest player he ever encountered.

Meanwhile, Pottios said Atkins was "just a mean, big, tough guy who played the hell out of the game. I mean, he was physical and destroyed offensive linemen and anybody who tried to block him—*and* the quarterback. If you talk to the players, they'll tell you, he was the toughest."

It's obvious that the majority of the toughest players of the time period were linebackers or defensive linemen. Few defensive backs of the era are worthy of mention alongside men like Jones, Marchetti, and Butkus, but Dick "Night Train" Lane is. If asked to select the top ten most-feared defenders, some fans might cram ten linebackers on their list. When the TV show *Top Ten* made their list, Lane, who hit with the impact of a blitzing linebacker, ranked second behind only Butkus.

Just watching Lane savagely take down ball carriers made opponents who were riding the bench wince—and it made receivers think twice about wanting to catch a ball on Lane's turf.

Not merely a brute, the proficient Lane set a record in 1952 by intercepting fourteen passes, doing that over a twelve-game schedule *and* as a rookie! Not only that, the total is still the best ever. Toss in the fact that his sixty-eight lifetime picks have only been surpassed by three men. Furthermore, Lane never played a game of college football (although he spent some time as a defensive back in junior college). After serving in two wars, he became a sort of pro "walk-on," showing up in Los Angeles asking for a chance to play for the Rams. They gave him a job at a cornerback spot even though he had never played there before. They had to like what they saw—at about six foot one and 195–200 pounds, he was as big as some NFL linemen of the day and much faster.

He made the All-Decade Team for the 1950s, touted as the best cornerback ever at that point. He entered the Hall of Fame in 1974, and he was on the NFL All-Time Team selected in 1994.

Raymond Berry said he seldom came into contact with Lane, and he was grateful for that. Berry commented, "He covered the other side of the field, on Lenny Moore, when we played against him. They were two super athletes. I used to say to myself jokingly, 'It's good they're up against each other. They deserve each other.'"

Marchetti observed, "Night Train was ideal for a defensive back, a guy that could come in and, if you don't catch the pass, he'll hit you to make sure that the next time you come in his area, you're going to be looking out for him and not the ball."

Face it, nobody wanted to cope with Lane's wrath. His two most famous and most feared tactics were the pain- and injury-inducing clothesline tackle and the tackling of ball carriers around their necks and heads. He often shot a forearm out, aimed at lifting the player off the ground. He twisted necks and wrestled opponents to the ground. Other times his tackles were head to head, under a ball carrier's jaw, like magnified shots from the Rock 'Em Sock 'Em toy. In street vernacular, Lane had an "I'm gonna jack your jaw" mentality, but the devastation he doled out was eventually too much for the NFL. Because of Lane the NFL outlawed necktie tackles and, some sources say, they also banned the face mask-yanking tackle due to Lane's actions (others say it was due to Hardy Brown).

They say Lane also invented the bump and run defense, and when Dick "Night Train" Lane bumped a receiver, both he and his route were disrupted, to put it gently.

Another defensive back who deserves to be mentioned with Lane was Larry Wilson of the Cardinals, a man who hurt many a quarterback, hurtling his 190-pound frame onto, almost *through* them with seismic results on his patented safety blitz.

Belu said, "I got to know Larry very well, and what a great person he was. He was one tough football player. He would come up and tag you!" He added that Wilson didn't actually concoct the idea for the safety blitz, "It began before him, but when the Cardinals did blitz him, he was so effective, he got all the accolades."

Wilson surely made the tactic into a weapon of mass destruction. Here's how it was born for Wilson. After observing Wilson play, the St. Louis defensive coordinator, Chuck Drulis, realizing what he had in Wilson, conceived the risky but rewarding strategy. As Pottios said, "Wilson was the first to receive notoriety for it, and I don't recall anybody using it as much as St. Louis did when they had Wilson there."

If any safety can blitz, what made Wilson the best at it? Belu said, "Tenacity and instinct. You can watch some safeties play and they don't come up with that tenacity. There are all different sorts of safeties. Some play up close to the line of scrimmage, used like an eighth man in a seven-man front to stop the run. Others can really cover ground, that have the speed to get the football, but they're not real vicious tacklers."

One Cardinal teammate, Chuck Bryant, said Wilson "got his nickname 'Wildcat' because that was the defense we ran when we shot the safety. We also called him 'Popeye,' because he looked like Popeye the Sailor Man, but he was tough as nails. He was one of the hardest hitting players I ever saw."

Blitzing as he did, at times Wilson absorbed painful blows from a blocker who picked him up. However, totally undaunted, Wilson's approach of sacrificing his body for the good of the team resulted in his dishing out more pain than he stoically accepted and in causing havoc for the opposition. It also resulted in many interceptions, including his league-leading ten in 1966.

Pottios stated, "I liked Larry, he was a guy who, boy, was very physical. I admired him. Until the offenses figured out how they were going to block that safety blitz of his, he had a free shot, which was great. But he got the hell beat out him, beat up quite a bit, but he always kept coming and he was a hard-nosed, tough guy."

Some media members even called Wilson *the* toughest player in football, and, remember, that label was attached to him in the era of Butkus, Lane, and company. Adept at open-field tackling, he took runners to the ground with pure tackling form, but he wasn't averse to applying blasts to a runner's torso.

Tough? In one game Wilson suited up despite doctors' admonishments, playing with both hands broken. On one pass, he blocked the ball, secured it after it deflected back to him, and returned the interception thirty-five yards—all with his hands firmly encased in casts.

His talent was enduring, too, as he made the All-Decade Team for both the 1960s *and* the 1970s. Not surprisingly, he also made the 75th Anniversary NFL All-Time Team.

Not all of the toughest players were defensive stars. Raymond Berry, who once called Unitas "the toughest guy on the football field when I played," added that he believed if his teammate "had been big enough, he could have been, say, a Hall of Fame linebacker."

Berry proved his point by telling a truly revelatory story of an unforgettable incident that took place in a game versus the Bears. "We played them twice a year in our division. They were 'The Monsters of the Midway,' and it didn't make any difference what kind of monsters they were, John Unitas was not able to be intimidated. They'd hit him in the mouth and he just spit out his teeth and he'd go back and beat you.

"We were playing them one time and somebody, a defensive lineman, came in and hit him right in the mouth and busted his nose. He didn't call time out because his nose was bleeding. What he did there on the field was he picked up some dirt, stuffed it up in his nose, got the blood stopped, and stepped back in the huddle—threw a touchdown pass. That's Unitas."

Another Baltimore teammate confirmed the story and added a few details. Andy Nelson recalled, "Unitas got a broken nose that day, and I remember him stuffing, I think it was some mud up his nose to keep it from bleeding, then he threw the touchdown pass. It was to Lenny

Moore. Johnny was a tough character. That's how he earned our respect—he played with injuries."

Sam Havrilak played with Unitas and said, "He *was* tough. Physically, he wasn't very imposing. Guys in those days didn't lift weights. They used training camp to get in shape, but he was a pretty tough guy who could take a hit. He stood in the pocket till the very last minute, he played with injuries all the time. He tore his Achilles tendon playing racquet ball, had surgery, and came to training camp when it wasn't even totally healed yet. He was out there practicing and it was bleeding through his sock." And that was years before major league pitcher Curt Schilling gained fame for taking the mound for the Boston Red Sox with a bloody sock.

Manny Fernandez, former Dolphins star, said that once after he had retired he was playing golf in a tournament in North Carolina. "I was addressing the ball on a par three and about to hit my tee shot when I got laid out by a cross body block. I mean, he laid me out. I was ready to fight. I turned around and it was Johnny U. He laid me out and just stood there laughing, 'Ha, ha, ha. I owed you that.' He was no spring chicken then—in the mid-to late 1980s. All I could do was go over and give him a hug."

Asked if he had, in fact, sacked Unitas over the years, Fernandez joked, "Never enough. He was one tough cookie. He'd hang in the pocket—that's why he got hit so often. I mean, I put a lot of shots on him, but not enough sacks, but he would hang on to the ball until the last second. Fearless. And accurate."

One opponent said he actually believed sometimes Unitas would purposely hold on to the football a second or so longer than he had to before releasing it. The reason? So he could absorb a hit from a defender and just laugh at the tackler.

In a contest against the Packers, Unitas had been tackled and was still on the ground when Johnny Symank, a defensive back, pounced on Unitas's chest with his knees. The impact broke three ribs, punctured a lung, and caused Unitas to be hospitalized.

With uncanny resiliency, Unitas missed just two games. Upon his return, and on the very first play from scrimmage, he heaved a fifty-eight-yard score to Moore and the Colts waltzed to a 34–7 victory.

Not surprisingly, the Unitas mentality can be traced back to his youth. John Ziemann, the president of Baltimore's Marching Ravens (formerly the Baltimore Colts Marching Band) became a close friend of Unitas. He stated, "John came from a tough area of western Pennsylvania, right outside of Pittsburgh. His mother was widowed at a young age so John had to get out and help support the family plus go to school. As a kid, he used to shovel coal in people's houses for, like, twenty-five cents to help make ends meet. It was a tough life, and a life that taught him that you have to get out and work for what you want."

Another tough quarterback was Otto Graham, aka "Automatic Otto," who seemed to win every game he played with automaton regularity. That led opponents to look forward to facing him the same way a condemned Frenchman anticipated his march to the guillotine. Graham accomplished some absolutely eye-popping feats.

He led his league in passing five times and in touchdowns thrown three times. In three seasons he completed 59 percent or more of his passes, and he led the NFL in that category four times, including his final three seasons.

Versatile, he was also a defensive back and a punt return artist. He even played pro basketball for the old Rochester Royals. And what a leader he was—from 1946 through 1955 he played in a remarkable ten consecutive championship games, a feat unprecedented and still unmatched. From 1946 through 1949, his Browns went 47-4-3 in regular season play, winning four All-American Football Conference titles in a row. Then, in the NFL from 1950 to 1955, the Browns won three of their six championship games. Over his dozen playoff games he registered a win-loss percentage of .750.

Longtime football coach George Belu commented, "Graham was more of a cerebral football player, in my humble opinion, than like a Fran Tarkenton who's going to beat you running all over the place. Graham was such an intelligent football player who knew everything about the game. I can remember a time when they hit him on the sidelines and ripped his mouth open. He had to go in and have about fourteen stitches, and he came back and played the second half of that game. You think of him as cerebral, just sitting in the pocket throwing, but, boy, he had some competitiveness and toughness to him. He has to be among the toughest quarterbacks ever."

Over his ten-year pro career, his teams posted a win-lose record of 105-17-4. He departed football in style after again winning the NFL championship in 1955. Going into the 2016 season, he still ranked number eighteen lifetime for touchdowns thrown and eleventh for the best percentage of his throws going for scores at 6.0 percent.

Bobby Layne was no slouch, either. The fearless Hall of Fame quarterback had a reputation for partying, yet being able to perform on the day after.

After Sam Havrilak retired, he became a dentist and Art Donovan was a patient. Donovan shared a Layne story with Havrilak. "The Colts were playing Detroit, and, of course Layne would skip curfew quite a bit—I kind of doubt if players do that anymore, but we did it quite a bit years ago. Anyway, Art tackled Layne. Layne didn't even wear a face mask until later in his career. Art was close to Layne's face and he said, 'Christ, Layne, your breath is terrible.' Bobby said, 'Well, it should. I was out until five in the morning drinking.'"

Donovan elaborated and told the story a bit differently, saying the sack came in the second half of a game in which Layne's line wasn't protecting him, making for a long day. When Donovan noticed Layne's breath reeked of alcohol, he said, "You must have downed quite a few last night." Layne grinned and replied, "Fatso, let me let you in on a secret. The way this game's going, I had to down a few at halftime."[5]

Marchetti said Layne was as tough as they come, "Oh, God, yes. I think he was a leader, too. I can remember one game we played. We were ahead by [almost] three touchdowns. For some reason Layne had been benched. With about five minutes to go in the ballgame, he comes out on the field. Right away I'm nervous because I had played against him a few years and I know what he does to the whole team when he comes on. He picks them up, puts them on his shoulders. He scored three touchdowns and beat us."

Marchetti shared another Layne story. "One day in Memorial Stadium, Bobby Layne was the quarterback for the Detroit Lions, and I got, I think it was, eight sacks. In those days they counted sacks a helluva lot different than they do today. One time he got so mad I could hear him cussing his tackle out, 'Goddamnit, if you can't block that son of a bitch, let him go, I'll get him.'"

Belu said that Layne may have been a character, "but, I'll tell you what, he could take some hits and he'd stay in that game. He had some toughness." Andy Nelson chipped in, "You had to fear all the quarterbacks; they all were good, playing professional football, you had to have talent, but Layne was a good one. He was tough on the field and off the field, too."

Layne, one of the pioneer practitioners of the two-minute drill, loathed losing. He led the NFL in points scored in 1956 with ninety-nine. In 1951 he was arguably the best, or certainly one of the very best, quarterbacks around, leading the league in multiple major categories.

He also excelled at leading people. Pottios played with Layne and called him, "Probably the greatest leader that I ever played with. He had this quality about him that when he spoke, everybody listened. I mean, it was amazing, he just had that ability."

From time to time he'd tell teammates to join him at a bar for some fun after practice. There would be no divisiveness or arguing between offense and defense under Layne. Pottios noted, "He used a little psychology to get us togetherness, to get the guys closer, interacting instead of [going in] every direction. He ran the show." As for the tales of his lifestyle, "That was true. He lived hard, he lived fast, but he could play football."

Mike Ditka, like John Mackey, revolutionized the way his position was perceived and how it was utilized, not that he wasn't a solid blocker. His 1,076 yards on catches in his rookie season, 1961, helped announce the start of a new trend for tight ends. In the days of the fourteen-game season, no tight end ever caught more than his seventy-five receptions in 1964. From the very beginning of his playing days, he was so good and so strong fans almost expected him to don a cape and a mask before performing his heroics.

"Iron Mike" and pain went hand in hand, but as rugged as he was, he dealt with it. He broke his jaw once in a car accident. His dentist told him he could either save his four loose teeth by having his jaw wired shut, which would mean Ditka would have to sit out for several weeks, or he could have those teeth extracted. Unhesitatingly, Ditka opted for having the teeth pulled.

Speaking of teeth, at the University of Pittsburgh Ditka studied dentistry, which led people to conclude that his hits on opponents on the football field caused the same teeth that he planned to someday work on as a dentist, to fall out prematurely—and violently.

Pottios's Notre Dame team played Pitt every year, back when players went both ways. "I played guard," said Pottios, "and I had to block him, and, boy, he just waited to unlock that forearm. You felt it."

Joe Walton was in his first pro season when Ditka was in his freshman season with the Panthers. The Pitt coach, John Michelosen asked Walton to help with his ends in spring football. "I remember Mike was one of my star pupils. I told Coach Michelosen, 'If you want to, you can play Mike anywhere.' He would have been a great linebacker; he would have been great at anything. He was an awesome football player who had the right temperament. He had size and speed. He actually was the prototype of today's tight ends."

Ditka clearly was as tough as they come. After he retired as a coach, he reflected on himself and his reputation, "I don't know how you define what toughness is. I never asked any quarter, I never gave any, but you come to a point somewhere along the way where you make conscientious decisions about who you are or where you're at, where you want to be and how you're gonna get there."

Ditka, who has a reputation of having solid values, said he got that from his parents. In a 2014 interview he said, "She's ninety-three. She's in a nursing home; her mind's good. She's terrific. But we were taught life is long and when I did wrong, I got my ass kicked. I was the oldest of four children. I was the example, and my dad did not spare the rod. He wore me out when I did things wrong, and that was OK. I didn't understand it then, but I understood it as I got into college and I started looking at other people because he gave me a value system and an understanding, 'You've got to do what's right. You *cannot* bend the rules.' You have to stay on the right side of what's right. Now, you say, 'What's right?' Well, what's right in the eyes of man and what's right in the eyes of God are two different things. Man bends the rules, they like to be flexible. I don't bend the rules. What's right is right, what's wrong is wrong. I believe in treating people the way I expect to be treated. To me, we don't have that attitude in America anymore." His values and upbringing are all a part of the man and of his toughness.

Gino Marchetti selected two Jims as the greatest, roughest running backs he ever faced—Jim Brown, and Jim Taylor of the Green Bay Packers. Brown, he said, was tough and could elude tacklers or run them over, but he did feel there was somewhat of a distinction between the two runners. "Taylor was different. If you took an elbow to Taylor, he'd give you one right back. Taylor was tough. He'd knock your block off on pass protection. He wouldn't duck his head or let you run around him. He was probably the greatest [pass] blocking fullback there was at that time, but he didn't get much credit, particularly on the Packers, because they were mostly a running team."

So, as far as blocking goes, Marchetti said Taylor was "maybe a little tougher than Brown." Still, when Marchetti heard critics say Brown didn't block, he replied, "If I carried the ball as many times as Brown did, I probably wouldn't block, either. Brown was built for speed, quickness, shiftiness. Taylor was built for power. I'd take them both."

The Packers under Vince Lombardi certainly did run to daylight, and fullback Taylor found holes as a gritty inside runner. Pottios noted, "Taylor was strong and he'd drop his shoulder—he'd run over you." True, but Taylor also made openings for his backfield partners with bruising blocks, often leading Green Bay's trademark power sweep.

Green Bay won the Mega Millions lottery in the 1958 draft when they selected Taylor in the second round, then acquired Ray Nitschke one round later. That entire draft produced just three future Hall of Famers, so the Packers certainly did clean up. The third '58 draft future Hall of Famer was Bobby Mitchell, shockingly a seventh-round pick.

Belu noted Taylor was out of LSU: "When I was coaching there, I got to meet and be around him. Even when he retired—he was living in Baton Rouge—he kept himself in such great physical condition. He had great pride in his play. He wanted to be the best that he could be. He had great toughness. When he carried the ball, he was a tough runner who would get you short yardage, and when he blocked, he came to block!"

Taylor was the first man to register five straight seasons with 1,000 tough yards gained on the ground, back when the 1,000-yard plateau meant more than it does today. In his peak season, 1962, he found the end zone an NFL-leading nineteen times and rumbled his way for 1,474 yards to become the only man to interrupt Jim Brown's streak of winning the rushing title. His 114 points led the NFL, as did his average of 105.3 yards rushing per game.

Taylor's main running mate at Green Bay was Paul Hornung. Belu said, "Of course everything you think about him was his nickname, 'the Golden Boy,' and he came across that way, but you talk about somebody who competed! When that whistle blew, Hornung came to play. I mean, all that pretty boy and Golden Boy—that was not the way he played the game."

Hornung's career was diverse and illustrious (although he and Alex Karras were suspended for the 1963 season for gambling on NFL games). Hornung set a record for the most points scored in a season as he ran, caught, and kicked his way to 176 total points in 1960, and he'd chip in 146 more the following season. The 176-point total stood as a record for forty-six years. A Heisman Award winner as a Notre Dame quarterback, he was the number one overall draft pick in 1957. He continued his winning ways in the NFL, notching an MVP Award in 1961 and four world championships

Pottios critiqued Hornung by saying, "He was just an all-around ballplayer—nothing out of the ordinary, but just damned good. He wasn't physical, he didn't have tremendous speed, but he was just super." Havrilak knew of Hornung's versatility, noting how good he was at the halfback option pass. "He played quarterback at Notre Dame. Of course he played in that famous Green Bay offense, and people don't realize it, but they probably only had about ten or fifteen plays a game. They executed them so well that they kind of dared the defense. They said, 'This is what were going to do, and here it is, and come on and stop us.' And most teams didn't in those days."

Pottios continued, "He and Taylor were a good combination. They just fit that program and the offense that Lombardi put in, along with Starr's passing. They were the guys who did the job, that's the best way to explain it. They did what they had to do. They were very disciplined."

Belu observed, "Another thing he had—and this is a real innate part of a great running back—was he could slip a block. He'd give you a limp leg like Jim Brown—when they'd come in to tackle him, he'd put his weight on his opposite foot and not have any weight on the foot they were going to hit, and they'd miss the tackle; or he'd shift his hips at the last minute to make them miss, or he'd roll with the tackle. Tacklers did not get a real clean shot on Hornung. And his pass-catching ability was real good, too."

Oddly, while many people tend to think of Taylor as the big fullback who would block for a smaller halfback in Hornung, they both weighed right around 215 pounds, and Hornung was two inches taller than Taylor.

A final thought on toughness: being rugged in the vicious world of the NFL can, of course, be an asset, but it has its drawbacks as well. When Tom Landry was a player his lip was split open, but he finished the game, naturally. Later when the trainer finally attended to him, he sewed the lip up, putting in stitches without the use of anything such as a local anesthetic. So much for sports medicine.

A more serious concern deals with head injuries. Andy Nelson of the Colts said in his day if a player sustained a concussion, team officials basically placed smelling salts under his nose then instructed him to tell how many fingers the trainer was holding up. Then, often after a brief time, the player was sent back into the game, to "play through it." Players knew they had to accept the risk of concussions—it was either that or get scoffed at and probably even lose their job. So serious injuries were often minimized, at times reduced to a joke shared with teammates who might say, "Oh, man, you just got your bell rung good," or, "Ah, that's nothing—just got your bell rung, that's all."

Rick Volk sustained a concussion in Super Bowl III and, even now, has few recollections of the game after he was injured. Volk said he can remember being in the hospital. "I had some things that happened to me—convulsions at the hotel. It took some time to get myself back to normal, but I had the whole off-season to sort of get my mind and my brain right. It really took a long time.

"That's why these concussion things that you see right now are serious, because you don't feel bad, but you're not really ready to go out and hit again because your brain might be swelled a little bit. You're more susceptible to getting knocked out easier. That's why they're really testing these guys now when they get hit, and hold them out for a game or two, and that's really probably the best thing."

Bill Malinchak said after he sustained three concussions in one season he was fortunate not to suffer another. Having three in one year was understandable for several reasons. First, and most obvious, is that people who play a sport such as pro football are, by the very nature of the game, prime candidates for getting concussions. Secondly, "Once you get one," said Malinchak, "they come easily, they come a lot easier like when I got kicked in the helmet and hit another time hit head-on.

That's when I was playing special teams as a wedge buster so you had to put your head in there. And I'm 195, 200 pounds, but you had to do it.

"At that time they weren't recognizing concussions—it was just called a 'dinger.' They'd give you smelling salts and, 'How many fingers do I have up.' Then they would evaluate if you could go in and play again. I don't remember at that time if I went back in. I don't think I did, but I'm not sure. I don't remember." He reiterated that he quickly sustained his three concussions, but added, "I didn't get any more. I only had three." Only a man who made a living doing a dangerous activity such as pro football would use the word "only" in conjunction with discussing his three concussions.

Furthermore, many a player from the old days now has mangled fingers, lingering pain, and much more serious repercussions from playing with serious injuries. A link between chronic traumatic encephalopathy (CTE) is now known to exist, and many former pro football players suffer, and die, from Alzheimer's disease.

Probably ignorance was bliss back in the 1950s and 1960s in one respect, as fans and players could take delight in watching the game's toughest players lay somebody out with a crushing blow without thinking about the human side of the equation and the long-range ramifications of the damage the tough guys doled out and absorbed. And there is no doubt about it; this golden era did feature some of the toughest players ever to don shoulder pads.

5

THE BEST OF THE REST

Not all of the interesting, noteworthy players from the decades of the fifties and sixties were Hall of Famers. Some, for example, were talented Pro-Bowlers who were famous, but not household names such as the previously discussed Jim Brown and Dick Butkus. This chapter is far from all-inclusive, but it does provide profiles of some quite interesting stars of the Glory Years, a select list of the rest of the best.

Take defensive back Pat Fischer, for example. The five-foot, nine-inch, 170-pound Fischer spent seventeen seasons with the Cardinals and Redskins. Belu said Fischer was in the mold of Johnny Sample in that he was "a small, undersized player that played with tenacity. In today's vernacular, he wasn't a great athlete, but I guarantee you, he was an athlete that reacted to the football and came up and hit, and he could play the ball very well for his size."

Bill Malinchak was on the same Redskins team with Pat Fischer. "He was a good friend of mine. As a matter of fact, he was my roommate at one summer camp at Carlisle, Pennsylvania, so we were close and he was a good guy. He was a very intelligent guy.

"The thing that jumps out at me with Pat is before games. I can remember early on, I guess this was probably my second year there, right before a game I tried to talk to Pat. I said something to him and he just refused to talk to anybody. He was getting so focused. He was totally focused—there was no way to say anything to him. He was visualizing everything he had to do, I guess, and that was it."

Fischer made the Pro Bowl three times, and his fifty-six interceptions have him tied with Lem Barney at number eighteen on the all-time list. Although he never led the league in any category, he came in second in 1964 with his ten interceptions and third another time. He also finished second and fourth for interception return yards. Steady and dependable.

Baltimore's Andy Nelson was another solid defensive back. He made the Pro Bowl in 1960, but wasn't selected as an All-Pro, and in 1959 he was First-Team All-Pro, but didn't get invited to the Pro Bowl. When asked how that played out, Nelson responded, "I don't know. I should have gone to the Pro Bowl three or four times.

"I guess I was handpicked by Vince Lombardi when I got to go in 1960. We played on the West Coast and Don Kellett, our general manager, had run into Lombardi at the airport when the Packers were coming in to play on the West Coast. He told Kellett he wanted me for the Pro Bowl, so I was picked by Lombardi and I was proud of that, I really was.

"In 1958 I had my best year, one of my proudest moments. We won the world championship and I contributed to it. That made me feel good. I led the league in return yardage, 199, I had eight interceptions. I should have gone to the Pro Bowl then and in 1959. In 1960 I had a fair year and I wasn't going then until I got picked by Lombardi."

Nelson said it seemed as if once a player was selected for honors such as playing in the Pro Bowl, he would go back often—much like how once a major league baseball player gets a reputation for being a good fielder he may win many Gold Gloves, sometimes virtually unopposed. "It was a great honor in our day to go to the Pro Bowl," continued Nelson, "but it doesn't seem to be now.

"Winners got $500, losers got $300. We won when I was out there, but to me, I wanted to show them what I could do. A different mind-set [from today's players]." Plus, of course, back then the $200 difference in the paycheck meant more to players than any gap between the winning and losing purse would to players in the game today. "We played hard for pride. You were representing your team, the Baltimore Colts, and I wanted to try to do the best that I could. In other words, I played as hard as I would play in any game during the season. I don't think they need the money [or are willing to risk injury] now."

At one point Otto Graham was working with Nelson on his quarter-back skills. Nelson recalled, "He said, 'Now, Andy, you've got a future as a quarterback here.' I said, 'I want to play. Who's going to play over Unitas? I'm playing defense.'

"But I was a defensive back. That's what was my game. I was known mainly for my tackling. Weeb Ewbank said I was the best tackler on the team."

Nelson's Colts won it all again in 1959. "Coming from a small school, Memphis State, that was a good feeling, and so was playing with guys like Raymond Berry, John Unitas, Gino Marchetti, Jim Parker, all the Hall of Fame guys. I was just proud to be on the team. I did my job and, of course, I wasn't perfect.

"I only weighed 170 pounds and wasn't the biggest defensive back, but I was wiry and didn't get hurt that much until the years caught up to me. In college I never came out of games. The Lord took me to the right place. I had a good career."

Baltimore's Bobby Boyd was another defensive back of note. He spent his whole career with the Colts (1960–1968). Born in Dallas, Texas, he defected across the border to play his college ball for legendary coach Bud Wilkinson at Oklahoma. After his days with the Sooners came to an end, he was converted to cornerback by the Colts from his former quarterback position.

In fact, when the Colts' two main quarterbacks, John Unitas and Gary Cuozzo went down with injuries in 1965, head coach Don Shula had to look down his bench in desperation to find a fill in. He gave the nod to Tom Matte, who had also played quarterback in college, at Ohio State, but he gave consideration to Boyd as well.

It only made sense to place Boyd in the picture—at Oklahoma he, like Matte, had been more of a runner than a passer, but he helped get the job done for the Sooners. In his first two seasons of seeing playing time, Oklahoma finished fourth and fifth in the final Associated Press polls.

Playing from 1957 through 1959, Boyd only threw the football 110 times for six touchdowns. Face it, though, at Oklahoma back then, *nobody* threw the football much. During Boyd's three-year stretch the team averaged a mere 11.1, 11.7, and 11.1 passes per game. He also ran for more than five hundred yards as a senior, and at the end of that season his Sooners owned a cumulative record of 27-5 during his tenure.

"Bobby Boyd protected me," Marchetti chuckled. "He was a left [defensive] halfback who played outside of me. Once the defense lined up, from the center over there [to the left] was Art Donovan, me, Bill Pellington, and then there was Boyd. He was a good defensive back, a lot of speed, he covered *a lot* of ground. He was a good ballplayer, a nice guy, and worked hard. We liked him a lot."

No wonder. Nelson was a veteran when Boyd broke in with Baltimore and said Boyd picked things up quickly. "I went over defenses with him and I could talk to him during the game, tell him what they were going to try to do to him. I think he ended up with sixty interceptions [actually, 57, tied number thirteen all-time through 2015]. He was tough, a good tackler and he could read offenses." Nine of his fifty-seven interceptions came in one season, 1965, when he led the league in that department.

Other observers of Boyd must also have liked him as he was selected to the Pro Football Hall of Fame All-1960s Team. His 994 yards on interception returns stood tenth best all-time going into the 2016 season. During the 1964 season he helped Baltimore make it to the championship game by returning nine interceptions for 185 yards, good enough to lead the NFL.

Boyd was also quite dependable, missing action in just three games over his nine years in the NFL. Even in his final season he was still going strong. He picked off eight passes and returned them for 160 yards, his third highest output and the sixth time he topped the century mark for yards gained on interception returns.

Rick Volk's career in the Colts secondary overlapped Boyd's for a few years. Volk was a fine player, an All-Pro and winner of a Super Bowl ring. Like all consummate pros, he gave a great deal of thought to playing his position. Naturally, he was well aware of how difficult his safety position was to play. As many have pointed out, a defensive back is doing the same thing a receiver does, but he is doing so in reverse, that is to say he is running backward, having to react to the receiver. "If you're playing a zone or a man, whatever it is," began Volk, "you've got a responsibility, and once you realize it's a passing play and the ball goes into the air, then you become a receiver is what you do.

"A lot of guys I see playing today, the defensive backs, they don't get their head around, they don't see where the ball is. The receiver does, he sees that the ball is short, he stops and the guy runs into him or runs by him, and the receiver turns and catches the ball. I always felt that if I could get my eyes on the ball, if I could see where it's going, I could play the ball and make adjustments like a receiver does. I know they run a lot of man coverage now, and they tell the guy to, 'Just stay with your man. Don't turn around and look—as soon as you turn around and look, he's gaining on you.'

"I don't know, it's just a different philosophy of playing defensive back, but we played more zone than we did man coverage, so it could be more of a situation in which your eyes are more on the quarterback and the receiver, both, and you react that way."

It probably boils down to whatever works best for you is what you should stick with. Volk definitely got the job done. He made the Pro Bowl three times and picked off thirty-eight career passes. He even came in fourth in 1968 for yards gained on punt returns. That same season, he returned one punt ninety-four yards, longest of the year.

Moving to the defensive line, there's Jim Marshall, who was the Iron Horse of the NFL. One source says he owned a streak of playing in 301 straight games, counting postseason contests. He played so long, his rookie season of 1960 (when he broke in with the Browns) was still in the era of the twelve-game schedule, and his final two seasons, 1978 and 1979, were years with sixteen games on the schedule. He also held the record for most lifetime fumble recoveries with thirty.

Teammate Fred Cox said, "I played with the only guy that picked up a fumble [in the NFL] and ran the wrong way with it, Jim Marshall. He was probably the greatest defensive football player in football annals who isn't in the Hall of Fame. He should be there. It's hard to believe that a man who played for twenty years without missing a football game and was an All-Pro isn't in the Hall of Fame. And it's strictly because we lost four Super Bowls."

Cox was correct about the fumble and he may also be right on the money about the losses in the Super Bowl. First, the defeats. While many experts contend that having the talent it takes just to get to the Super Bowl is laudable and should be a huge plus on one's resume, too many Americans are consumed with labeling things using only black and white markers. That way of thinking argues, "You're either a winner or you're a loser."

Marshall shares the same fate as Buffalo Bills quarterback Jim Kelly, who took his team to four consecutive Super Bowls only to leave each one with another tally mark in the loss column. In his case, though, voters considered his entire body of work and elected him to the Hall of Fame. Marshall may never get in.

As for Marshall's Wrong Way Corrigan Act, in a 1964 contest against the San Francisco 49ers Billy Kilmer, in his days before he became a starting quarterback, caught a pass from George Mira, but fumbled the football. Alertly, Marshall scooped the ball up and huffed and puffed his way into the end zone on a sixty-six-yard jaunt.

However, it was not to be a happy trip, as he had become disoriented and ran into the Vikings' own end zone. Upon arrival, he fired the football out of bounds to celebrate his having put six points on the board. Unfortunately, in reality he had placed two points on the San Francisco side of the scoreboard as the play was ruled a safety. Moments after his celebratory toss, a 49er trotted over and patted the perplexed Marshall on his back. Who knows, perhaps such a moment did enter the minds of some Hall of Fame voters, as Cox believes.

If so, those voters were shortsighted. Marshall was much more than his actions of one moment. Those in the know, such as Miami offensive lineman Doug Crusan, who had to play against Marshall, are cognizant of his abilities.

Crusan said, "He was quick. He was the smallest of their front four. Eller was a heckuva pass rusher, [Gary] Larsen was at tackle, then Page was across from our left guard and Marshall who was across from me— so that's what I faced when I played Minnesota. Marshall was a very, very good player who belongs in the Hall of Fame."

Gene "Big Daddy" Lipscomb was considered to be huge in his day (hence the nickname); he was six foot six and made scales groan with his 284-pound weight.

Former linebacker Myron Pottios commented, "I liked him. I tell you one thing, he had the speed and the quickness. In fact, I think 'Big Daddy' was the fastest defensive lineman that I ever played with, and I played with Deacon Jones who everybody says was the fastest, but I think 'Big Daddy' would beat him in a forty-yard straight-on race. It would have been a good race because both were big men and had great speed."

Lipscomb was a Pro Bowl defensive tackle three times during his career, which spanned the years 1953 through 1962 with the Rams, Colts, and Steelers. He was also a member of two championship-winning teams with the Colts in 1958 and 1959.

Raymond Berry called Lipscomb a huge force and huge asset for Baltimore. "He was quick with great upper-body strength, a heckuva defensive tackle. We got him in a trade from the Rams. How in the world they let go of him has only one explanation—they had so much talent in those days they didn't realize what they were doing."

Intimidating in every way, he was a fierce tackler. One time he explained his style of bringing opposing players down: "I just wrap my arms around the whole backfield and peel 'em off one by one until I get to the ball carrier. Him I keep."

The behemoth Lipscomb came straight to the NFL from the streets and sandlots of Detroit, never having played in college. Tragically, in 1963, he was found dead with needle marks above veins in both of his arms with a syringe near his body. He was thirty-one years old.

Miami's Manny Fernandez, who played at both the defensive tackle and end spots, began his career at the end of the 1960s and said he is most proud of simply "making it as far as I did." Make no mistake, he made it quite far, making it to three Super Bowls, winning it all twice.

Of course, in one of the Dolphins' championship seasons, 1972, they rolled to a perfect 17-0 record, and their win-loss record for their two consecutive Super Bowl champion seasons of 1972–1973 was at an unheard of, nose-bleed altitude of .941, based on their cumulative 32-2 record—and Fernandez was right in the middle of the action. In those seasons, as was the case for most of his NFL games, he manned the left tackle spot, playing with players who were not future Hall of Famers, perhaps, but were very good, making for a solid unit. Because of their lack of ink and fame, the Miami defense was dubbed the "No Name Defense."

It's funny how, even over a long career—and Fernandez lasted eight years in the NFL—individual plays stay in a player's memory bank. Fernandez recalled, "There was a big fullback for New England and one day they threw a little swing pass to him, and I had a clear shot at him, and boy, I mean, I just knew I was going to drill him. Well, I did, but it was sort of a mutual drilling. He caught me with his knee in the side of the head and the next think I knew, it was the next morning and I was calling the trainer to see who won the game. I kind of lost a day-and-a-half."

Fernandez said another time in the Super Bowl against the Washington Redskins he got clocked—this time by a teammate. "Nick Buoniconti put my lights out. I had a hold of Larry Brown and Nick was coming in to put the killer on him. Hit me instead. I did hang on to Larry—we both went down, but I don't remember [anything else] until the second half of the fourth quarter of that game, Super Bowl VII."

Despite those painful memories, Fernandez enjoyed a fine career. In half of his seasons he was named to a first or second team on various All-Pro squads such as the UPI, which he made three years in a row.

Next, there's Rosey Grier, who played both tackle and end, and did his job well. Joe Walton played with Grier in New York. "He was always singing songs and playing his guitar and everybody used to tease him that he was going to be in show business, and that turned out to be right." Grier not only entertained audiences with his musical talent, he appeared in movies and on television—although being cast in movies such as *The Thing with Two Heads*, he wasn't exactly Oscar bait.

Walton resumed, "He was a helluva ballplayer. For a man his size he could run." He could also win. Over a seven-year period the two-time All-Pro Grier played in five title games. Incidentally, he also was the person who taught the head slap to Deacon Jones.

Aside from his involvement in the field of entertainment, he also became an ordained minister in 1983. A genuinely nice man, he made it a point to love others and try to help those who were down on their luck. Also active in politics, he became a bodyguard for Robert Kennedy during his 1968 run for the presidency. In fact, Grier said he wrestled the gun away from Sirhan Sirhan after the assassin had shot Kennedy.

Sam Havrilak broke in with the Colts at a good time, giving him the opportunity to play with some stars who, while aging, were still solid members of the team. That includes, of course, Johnny Unitas, Lenny Lyles, Fred Miller, Jimmy Orr, Jerry Logan, and Billy Ray Smith.

One young, big-name Colt defensive lineman was Bubba Smith, only twenty-four years old when Havrilak joined the Colts and met Smith in 1969. Havrilak chortled, "Bubba used to call me 'Hon-due,' because he thought my last name was Havlicek, the same as the Boston Celtic star. So for the first year or two I was there, instead of calling me 'Hondo,' because that was Havlicek's nickname, he would call me 'Hon-due.' After a while, we were on the training table one day and he says to me, 'You know I thought your name was Havlicek, so I've been calling you Hon-due.' I told him he could call me what he wanted—it makes no difference."

When you stand six foot seven and weigh in at 265, you can probably call anybody anything you like and get away with it—it'll make no difference at all. Smith, with a perfect nickname for a Texas-born player, had already established himself as a force at Michigan State. Charles Aaron Smith was a Consensus All-American in 1965 and 1966 and became the first overall draft choice in 1967.

Havrilak continued, "But he was a heck of a football player. In those days people weren't really weight-lifting strong. From that standpoint Bubba wasn't really that strong, and neither was Ted Hendricks, but they had such great football skills, with such great leverage they were able to make a lot of plays. Bubba probably had trouble bench pressing his own weight, which was about 275."

Havrilak appreciated the Colts giant defensive end, but said of the Glory Years, "One thing that you loved were the linebackers in those days. Lee Roy Jordan was the middle linebacker for Dallas, and he only weighed about 205 pounds. He was very, very small, but the defensive line was so good that they kept all the offensive lineman off of him so he could make a lot of plays."

Despite a lack of size, Jordan was inducted into the College Football Hall of Fame in 1983, seven years after he played his final NFL game. He was born in a town with a name that, as a verb, could go hand in hand with Jordan—Excel, in the state of Alabama. At Excel High School he was a fullback. He then stayed in state to play his college football at the University of Alabama for the man who for quite some time was the winningest coach in the game, Paul "Bear" Bryant. Jordan, a center and linebacker at Alabama, was a part of just the second recruiting class of Bryant's.

Jordan won the MVP in two of the three bowl games he played in. On New Year's Day of 1963, in his final game in an Alabama uniform, he was ubiquitous in the Orange Bowl, making a simply amazing thirty-one tackles in a 17–0 whitewashing of Oklahoma. The All-American even came in fourth in the Heisman Trophy voting. The previous season his Crimson Tide squad won the national championship with a perfect 11-0 record.

The Cowboys liked him a lot, relatively small size and all, and made Jordan their first-round draft pick (number six overall) in 1963. In most of the seasons he played he was, in fact, the smallest middle linebacker in the NFL. Incidentally, he was also drafted by the AFL's Boston Patriots, but shunned them and their cold-weather clime. He would be a mainstay to the defense of another legendary coach, Tom Landry, all the way through the 1976 season.

In a 1971 contest he was all over the field, compiling a team record twenty-one tackles against the Eagles. Two years later against the Bengals, he picked off three passes, one of which he took in for a score, from Kenny Anderson—all in the same quarter and all within a period of five minutes.

For a few years he was at the right linebacker spot before settling into, and shining at, the middle linebacker position. The move to that spot coincided with the era when Dallas ceased being a weak, relatively new team to the NFL and became a perennial powerhouse. Decades after Jordan quit, he still stood second on the franchise's list for career tackles, winding up with 743 solo tackles. His combined total of solo tackles plus the tackles he assisted on (1,236) is also number two on the all-time Cowboys list.

He made it to the postseason almost annually—playing in a total of nineteen playoff games—for "America's Team," and made it all the way to the Super Bowl on three occasions, winning it all once. All of those feats helped make him just the seventh Cowboy ever to be honored in the team's Ring of Honor.

Bob Hyland said, "Jordan was a guy who knew that Dallas defense as well as anybody. Jordan knew how to shield himself with his defensive linemen so he had a clear path to the ball carrier. He was a very good tackler, a very good player. He was their vocal leader on defense. I think everybody respected Jordan."

Pottios said Jordan "was a good ballplayer, tough, but not in the same destructive way that Butkus was. For a middle linebacker, he was small, like Nick Buoniconti." Green Bay runner Chuck Mercein added, "He was especially good for his size. He had great mobility. It was an honor to play against him."

"Hell, you had to see him," said former running back and wide receive John Isenbarger. "He would take his fake teeth, or at least one, out so when he opened his mouth there was just a gap." That intimidating sight was one Jack Lambert would later emulate.

Another fine Dallas linebacker was Chuck Howley. He played alongside Jordan from 1963 through 1973, the year of Howley's retirement. Actually, though, he began his career in 1958 as a member of the Chicago Bears, the team that drafted him out of West Virginia University in the first round as the seventh overall pick.

As a Mountaineer guard and center, he made All-Southern Conference three times and was that conference's Player of the Year in 1957. His skills helped West Virginia go 21-8-1 over his three years playing at the varsity level. He is believed to be the only man to attend that university and earn letters in five sports—football, track, swimming, wrestling, and gymnastics.

Moving to the NFL, he played in twelve games as a rookie with the Bears and in just three more contests the following season due to a knee injury he sustained in Chicago's training camp. That injury caused him to sit out all of the 1960 season.

Moving to the Cowboys in 1961, his career took off. In 1968, for example, he ranked tenth in the league with his six interceptions, and most of the players with more interceptions were defensive backs, not linebackers. Career-wise, he picked off twenty-five passes, returning them for 399 yards.

Like teammate Jordan, Howley also has his name emblazoned in the Cowboys Ring of Honor, which ran around Texas Stadium and is now on display around the AT&T Stadium in Arlington, Texas. Howley's name was added in 1977 following only three other Cowboys: Bob Lilly, Don Meredith, and Don Perkins. Through 2016, fewer than two dozen Cowboys have been so honored.

Without a doubt, his single most impressive honor was the MVP trophy he earned for his play in Super Bowl V. Sadly for Howley, the award is tarnished in that the Cowboys lost the game, making him the only member of the losing team to take home MVP honors. "He played well," said Havrilak of Howley's Super Bowl showing. "I think he had an interception, maybe two, and had a bunch of tackles."

Havrilak was correct, but he could have added the fact that the Cowboys star also recovered a fumble. Howley's first interception on a pass from John Unitas came in the opening quarter and led to the game's first score, a Mike Clark fourteen-yard field goal. At the start of the fourth quarter, Howley picked off an Earl Morrall pass, but it didn't figure in the scoring, and the Colts went on to win it on a thirty-two-yard boot by Jim O'Brien with nine seconds left to play in a 16–13 contest. Fortunately for Howley, he and his Cowboys returned to, and won, the Super Bowl the subsequent season.

Mercein called the six-time Pro Bowl pick "a great linebacker. I respected the heck out of his ability." And Bob Hyland said Howley, "fit the mold that Landry was looking for—a guy who plays defense first then reacts as a football player."

However, it was John Isenbarger who more bluntly summed up Howley. "He knocked the shit out of me. He was a fabulous linebacker. Everybody on the Cowboys was All-Pro."

Cleveland had a good one, too, in Jim Houston. Tom Matte said Houston, a thirteen-year vet who seldom missed a game, was a very versatile football player. A linebacker in the NFL, Houston was one of Matte's receivers when Matte quarterbacked the Buckeyes. "He was a tremendous football player."

Another Ohio State teammate, Chuck Bryant, said, "Jim and I were roommates. He never came off the field. He played defensive end, tight end, and when he went into the pros, he concentrated on the down defensive end [then linebacker position]."

A Pro Bowl player four times, Houston had a nose for the football. His hometown fans didn't find that a bit surprising as Houston's roots are entrenched in a locale steeped in football tradition, Massillon, Ohio. High school football there dates back to 1894 and the Tigers' most famous coach was Massillon High alum Paul Brown. He guided his old high school for nine seasons, winning six state championships while putting up an admirable record of 80-8-2. The school has produced twenty-three professional football players.

Myron Pottios, who was drafted by the Oakland Raiders and the Pittsburgh Steelers, decided to stay close to his western Pennsylvania roots. Thus he began his career, coming off the Notre Dame campus, as Pittsburgh's middle linebacker in 1961. He did so with a solid impact, making the Pro Bowl team in each of his first three seasons, 1961, 1963, and 1964 (he did not play in 1962). What's especially noteworthy about this is the fact that not only was he on that squad as a rookie, but when he was named to the Pro Bowl the third time, he had only played in half of his team's fourteen games.

The following season, 1965, he also played sparingly—in just six games. Pottios said that the first of the two head coaches he played under in the NFL, Buddy Parker, was a good coach, but the Steelers just couldn't seem to click. In Pottios's final two seasons in Pittsburgh they finished next-to-last and last in their East Division, going 7-21 those years, capped by an abysmal 2-12 season in 1965. However, all that was about to change, as he would no longer have to endure playing on, for the most part, losing teams.

Most of the fame Pottios earned came soon after his days with the Steelers, when he played under George Allen—first with the Rams from 1966 through 1970, then with the Redskins from 1971 until his final NFL season, 1973.

In just the second season with Los Angeles for both Allen and Pottios, the team soared to the playoffs on a gaudy 11-1-2 record. The Rams' staunch defense was fortified behind their great line by a fine linebacking crew. Allen stationed Pottios in the middle, between two very good linebackers, Jack Pardee and Maxie Baughan.

When Allen was fired by the Rams, he moved on to take the head coach position with the Washington Redskins for the 1971 season; one of his earliest moves was to acquire Pottios. Allen, who favored having veterans on his team over young players, turned his team into what became know as the Over-the-Hill-Gang.

Allen knew he should build another tough linebacking unit, and he did. This one featured Pottios and Pardee together once more, Chris Hanburger, and Dave Robinson at times. The somewhat underrated Pottios helped the Redskins make it to postseason play right away in 1971, and again in each of the next two seasons before he retired.

During those three years, Washington's overall regular season record was 30-11-1.

In fact, Pottios was a member of the Redskins when they made it to Super Bowl VII at the end of his 1972 season. It took the runaway train Miami Dolphins (17-0 on the season) to stop Washington from reaching the apex of the NFL that year.

Pottios's credentials are solid. For example, in 1968 he ranked third in the NFL for fumble recoveries, calling his ability to find the football "a combination of skill, luck, and being in the right place at the right time, and it's hustle. The more you're hustling around the ball, your chances of something good to happen are going to be in your favor." Over his thirteen-year career, Pottios caused plenty of good things to happen for himself and for his teams.

Incidentally, when he departed from his original team, good things were destined for the Steelers. Pottios's presence on that team was the start of what would become a great defensive unit. Then, another early part of the Pittsburgh defensive puzzle fell into place when linebacker Andy Russell joined the Steelers in 1963. This was a team just beginning to build an NFL empire. Some experts trace the genesis of the great Steel Curtain defense, with a focus on a long line of stellar linebackers, back to Pottios with a nod of recognition also going to Russell. The other great linebackers such as Jack Ham and Jack Lambert would follow.

Switching to running backs, there's the very valuable Jim Kiick, a Dolphins running mate of Larry Csonka and Mercury Morris. Miami teammate Doug Crusan said, "Kiick was a character. Funny. He and Zonk were best of friends, 'Butch Cassidy and the Sundance Kid,' and you had Merc, the third one who would alternate with Kiick. Kiick was a very good pass catcher coming out of the backfield and they threw to him a lot."

In 1972, the Dolphins became the first NFL team ever to boast of two 1,000-yard rushers. Csonka rumbled for 1,117 yards and Morris darted for exactly 1,000. For the record, Kiick added 521 more on the ground, the year they ran the table, winning the NFL championship with an unblemished 17-0 record.

Oddly, before firmly securing his 1,000th yard, Morris had only been credited with 991 yards. However, five days after the regular season's end, a statistician's error that had cost Morris nine yards was unearthed. When those yards were added back into his total, Morris wound up with exactly 1,000 yards rushing.

Dan Reeves was an important player long before he became a successful NFL head coach. He signed with the Dallas Cowboys, not as a highly touted, early-round draft pick, but as a free agent just out of college in 1964. The NFL and AFL had selected more than five hundred players in their respective drafts, and Reeves was spurned by everyone. By the time he retired, though, having played his entire career with the Cowboys, he stood number five on the team's all-time rushing list.

Hardly a flashy runner, the Rome, Georgia, native was, nevertheless, steady. He rushed for 757 yards and tacked on an additional 557 on catches in 1966. Those statistics meant he led his team, better than veteran Don Perkins, for ground gains, and he trailed only Bob Hayes for yards gained on receptions. Also that season Reeves's eight touchdowns scored on runs was tied for the second-highest total in the NFL, and his eight additional touchdowns on pass receptions placed him behind only five players in this department. Furthermore, his total of sixteen TDs ranked him first in the league that season (tied with Cleveland's Leroy Kelly).

Thanks in part to Reeves, 1966 also marked the first time the Cowboys won a division title. As a matter of fact, it was the first time the Cowboys ended a season above the break-even mark. Finishing the season at 10-3-1, Dallas then battled Green Bay for the NFL title. Reeves came through with a touchdown run, but the Cowboys fell seven points short of the champion Packers.

In his prime Reeves, a true all-purpose back, was good for about four yards or so per carry and around thirteen yards per reception. Reeves lasted eight seasons (1965 through 1972) in the NFL, easily beating the average length of tenure for running backs. In 1968, he suffered the same knee injury sustained by Gale Sayers, yet Reeves continued contributing to the Cowboys winning ways, playing in thirteen or more games in each of his remaining seasons in the league.

He continued to make a living from football long after his days as an active player ended. Actually, for the final three seasons with the Cowboys his football acumen was so highly regarded he was selected to serve as a player/coach. Then, before getting his first head coaching job, he was an assistant coach. At the age of thirty-three he was named Tom Landry's offensive coordinator.

As a head coach, Reeves won 190 games over twenty-three seasons. He won three AFC championships and one in the NFC. At Denver, he took his team to the playoffs in six of his twelve seasons, won five division titles, and made it to the Super Bowl three times of the four total times a Reeves-coached team made the trek to the Super Bowl.

He was so sought after, when his stay with one team was over, he immediately bounced back with another, coaching from 1981–2003, first with the Denver Broncos, then the New York Giants, before concluding his clipboard days with the Atlanta Falcons.

Reeves set a somewhat obscure record by appearing as a player or coach in nine Super Bowls—five with the Cowboys, three with the Broncos, and one with the Falcons. As a player, his Cowboys made it to postseason play in every season he suited up. While he did play on the losing end of Super Bowl V against Baltimore, he was a member of the resilient Dallas team that won Super Bowl VI in a 24–3 romp over Miami.

Sam Havrilak said Reeves, with a record of 14-of-42 as a passer over his career for an average of 26.4 yards per completion, was among the very best ever at throwing the halfback option. Tom Landry, who coached Reeves, put him right up there with Frank Gifford. Green Bay's Mercein naturally favored Hornung, who completed 24-of-55 passes for five TDs. "He was a quarterback at Notre Dame, so he could throw the option very well," said Mercein, "and Donny Anderson was good at it, but we didn't run him on it that much. Probably Reeves was best known for it—he was a quarterback also, at South Carolina. He was a gritty, tough football player and that was certainly an extra ability that he had."

Perhaps the biggest pass Reeves ever threw, albeit in a losing cause, came in the Ice Bowl, the NFL championship game between Dallas and the Green Bay Packers on New Year's Eve of 1967. Down by a score of 14–10 in the fourth quarter, Reeves hurled a pass to wide receiver Lance Rentzel for a fifty-yard touchdown strike. Sadly for the Cowboys, they held their lead until the final seconds of the game when Bart Starr made his famous sneak into the end zone. His plunge gave the Packers a 21–17 win and a trip to Super Bowl II.

Alex Webster, aka "Big Red," finished in the top ten in the NFL for yardage and touchdowns as a runner four times from 1955 to 1964. However, in the two seasons before he joined the New York Giants, he was with the Montreal Alouettes. There, in the Canadian Football League, he once was the league's leading ground gainer and MVP.

He had been drafted by the Washington Redskins in 1953, but as somewhat of an afterthought—he wasn't chosen until the eleventh round, way down low as the number 123 overall selection, and they soon cut him. The Redskins hadn't even given Webster a shot as a runner—after trying him on defense for a while, they set him loose before they even broke camp.

Webster was a powerful runner who also had good hands—in 1962 he had a personal high of forty-seven catches. When he did join the New York team he was instrumental in the Giants winning six division titles and one NFL championship during the Glory Years. At six feet, three inches, and right around 225 pounds, he was considered to be a burly running back, yet he could handle all of the duties of both half-back and fullback. For example, he was adept at open-field running, blocked well, and was ideal in short-yardage and goal-line situations. His main problem in the Big Apple may have simply been the fact that he was overshadowed by Frank Gifford.

Webster used his power and size to amass yards and records for the Giants—when he retired his 1,196 carries, his 4,638 yards, and his thirty-nine touchdowns via runs were all franchise highs, better than Gifford's output. Along the way, he enjoyed a personal season high of 928 yards rushing, as a fullback, in 1961, the first of two seasons in which his total yards from scrimmage eclipsed the 1,000 mark.

Webster's single-season best for touchdowns scored came in 1956, when he averaged almost one TD per game played. That was the same season his Giants won it all, trouncing the Chicago Bears in the title game, 47–7. That day Webster helped illuminate Yankee Stadium and its 56,836 fans in attendance by scoring on two short runs and grabbing five passes for seventy-six yards, including one reception that resulted in a fifty-yard gallop.

Teammate Joe Walton said, "I think we were playing the Steelers at Pitt Stadium [in the early 1960s]. I was downfield and he caught a screen pass and he was trying to run for the touchdown. I kept blocking the defensive back and Alex would follow me. I'd block him again, and Alex would still follow me. Finally, another guy came and tackled Alex and he said to me, 'If you'd have gotten out of my way, I'da scored.'" Walton let out a chuckle, "It was all my fault. OK, Alex. But he was a tough redhead, I'll tell you that.

"Alex Webster became a head coach of the New York Giants in 1969. I was scouting still and he asked me if I would come and help coach as well. So Alex is the guy that really got me into coaching."

Bob Hyland noted that Webster, "was unusually big for a running back in those days. He could do the whole thing—catch the ball, run with the ball, and he could block like a guard." Given all of the East Division titles and the one NFL championship Webster helped engineer, Hyland could have added, "Webster could also flat out win."

Ken Willard is the answer to an interesting trivia question: What San Francisco running back was selected in the 1965 NFL draft as the second overall pick, meaning he was chosen ahead of both Dick Butkus, the third pick that year, and Gale Sayers, the fourth selection. Only Tucker Frederickson of the Giants, who was a decent but not great player for six seasons, was drafted ahead of Willard.

Willard's background is interesting and colorful in other ways. The Boston Red Sox tried to get him to agree to a healthy contract, reportedly with a $100,000 bonus to sign, to play pro baseball. Instead, Willard played college football and baseball for the North Carolina Tar Heels, where he led the Atlantic Coast Conference in homers two times.

As a member of the 49ers, John Isenbarger got to see Willard, a good blocker and a four-time Pro Bowl pick who played in the NFL from 1965 to 1974, close up. "He was our fullback. He was like Jim Taylor of the Packers. They were just going to get three or four or five yards. I never saw him run more than twenty yards, ever. He just wasn't that type of runner." For the record, prior to Isenbarger's joining the 49ers, Willard did break off a sixty-nine-yard run in 1968.

Very steady, Willard accounted for about fifty yards per game on runs, grinding out almost four yards per carry while running rather sparingly. He averaged twelve rushes per game lifetime, but in his best seasons he was called upon to carry the ball more than sixteen times each game. Over his first four seasons in the league he was in the top five running backs for yards gained on the ground, finishing fourth as a rookie, then fifth the next year, and second two years after that.

One year, 1968, he ran quite a bit and ended the season with a career high 967 yards, tantalizingly close to the 1,000-yard plateau. He supplemented the San Francisco offense (John Brodie, John David Crow, Gene Washington, et al.) quite well by usually scoring around eight touchdowns a season during his prime years.

In addition to his value as a lead blocker and reliable runner, Willard also came through as a fine receiver, often on little flares and screen passes. In his sophomore season in the NFL he nabbed forty-two passes, a career high. Over his career he averaged almost exactly eight yards per catch. In all, he ran for 6,105 yards and caught 277 passes for 2,184 more yards.

Under head coach Dick Nolan, Willard saw action in postseason play in 1970 and 1971. Both years the 49ers won their opening round before losing the Conference Championship to the Cowboys. In the first round of the 1970 playoffs, a narrow 17–14 victory over the Vikings, Willard was responsible for more than one hundred yards in total offense, in what had to be his most important contribution ever.

He ended his career with a brief stint with St. Louis, helping the Cardinals any way he could. The team did make it to the playoffs in his one season there, 1974, but by then he had run out of steam and was used to carry the ball just once in a 30–14 loss to Minnesota.

Like many of our non-Hall of Famers, Willard may not have been great, but he was very good and much in demand. Willard, said Isenbarger, was similar to prototypical fullbacks such as Bill Brown and Tom Woodeshick. Such players often don't receive a lot of hype, but they're quite valuable. "And they were durable. They might have got hurt, but I don't remember them missing many games," concluded Isenbarger. Willard's first seven seasons featured him *not* starting only once.

As for Bill Brown's durability, he started twelve or more games in seven straight seasons. Not only that, when taped, suited up, and unleashed from the locker room, Brown wanted the ball. In 1966, he cradled the football under his strong arms 251 times. That total not only topped men such as Sayers, Leroy Kelly, and Jim Taylor, it led every other runner in the NFL. Brown was even used to run back kickoffs—not often, but one of his twenty-one career returns went for a seventy-eight-yard touchdown.

Like Willard, Brown's college background was interesting. He attended the University of Illinois where he made the All–Big Ten team at his fullback position. He also excelled at another sport, winning his conference's championship in the shot put event. He also set a school record in that event when he once heaved the shot put an inch and a half shy of fifty-five feet, but it was his football press clippings that helped make him a second-round draft pick in 1961.

Mercein succinctly said, "I admired him as a punishing runner and a tremendous blocker." He nailed that description, as Brown, playing exclusively for the Vikings thirteen seasons from 1962 through 1974 (after spending his rookie season with the Bears before they traded him), was in the top ten five times for the most times carrying the ball, all in a row from 1964 to 1968.

On four occasions Brown ended a season in the top ten for rushing yardage with a personal high of 866 yards in 1964. His 5,838 lifetime yards on carries is still in the top one hundred all-time. If he is a somewhat overlooked player from his era, it's not his fault, as he also was among the top runners for touchdowns scored on the ground five times and his seventy-six career scores ranked number sixty-three through 2015. In four of his seasons his average of yards gained on runs per game put him in the NFL's top ten. He helped his Vikings make it to the Super Bowl in three of the four seasons they made it that far. Realistically, though, he was on the decline in those years and didn't contribute as much as he had during his peak seasons.

In his prime, Brown did get recognition, even if it perhaps wasn't on a par with big name halfbacks, for example. He was a four-time Pro-Bowler, making that squad in 1964, 1965, 1967, and again in 1968.

In 1964, he even caught nine passes for touchdowns, fourth best in the league. That season Brown's all-purpose yards, a gaudy total of 1,637, trailed only one other man, another rugged runner with the same surname—the great Jim Brown (1,786 yards in all).

Viking placekicker Fred Cox remembered Brown quite well. "Bill was funny, a guy that would go out and you would have a two-and-a-half hour, full out practice, and go back to the dorm where everybody else was in their bed, trying to get some rest and Bill's going up and down the hall trying to get a card game started.

"The guy absolutely lived to play football. The good part about him was that he was a guy that, when he retired, he didn't leave football and get a job. The truth of the matter is, and he would admit it, fifteen years after retiring if you would have given him a uniform, he would have covered kickoffs—that's how much he loved the game."

Chuck Bryant played with Tom Matte at Ohio State and called Matte, whose father played professional hockey, a great athlete. He supported that contention with an OSU recollection involving head coach Woody Hayes. "In a game against Indiana our quarterback got hurt. During halftime Woody took Tom outside to a practice field and showed him how to play quarterback, and he came in and played quarterback in the second half."

Matte may not have lit up the sky with passes under Hayes, who took a very conservative, run, run, run offensive approach to football, but Matte did a great job. Hayes had a penchant for keeping the ball on the ground, where there are fewer things that can go wrong (a fumble) than can go awry on pass plays (sacks, incompletions, and interceptions). The Hayes philosophy, of course, gave birth to the quote, "Three yards and a cloud of dust." Still, over Matte's OSU career he threw the ball 146 times—of course he ran it much more often, 868 times. In 1960, he finished seventh in the voting for the Heisman Trophy. "I ended up as an All-American," he said. "Surprisingly, I was the number one draft choice for the Baltimore Colts as the seventh player taken overall."

Matte was being modest about his lofty selection being a surprise—his quarterback rating in college was 140. By way of contrast, Joe Montana's rating at Notre Dame stood at around 125. Matte laughed and said, "Well, the reason why I had such a high quarterback rating was we didn't throw the ball that much because we had established such a great running game. So they had to respect the running game, so the coverage sort of opened up behind them there.

"But I have small hands, I couldn't hold the football. With my small hands, throwing the ball and getting a spiral on it was an accomplishment for me. But I also played defensive back, I was the punter, I was the kickoff return, I was punt return. I was going sixty minutes. I think that's why the Colts drafted me, because I was good at everything, not great, by no means, but I was good at everything I did. And I could play all these different positions, so they said, 'Hey, we need a versatile player.' So that's what Weeb Ewbank thought about when he drafted me; he wanted me to be a Paul Hornung."

Another of Matte's Colt head coaches, Don Shula, was delighted and relieved to have Matte on his team when a 1965 quarterback calamity hit his team. Starter John Unitas went down first, out of the Colts lineup with a leg injury. Then in the next-to-final game of the season, his backup, Gary Cuozzo, was lost to the team with a separated shoulder. Who, Shula wondered, could he turn to? The answer was college option quarterback Matte.

Matte was rigged up with a makeshift plastic wristband which listed the plays he was to run, and Matte relied on that as a cheat sheet. Passing the football just twice while running for ninety-nine yards, Matte led the Colts to a 20–17 win over the Rams in the final game of the season to thrust Baltimore into the division championship game against Green Bay. The winner would advance to the NFL title game.

Unfortunately, despite Matte going 5 for 12 in the passing department, and despite holding a 10–0 lead at the half, the Packers prevailed, 13–10, winning in overtime on a Don Chandler field goal. Interestingly, though, the Packers had to kick a field goal earlier, with only 1:58 left to play, to send the game into overtime. Although the kick was declared good, Chandler himself has said it wasn't. Had the referees got the call right, Green Bay doesn't beat Baltimore in overtime, and the Matte-driven Colts win it, 10–7, to advance to the NFL title game. What a story that would have, and should have, been.

Matte said he was proud that when the NFL films "came out with the ten most versatile players who ever played in the National Football League, I was number ten—that was the epitome for me. I was playing defense, playing safety back there as a free spirit and I could read the plays pretty well. So Weeb used me back there and Don Shula did in an emergency situation if anybody got hurt. Of course I was playing half-back behind Lenny Moore, and when Lenny retired I stepped in."

Matte said that when he was called on to throw the football one of his targets was Jimmy Orr. "He always talked in that southern Georgia drawl, 'You know, Matte, you're going to make receivers obsolete if you keep playing quarterback.' That was a great line. I loved it.

"And I was a pretty durable back. I didn't have too many injuries. I only screwed up my knee one time in 1970, and that was the only thing that really was bad. Oh, I shouldn't say that—my rookie year I crushed a couple of vertebra in my neck and missed quite a few games, but I came back after that." That's the nature of the violent world of the NFL. When a player nearly forgets a serious neck injury and feels that screwing up a knee along with the vertebrae issue isn't all that bad, that says a lot about the risks of playing pro ball where, truly, only the strong (and lucky) survive.

Lenny Moore chimed in on his teammate, "Tom Matte was behind me, and he was good. He was a good all-around guy to have—you want guys like Matte that can do more than one thing. Matte also learned how to do some quarterbacking—I mean, you can't go from running back to doing the quarterback job. That takes ability and a lot of talent. Those are two entirely different positions, and Tom did that, and did it well."

Matte was so talented coming in, Moore said he didn't have to teach him much about the running back position, "the basic ingredients of what makes a decent running back—how to cut in certain areas, for example. And the reason I can't get into deep specifics, was because mine was God-led. He had given me the talent and the ability that I didn't even know what I was doing." Moore contended that it was difficult for him to pass on the how-to's when things came so naturally to him in the first place. "If somebody asked me, 'How do you do this?' I'd say, 'Do what?' They'd say, 'Well, how did you make that cut?' I said, 'I don't know. It's just instinctive.'"

Like Matte, Emerson Boozer was very valuable to his team. He was in the same Jets backfield with Matt Snell for seven seasons from 1966 through 1972, forming a fine combination. Basic statistics often don't tell the entire tale when it comes to a runner such as Boozer who, among other talents such as his speed, was a very good blocker.

Still, he did manage to create some tangible statistics. For instance, he led his league in rushing touchdowns in just his second season when he rolled into the end zone ten times. He also scored three more times on pass receptions, and his total of thirteen touchdowns also led the league. What makes those feats even more monumental is the fact that due to a knee injury he compiled his thirteen scores in just the first eight games of the year. They would be, in fact, his only eight games of the year. Who knows what a healthy Boozer would have achieved that year.

In that 1967 season, thanks to Boozer and star teammates such as quarterback Joe Namath, Don Maynard, George Sauer, and Snell, the Jets went 8-5-1, marking an improvement of two wins and one slot in the standings, up to second place in the East Division. The steady march toward the top came to fruition the following season when the Jets stunned the Baltimore Colts in Super Bowl III.

Boozer, born on Independence Day in 1943, was named to the Pro Bowl in both his rookie season, 1966, which is quite a feat, and again two seasons later. A workhorse of a halfback, he twice finished in the league's top 10 for the most carries in a given season and for total rushing yardage.

When the football got close to the goal line, he really began to clamor for a chance to hit pay dirt—in five of his ten years in the pros, all spent with the Jets, he ended the season among the best ten players when it came to scoring on runs. Through the 2015 season, Boozer's fifty-two rushing touchdowns placed him at sixty-fifth all-time, perhaps not quite as many TDs as leader Emmitt Smith (164), but more than Hall of Famers such as Paul Hornung, John Henry Johnson, and Floyd Little. In 2015, the Jets decided to honor Boozer for all he had accomplished by finding a place for him in their Ring of Honor.

Boozer is also the answer to a very obscure trivia question as he was the first player ever to score a touchdown during a regular season sudden death game. Under the new overtime rules that came into place in 1974, on November 10 he pulled down a five-yard pass from Namath to knock off the cross-town Giants, 26–20. That score opened a new door—since the new rule was established, more than five hundred regular season contests have been decided in overtime play.

Miami's defensive star Manny Fernandez shared a great Boozer story that, coincidentally, also involved a Jet, Sherman Plunkett, who had attended the same college (what is now called the University of Maryland Eastern Shore) as Boozer. Fernandez's Dolphins were playing the Jets, and on one run Fernandez zeroed in on the five-foot-eleven 195-pound Boozer. "I had a clear shot at him. He was coming out of the backfield and we were coached second man out of the backfield, you had to either cover him or knock him down. The easiest way to knock him down was to clothesline him which was legal in those days. And I strung him up. Gave him a good clothesline. He followed me all the way back to the huddle cursing me, telling me, 'What goes around, comes around, rookie. I'm gonna get you.'

"Now, sometime later in the game I came around that big offensive tackle of theirs, Sherman Plunkett, who weighed about 370 pounds [actually, 290], and Emerson was hiding behind him. As I came around, he popped me under the jaw with his helmet, knocked out a molar, and just stood over me, pointing his finger and laughing, saying, 'Hah, hah. Told you I'd get you, rookie.'" It was a clear case of, "Welcome to the NFL, rookie."

Lenny Moore knew a solid, valuable runner when he saw one, and he had the opportunity to see one daily with the Colts in Alan Ameche. Nicknamed "The Horse," Ameche is most famous for scoring an unforgettable touchdown on a one-yard plunge over right tackle to give Baltimore a dramatic sudden-death win and the NFL championship in 1958. Moore, a great runner out of Penn State, said, "I played against Ameche when he was at Wisconsin. He was something else, man. He was the perfect size of a fullback, right about 220, 225. He was a great blocker, tough runner—good for that nasty one, two yards, oh yeah."

At Wisconsin, Ameche led the Badgers to the Rose Bowl to conclude the 1952 season, and won the Heisman Trophy for his 1954 work as a running back and linebacker. When he left the Madison campus, he did so as the most prolific running back in NCAA history with his 3,345 yards gained on the ground. He also became the third player picked overall in the 1955 draft.

The movie *Diner* featured a character quizzing his girlfriend on Colts trivia, and one of the questions he asked her was, "What was the longest run from scrimmage by a rookie in his first game?" The answer was the seventy-nine-yard jaunt by Ameche in the team's season opener in 1955.

Ameche was much more than a one-trick pony, much more than the answer to any trivia question about his 1958 game-winning run or that long rush from scrimmage as a rookie. Throughout his rookie season he showed that he belonged in pro football as he led the league in rushes, rushing yardage with 961, and total yards from scrimmage at 1,102.

He also tied Chicago's Harlon Hill for the most touchdowns scored that year. Through the 2015 season, his average for yards per game carries places him at eighty-sixth best ever. He only played six years, from 1955 through 1960, but he made four Pro Bowl teams and, more impressive, he was named to the Pro Football Hall of Fame All-1950s team.

Raymond Berry believes Ameche quit even though he was only twenty-seven because he got fed up with how he was being treated on the Colts. Plus, having invested in a string of McDonald's-like hamburger restaurants with Gino Marchetti, Ameche was financially set. Berry also stated, "His I.Q. must have been off the board. He also had the greatest sense of humor you could ever hope to have.

"Of course he was also a tremendous football player. He had speed and quickness, size and power. Plus, he could catch the ball, especially on the flare and swing passes that we used, making him the whole package. The defense could not completely blanket our wide receivers because that would turn him loose on a flare, and he'd take it and kill you running after the catch. He was one of the most talented people I've ever been around, multitalented."

Continuing with Pro Bowl tight ends, Jerry Smith's story is an incredible one. As was the case with Merlin Olsen, when Smith was at San Lorenzo High School in California, a football coach asked him why he was even bothering to tryout for the team, saying that he would never be any account as a player. As was also the case with Olsen, Smith became determined to prove the coach wrong. A few years later Smith was attending Arizona State University and, in 1965 he was drafted into the NFL.

However, as a lowly ninth-round selection, he once again had to prove himself. He did. In just his third season, 1967, Smith was selected to the Pro Bowl for the first of two times. In 1969, he upped the ante by being named to First-Team All-Pro honors. He was so good he lasted from 1965 through the 1977 season and spent that entire time with just one team, the Washington Redskins. Appreciating all he did for the team, the Redskins added his name to their Ring of Fame, and he has been called one of the eighty greatest players in the history of that franchise.

Smith's finest season was probably 1967 when he finished second in the league with his sixty-seven catches and second with his twelve touchdown catches. He accounted for an impressive 849 yards on receptions as well. During his prime seasons he was typically good for around 575 to 700 yards with that peak season of 849 thrown in the mix. Likewise, he was usually good for tearing off around 13 yards every time he caught the football, with a personal zenith of 16.8 yards per reception coming in 1972.

Smith was fortunate to have been coached by some huge names in Washington. The first of three such head coaches was Otto Graham for three seasons (1966–1968). He was followed by Vince Lombardi for one year, 1969, the only season Lombardi coached a team not named Packers. Finally, Smith played under George Allen from 1971 through the end of his career.

Myron Pottios called Smith "a good all-around ballplayer. Not physical, but he did the job and had good hands, speed, and quickness."

Smith used those assets and not only proved his high school coach wrong, it can be argued that Smith reached (or should have reached) the pinnacle of pro football, that he deserves to be in the Hall of Fame. Everyone recognizes the greatness of fellow tight ends John Mackey and Mike Ditka who waltzed into the Hall, so a statistical comparison with Smith is only fitting.

Mackey caught 331 passes for 5,236 yards and thirty-eight touchdowns. Ditka caught the ball 427 times for 5,812 yards and forty-three touchdowns. Over Smith's career he was on the receiving end of 421 passes and crossed the goal line sixty times to set a record for tight ends. It took twenty-seven years before another tight end, Shannon Sharpe, surpassed the sixty touchdowns record. Smith's catches also accounted for 5,496 yards. The argument for Smith's inclusion in the Hall of Fame is as logical as a syllogism. Even though he became eligible for Hall consideration in 1983, he was on that organizations' preliminary list just twice, 1983 and 1987, and he never made it to the finalists list.

Some speculate Smith has been a Hall outcast due to his sexual orientation in a time when homosexuality was one of the country's most dreaded taboos and homophobia ran wild. Smith never came out publicly to declare that he was gay, but he did let it be known he had AIDS, the disease that took his life in 1986. Even now, his chances of ever making it into the Hall of Fame seem as remote as the very era in which he starred.

John Isenbarger spoke of a 49er teammate, wide receiver Danny Abramowicz, who initially was with the Saints (1967 through part of 1973).

"He was another guy who couldn't beat you in a race, and he didn't have the quickness of Biletnikoff, but because we had Gene Washington on one side and Ted Kwalick as the tight end, Dan got a lot of balls. He was a really good guy and he had great hands. I didn't see him, Washington, or Kwalick drop many footballs if they were in their hands."

In fact, in 1969 Abramowicz sat atop the NFL with his seventy-three receptions, despite often running the forty-yard dash right around the five-second mark. That year he also piled up 1,015 yards, a personal best, on his catches. That's not too shabby for a player who saw 419 other men drafted ahead of him.

At one time, Abramowicz held the record for the most consecutive games with at least one reception. The streak ran 105 games, breaking the mark of Lance Alworth (96), and began during the seventh game of his rookie season, 1967, when he earned his first start. He quickly rewarded his coach, Tom Fears, by catching twelve balls for 156 yards. From there it was off and running. Overall, he played in 111 NFL games and had at least one catch in 109 of them as the streak extended through at least part of every one of his eight pro seasons.

"When he was with New Orleans," said Isenbarger, "he was about all they had." That was largely due to the fact that his quarterback, Archie Manning (and earlier Bill Kilmer), "was on his back more than he could look downfield. Dan had to run a lot of five-yard 'outs.'"

Both Joe Walton, an NFL player (1957–1963) for the Redskins and Giants, as a twenty-first overall draft pick, and his father, Frank, coached in the NFL, a rarity. Frank played for the old Boston Redskins in 1934 and then didn't play again until 1944, after World War II had broken out and NFL rosters were depleted due to many players leaving the States to fight overseas.

It was a time when pro sports were desperate to fill their rosters. In major league baseball some old-timers such as Pepper Martin came out of retirement. He had retired after the 1940 season but returned to join a depleted St. Louis Cardinals roster in 1944 at the age of forty. Walton remembered one desperate move two teams made during the war. "The Steelers and the Eagles even combined their teams," said Walton. That gave birth to the 1943 squad with the unlikely, unofficial nickname of the Steagles.

The Waltons are from Beaver Falls, Pennsylvania, the same town that produced seven other pro players including Jim Mutscheller and Joe Namath. In Joe Walton, they also produced an NFL head coach. Joe had that job for the Jets from 1983–1989, but had earlier made headlines when he was on the receiving end of three of Y. A. Tittle's record-tying seven touchdown passes in a single game.

Walton began his NFL days as a split end, but he also played some defensive back for the Redskins, switched there from his normal college position during his rookie season, 1957. He later switched to the tight end spot. "See, when I played tight end, I wasn't very big, but what they did in the beginning, when they went to the tight end formation, they converted wide receivers. I had done a lot of blocking at Pitt so I was a perfect choice to move—that's how I got moved to tight end."

Walton scored nine times as a rookie, and he ended his career with a lusty average of 14.8 yards per catch, exactly the same average as Frank Gifford, Ollie Matson, Terrell Owens, and Jerry Rice. Not bad.

Jimmy Orr's career with Baltimore, covering 1961 through 1970, was also noteworthy. Gino Marchetti stated, "Jimmy Orr had a phenomenal pair of hands." Then he chuckled, "He had the body of a girl. He wasn't very strong. If you looked at him when he walked in the locker room, you'd think sometimes he was going to fall apart, but whenever there was a ball near him, he got it."

Sam Havrilak added of the five-foot-eleven, 185-pound Colt teammate, "Orr was a tremendous receiver. He wasn't that big. I tried out as a quarterback one season, he comes up to me before our first scrimmage and he looks at me and says, 'I want you to remember one thing, son, don't ever lead me into trouble,' meaning don't throw the ball where he was going to get hit. Don't lead him [with a pass] into a defensive back."

Another Colt, Tom Matte, said, "Jimmy Orr was my roommate—he was a crazy man, but I'll tell you one thing—he was one of the all-time great receivers in the NFL. Nobody even knows it, but I do, so did John [Unitas]."

Matte went on, "You can go back and take a look at what they call the corner pattern, and he'd have those defensive backs turned inside out, they could never protect. And he'd set that thing up all during the game, and John [Unitas] would say, 'You ready?' And he'd say, 'I got 'em ready.'"

Yet another Colt teammate, Lenny Moore, had more praise for Orr. "He was something else. He was an excellent wide receiver, he could do it. He was another one that spent a lot of time with Johnny U. because he knew that with the talent that he had, it would be enhanced by working more with him than had he not worked as diligently with him."

Accolades aside, what many fans want to know is this: what numbers did he put up? Well, Orr may not be a Raymond Berry, but his statistics would put many a receiver to shame. Even before his personal glory years with the Colts, Orr stood out with a Steelers team, which hovered just a bit over .500 during Orr's three seasons there, from his rookie season of 1958 through 1960.

For example, in his debut season he actually led the league in average yards gained per catch with what would remain his personal best production, 27.6. Orr would lead the NFL in that category two more times, and he had four seasons with an average of 20 or more yards per catch over his career.

Obviously, he was a threat to go deep with men such as Johnny Unitas firing the football his way. In fact, his 7,914 lifetime yards on receptions through 2015 still placed him among the NFL's elite 100. More impressive is the fact that Orr's 19.8 yards per catch is still the eighth best ever for a career, ahead of a truckload of Hall of Famers such as Lance Alworth, Don Maynard, and Elroy "Crazy Legs" Hirsch, and Orr's average is a mere two-tenths of a yard behind the speedy Bob Hayes (number six all-time). For the record, the top man in this realm is Homer Jones at 22.3 yards per reception. Over Orr's thirteen NFL seasons he wound up in the top ten six times in this department, two seasons more than Jones accomplished this feat.

Orr made the second team on the All-1960s Team as selected by Pro Football Reference, and he was also named to two Pro Bowls, in 1959 and again in 1965, the same season he made the All-Pro First Team.

Yet many people, as if playing a word association game, think of one thing when they think of Orr—a Super Bowl III fiasco for the Colts. Quarterback Earl Morrall called for a flea flicker, which baffled the New York Jets defense. The trick play unraveled like this—first Morrall handed off to Tom Matte who then lateraled the football back to Morrall. By that time Orr was wide open—so wide open, in fact, he was waving his arms, desperately trying to get Morrall's attention. Despite Orr's gesticulations, Morrall never saw him and instead threw an interception. If he had hit Orr, the score at the half would have been tied instead of 7–0 in favor of New York. Could the Colts have won had this play worked instead of suffering a humiliating 16–7, monumental upset? Obviously, nobody knows or ever will, but the image of Orr, alone near the end zone, remains an unforgettable Super Bowl memory.

Joe Kapp was an interesting quarterback. His stint in the Canadian Football League ran from 1959 through 1966, before he played in the NFL from 1967 to 1970. He was the only quarterback ever to play in the Rose Bowl, the Grey Cup (the CFL championship), and the Super Bowl.

George Belu was a tight end in the CFL from 1961 to 1964 and said Kapp "was one tough football player. When we played him, he was not your typical quarterback."

In 2011, Kapp reaffirmed that when he attended a CFL alumni luncheon, a perfect setting for old-timers to renew acquaintances. The only problem was Kapp, at the age of seventy-three, got into a nasty fight with another former player, Angelo Mosca, also seventy-three, whom he had feuded with back in the day. Mosca had once wrestled under the nicknames "King Kong Mosca" and "The Mighty Hercules." The grudge fight at the luncheon included not just swinging fists, but a swinging cane by Kapp's pugilistic opponent.

Lifetime in the NFL, he threw more incompletions than completions and, worse, more interceptions (sixty-four) than scores (forty), and his record as a starting quarterback was just 24-21-3. He threw forty touchdowns in fifty-one games, but in one game, this unlikely candidate to tie an astonishing record did just that, throwing for seven touchdowns.

In just one game he registered what would be 17.5 percent of the touchdowns he would throw for his entire NFL career. To this day, he shares the single-game touchdown passes mark with men such as Sid Luckman, George Blanda, Y. A. Tittle, and, most recently, Drew Brees. Kapp's arm accounted for all but three of his Vikings points (other than the extra point kicks) in a 52–14 rout of the Colts. He hit on twenty-eight of forty-three throws for 449 yards, and, interestingly, hit six different receivers for scores (Gene Washington snared two TDs).

Fred Cox said, "Joe Kapp was only with us [the Vikings] a couple of years, but he was a whole story unto himself. He did more with less athletic skill than any person I ever knew. Joe, as far as I know, still holds the record for the most touchdown passes in a game with the Vikings, and yet, I kid you not, when he would warm up he couldn't break a single pane of glass. That's how bad his arm was, but if you wanted to talk about somebody that was tough—he was tougher than nails.

"He was so tough, I'm not sure how smart he was, that in '69, the last game we played, we lost to Atlanta and there was always a party, and he and Lonnie Warwick, our middle linebacker who was a Golden Gloves boxer, got into a fistfight over whose fault it was we lost the game. Joe said it was the defense and Lonnie said it was the offense.

"The next day the two of them show up at practice, both wearing dark glasses because they both have black eyes. That gives you some idea of how tough a man Kapp was. He's a quarterback taking on a Golden Gloves boxer and he did just fine.

"Joe made a lot of mistakes when he was playing, but you could never tell because he would spin around and go the wrong way and miss a handoff, then he just innately kept spinning and run right up the middle with the ball, probably gained twelve yards like it was some kind of planned play, but it wasn't.

"We were playing the Cleveland Browns in the championship game and he did that, and instead of going up the middle, he sprinted outside and when he did, they had a really big linebacker that Joe literally knocked cold. He hit him and ran over him, knocked him out—that was the essence of Joe Kapp."

Roman Gabriel was a big quarterback at six feet, five inches, 220 pounds, who was extremely difficult to bring down. Perhaps even the bellicose Kapp would have had trouble decking Gabriel. Highly coveted coming out of North Carolina State, Gabriel was the first overall draft pick of the Raiders in the 1962 AFL draft, and the second overall pick by the Rams. He played the bulk of his career for the Rams, where he became a highly accurate passer—only 3.3 percent of his passes were picked off, and several times he flirted with a 60 percent completion rate. His 201 passes for scores stood number forty all-time through 2015.

Rams teammate Myron Pottios said, "He was very physical. He worked out a lot and was in good shape. He's another guy that dedicated himself to making himself a much better player, and it paid off for him. When George Allen came there [to the Rams], things just turned around for him. He believed in George and his system and he did what he had to do. As a result he was an MVP [1969], and it panned out very well for him."

Gabriel is the son of a Filipino immigrant, making him the first Asian-American to start an NFL game. Keep in mind, though, he was born in North Carolina. One joke which he played didn't turn out very well. Chuck Bryant, Gabriel, and other college players representing the East were on a bus prior to playing in a summer All-Star college game in Buffalo, New York. Bryant said, "We got on a bus in Buffalo going into Canada. We got there and the border guard stopped us and asked if any of us were born outside the United States. Well, Gabriel got up and said, 'I was born in Red China.' Oh, my! We were there for two hours before we could go on to Niagara Falls for our lunch."

John Brodie was a great quarterback who, today, seems very underappreciated. Talented enough to win an MVP Award, he amassed 214 touchdown strikes (number thirty through 2015) and 31,548 yards through the air, still ranking him in the top forty. Sam Havrilak said that Brodie threw about the prettiest passes he ever saw.

Former 49er teammate John Isenbarger shook his head. "I still can't believe he's not in the Hall of Fame." He's not alone in thinking that. "I mean, he was an MVP and held all kinds of records. There are a lot of quarterbacks in who have less numbers than John did." Isenbarger feels it's unfair to compare Brodie, who played during the days of twelve- and fourteen-game schedules, to men such as Aaron Rogers and Peyton Manning.

Isenbarger said Brodie was "an amazing athlete. He was a scratch golfer who went on to be a professional golfer and even won on the senior tour one time. He was a great tennis player and bowler. He played basketball in high school, too." Brodie also was a television broadcaster, covering golf and football for many years.

Isenbarger respects Brodie as a player and as a person. "He had a wonderful family. He lives in Palm Springs with his wife, Sue. One of his daughters was on *The Bachelorette* several years ago," he said in a 2016 interview.

There are many more reasons to respect Brodie, as is evident with a closer look at his career. Always based on the West Coast, beginning with his high school days at Oakland Technical School, he played his college ball at Stanford, but he was not offered a scholarship, and, in fact, he tried out for and made the freshman team, but didn't start.

It was an enormous waste of talent. Just three years later as a senior he led the country in passing and total offense and his name was on the roster of most of the All-American teams. In the East-West Shrine game and the College All-Star game he was named the MVP, outshining men such as Jim Brown and Paul Hornung.

Having finally established the fact that he was better than a mere college walk-on, he was the third overall pick in the 1957 NFL draft. It was a move the 49ers would never regret. Brodie went on to play his entire career, a very long one, 1957–1973, with them. The possessor of a great arm, he wound up leading the NFL in twelve categories according to Pro Football Reference. Some of those categories were a bit obscure such as adjusted net yards gained per pass attempt, but most of them were major ones.

For instance, he sat atop the NFL three times for the highest total of completions in a season, and three times for the most passing yards, with a personal peak of 3,112 in 1965. That year he made a clean sweep of numerous departments, such as the most fourth-quarter comeback scoring drives, most pass attempts, most completions, most touchdown passes (30—he would lead the NFL again five seasons later), and the best completion rate (61.9 percent), which marked the second of the two times he led the league in that impressive stat. He even posted the best quarterback rating in 1970 at the age of thirty-five.

He had shown signs of great things to come as early as his second season in the NFL, 1958. Beginning as an understudy to the great Y. A. Tittle, Brodie hit on 59.9 percent of his 172 passes that season, a year in which he briefly was handed the quarterback job over Tittle, who had slumped a bit during the exhibition schedule. On the opening weekend Brodie notched the second win of his seventeen-year career (as a rookie he started and won one game), going 19-for-28 for 244 yards. He would go on to win seventy-two more games as a starting quarterback. By 1961 it was clear that Brodie, nine years younger than Tittle, was the go-to guy for San Francisco, for then and for the future. Tittle was swapped to the New York Giants.

Tittle, who had started just twenty games over the previous three seasons, got revitalized in New York. Over his first three years there, he helped the Giants get to three consecutive championship games, and he racked up records of 8-1-1, 12-2, 11-2 over that span, but the thirty-eight-year-old Tittle was through after the 1964 season, when his Giants plummeted to a 1-8-2 record with him as the starting quarterback. Brodie, meanwhile, would guide his team, and do it well, for many, many years to come.

Billy Kilmer was an intriguing football player who wound up finding his niche as a fine pro quarterback, one who inspired loyalty among his teammates. He was also talented enough to take his Redskins to seven playoff games, including a Super Bowl.

Bill Malinchak was a teammate of Kilmer's and said he had "the greatest personality. I not only remember Billy on the football field as a great leader, but on the plane coming back from games or on the bus. He would walk through the bus and sit down with you, talk with you, go to the next seat and talk to guys. I remember Billy very fondly because he was that kind of guy. He didn't sit with just one guy in the plane. He had so many friends and he always had a smile on his face. He was a wonderful friend. He brought the team together, always.

"He was the kind of quarterback that everybody loved. And he was a tough kid, a tough quarterback. At UCLA he had run out of the single wing formation, I think. He ran the ball a lot."

As a matter of fact, in his senior season he dashed for 803 yards, averaging 4.5 yards per pop. He also accounted for 1,086 yards passing and came in fifth in the Heisman voting.

In fact, when Kilmer was drafted by the 49ers, they didn't exactly envision him as a quarterback. As a rookie in 1961, he didn't start a game, threw only thirty-four passes, completing nineteen for 286 yards and no touchdowns. He also completed four passes to opponents. So the 49ers rarely used him as a passer. Over his next three seasons with San Francisco, his final ones there, he threw just forty-three more passes for two TDs. In all, with the 49ers, he started just ten games and saw action mainly as a runner—he rushed for 509 yards in 1961, 478 the next year, then languished, seeing little action before moving on to New

Orleans for four seasons. It was there that he finally was employed with regularity as the quarterback. He'd complete his career with Washington from 1970 to 1978, still playing a bit at the age of thirty-nine.

"When he got to Washington," said Malinchak, "he was pretty banged up and wasn't running a lot, but he was quite a runner at one time." Nevertheless, the resilient Kilmer still managed to lead the NFL in touchdown passes (nineteen) one year, and six times he wound up in the top ten for TD throws. In an additional seven seasons he cracked the top ten for quarterback rating.

Purists and announcers chided the appearance of his throws, comparing them to wobbly ducks in flight. Malinchak said, "They're comparing it with Sonny Jurgensen, who probably threw the nicest passes in the NFL, and Billy who threw some ducks, but he would always get it there. He was a competitor. It wasn't pretty, maybe, wasn't the prettiest pass, but it was very effective. It just wasn't up to the way Jurgensen threw."

Don Meredith, a nine-year "lifer" with Dallas, was the winner of the 1966 NFL Bert Bell Award as the top player of the season. Apparently later on the voters for a bigger honor considered him to be a notch below Hall of Fame caliber, but he nevertheless enjoyed a fine career. In fact, only ten players ever threw for a better lifetime average of yards per completion than his 14.7.

Flashback to his early days with the Cowboys. As an expansion team in 1960, the Cowboys were outfitted with castoffs and question marks, players other teams were gladly willing to give up. As such, Meredith's early teams were miserable, ragtag groups, and he was far from being a "Dandy" Don.

Being an expansion team back then was a sort of death penalty to an NFL club, and the Cowboys must have felt as if they were living on a grimy Texas death row. Meredith took his lumps early on, with opponents' defenses administering many of those debilitating lumps while he labored behind a line that all too often couldn't protect him very well. In 1964, he played while under the severe handicap of shoulder and ankle sprains, a rupture of a stomach muscle, bone bruises, and torn knee cartilage. Meredith and the Cowboys would not get a stay of execution and enjoy a winning season until their seventh year in existence, 1966.

Early on, the perception of Meredith by many observers was negative. A standout and a true winner in his native Texas at Mount Vernon
High and in college at SMU, his record as a starting quarterback
through his first three NFL seasons (1960–1962) was 4-7-2, hardly lustrous. It wasn't until his fifth season that he was responsible for a record
above .500, with Dallas at 5-4-1 under his leadership.

Once he gained experience, and more important, a solid crew of
players around him, his stock soared. From 1965 through his final season, 1968, his starting record was a highly commendable 34-13-1.
Translated, that means he won 71 percent of all his starts.

If Meredith had had better protection, he would not have had to
endure so much pressure from defenses or as many bumps, bruises, and
very serious injuries that he did. Who knows how many more games he
would have won if he hadn't called it quits after the 1968 season when
he was just thirty-years old—although a very battered thirty-year-old to
be sure. In any event, he did leave behind some impressive numbers.
Twice he led the NFL in yards gained per pass completion, and in
eighty-three career starts, he accumulated 17,199 yards.

Perhaps Hall of Fame voters held his record in playoff games against
him, ignoring the fact that he took what had been a horrible franchise to
postseason play in just a handful of years. His Cowboys made the
playoffs three seasons in a row from 1966 to 1968, but his record in
those contests was 1-3.

In Meredith's defense, in the team's first trip, during the franchise's
first winning season ever, the Cowboys just weren't quite ready to be a
championship-caliber team, yet the only thing that stopped them from
winning it all was the juggernaut Packers team of Vince Lombardi. And
even then, Dallas played them down to the wire, losing to a great team
by only seven points, 34–27.

They came oh, so close again in 1967, only to prove the cliché that
close only counts in horseshoes and hand grenades. Still, if Bart Starr
had slipped on the tundra that was Green Bay's Lambeau Field instead
of being able to follow his blockers and quarterback sneak the football
into the end zone on the Packers last play of the title game, Meredith
and his Cowboys would have emerged from the game that became
known as the Ice Bowl as NFL champs.

Nobody seems to remember that just to get to that title game Meredith's Cowboys shellacked the Cleveland Browns, 52–14, in the Divi-

sion Championship game. Meredith was brilliant, leading Dallas to four first-half scores, two on his contrasting-in-length passes of 3 and 86 yards, to put the game on ice, 24–0, before Cleveland could muster a score. Meredith hit on eleven passes and threw just two that didn't find their mark, good for 212 yards.

In his final playoff game, the 1968 Division Championship game which was also against the Browns, Meredith, who had taken his team to a 12-2 regular season slate, did have an off day. Cleveland prevailed, 31–20, and Meredith hobbled off into the Texas sunset.

He wasn't entirely through with football, though. In addition to enjoying a career in acting, he probably became more famous for his days in the television booth alongside Frank Gifford and Howard Cosell than he did as a Cowboy. The popular Meredith changed the landscape of football broadcasting with his witty irreverence, his humor, and his unparalleled ability to at least partially deflate the Goodyear blimp–sized ego of Cosell.

Raymond Berry was a coach for the Cowboys when Meredith was with the team and called him a great natural talent. "Those kinds of guys are born with an ability to throw that ball accurately, and Meredith could throw any type of pass there was. On top of that, he was one of the most interesting extroverts you'll ever be around. When you're talking about Don Meredith, you're talking about a multitalented guy." As usual, Berry was 100 percent correct.

Early in his career Meredith could have used a man like Doug Crusan, who was a fine offensive lineman in the late 1960s and helped protect many a Miami Dolphins quarterback from 1968 to 1974. Interestingly, and coincidentally, Crusan was a contemporary at a small school, Monessen High School, of three other men who would later play in the NFL—Eric Crabtree, Havrilak, and Malinchak. Havrilak and Malinchak actually grew up directly across the street from each other. In the meantime, Crusan and Havrilak both made it to, and won, Super Bowl games.

And boy did Crusan make it to the Super Bowl. Over a three-year stretch, his Dolphins went 44-6-1 and went to the Super Bowl each season. Even better, over a two-year span they went 32-2 and *won* two Super Bowls including the one captured by the 1972 undefeated squad.

That season was probably Crusan's best, as he made Honorable Mention All-AFC.

The Dolphins used a first-round draft pick on Crusan, which paid big dividends, as he and other offensive linemen including Larry Little did a great job. During Crusan's rookie season of 1968 Bob Griese was sacked twenty-one times. "Some poor quarterbacks get sacked forty times now," said Crusan. "So twenty-one's not too bad."

Crusan said offensive linemen know when they've done their job, and it's rewarding when they open a hole for a runner or give a quarterback an eon to find and hit an open man. Carrying out their duty well gives them a feeling of self-satisfaction, knowing that "the culmination of doing your job is a heckuva nice run or a touchdown pass. It means that everybody worked together, and that's what a team does."

Crusan explained that after his first two seasons with Miami, Don Shula was brought in "and the offense was changed. We went with more quick passes and, of all things, they traded for Paul Warfield and brought in a tight end, Marv Fleming from Green Bay." Those moves certainly didn't hurt the Dolphin offense.

Crusan spoke about the difficulty of his Dolphins greatest accomplishment, winning back-to-back championships. "It's very hard because everybody's laying for you—everybody wants to beat the Super Bowl champions. So we were 17-0 in '72 and we're 15-2 in '73, and the way I looked at it, everybody was playing their best game against you."

Now, in theory, a professional team should play their best every time they play, but athletes are human and get extra pumped up in certain situations. "Absolutely," said Crusan who clearly experienced this. "That would be a real notch [for opponents]. 'Hey, look what we did. Besides winning the game, we beat last year's Super Bowl champs.' It's a real mind changer kind of thing, it's good for confidence."

The Colts starting center in 1958, the season they won the NFL title in the Greatest Game Ever Played, was Buzz Nutter, whose real name was Madison Monroe Nutter. A onetime Pro-Bowler out of Virginia Tech, Nutter was, in fact, the first player from that college to be drafted into the NFL. He must have been good there because his team wasn't helping him get many headlines—the Hoakies were 0-10, 2-8, and 5-6 over his final three seasons at the school. In 1985 Virginia Tech would recognize his ability by inducting him into their Hall of Fame.

He may have been drafted into the NFL by the Washington Red-skins in 1953, way down in the twelfth round, but he didn't stick with the team. He spent one year working in a steel mill before the Colts picked him up. He not only was a part of the 1958 championship team, the next season Baltimore repeated and Nutter earned another glimmering ring.

Many of his teammates saw Nutter as an anchor for Baltimore. "He was excellent—he was *the* center," said Lenny Moore, who shared insights on seldom-discussed duties of a center. "Quarterbacks and centers really have to work together because they got to make sure they are in sync. They have to do a lot of work together to make sure that their timing is together. In case you have to have a check off, you have to make sure that you make the check off calls on the right signal.

"They have to be alert at all times, listen to what the quarterback says, make sure that they snap the ball to the quarterback in the same way every time, even if they have somebody on their head that is probably going to knock the hell out of them. They got to make sure that they're doing their job first."

Nutter did all of that, and he seemingly got better as he got older. His selection to the Pro Bowl squad came when he was with the Pittsburgh Steelers in 1962 at the age of thirty-one. That same season one poll selected him for their second-team All-NFL unit. The Steelers had picked Nutter up in a trade in which Baltimore had sent Nutter and Big Daddy Lipscomb their way in return for Jimmy Orr, a fine wide receiver.

Nutter would keep his job with the Steelers through 1965, when the Colts reacquired him for one last fling. That season he was a cog in Don Shula's Baltimore machine, which rolled to a 10-3-1 record, good enough to tie for the top berth in the Western Division.

After he had played the last of his 153 games as a pro, Nutter stayed in Maryland where he operated a beverage distribution company, which he aptly named Center Distributors.

Finally, a look at the kicking game through the eyes of a man who plied his trade for an NFL eternity, and is still listed as the twenty-ninth most prolific scorer of all time. Fred Cox was the placekicker for the Minnesota Vikings from 1963 to 1974. Coincidentally, he and Joe Montana come from Monongahela, a small town in western Pennsylvania, and, in fact, both grew up on the same block, though years apart.

Pottios, also out of western Pennsylvania, played against Cox in high school, in college, and in the pros. He said Cox was more than merely a kicker. In fact, at Pitt, Cox was also a halfback and a defensive back. "He was tough," said Pottios. "He was always big, stocky, put together well. When you tackled him you knew he was a good, strong, physical ball player."

Over Cox's career, he never missed a single game. Even now, he remains one of the greatest kickers ever—Cox even punted as a rookie, and came in sixth for punting yardage. Using the traditional straight-on style he learned as a kid, he may not have booted the ball as far as today's soccer-style heavy hitters, but Cox came through, and his longest field goal ever sailed some fifty-three yards.

Always dependable, he put up a career percentage for kicking points after touchdowns of 96.3. That included a stretch of five seasons of perfection, kicking with robotic-like precision. He felt that kickers who missed the close-in field goals let their teams down and they would often collapse after such misses.

He was also proud of his knack to split the uprights when the game was on the line. "For some reason I was blessed with the ability to have phenomenal focus. In fifteen years I missed two kicks to win a game."

When Cox, a teammate of Ditka at Pitt, retired, his 282 field goals ranked second all-time, trailing only the ageless George Blanda. His 1,365 lifetime points scored made him just the third player, after standouts Blanda and Lou "the Toe" Groza, ever to top the 1,300-point plateau.

Cox, a veteran of four Super Bowls, led the NFL in field goals made three times, once for field goal percentage at 70.3 percent, and the Pro-Bowler's 121 points in 1969 and his 125 the following season also topped all kickers. Additionally, from 1970 until 2001 he held the record for kicking field goals in thirty-one consecutive contests, and he was the record holder for scoring in the most consecutive games, 151. It's only natural that he was voted one of the fifty greatest Vikings.

Toss in two other little known facts about Cox: (1) He is the creator of the Nerf football, coming up with the idea of a foam ball in order to help kids avoid sore legs. (2) Cox pointed out the other incredible, obscure fact. "It's crazy that I only kicked four field goals as an amateur.

That's counting high school, everything. Three in one game against Notre Dame, and none at all before I was a senior, but then I went on to play fifteen years in the NFL as a kicker."

As a kid, Cox played a lot of soccer. "You can actually kick a soccer ball farther than you can kick a football. Even when I was in high school, I could kick a soccer ball eighty yards. You just kick it like a kickoff in football off the ground."

His soccer background helped him when he was with the Vikings. "I used to kickoff soccer style on occasion whenever head coach Bud Grant would want me to. When he was coaching football in Canada, he had a soccer kicker."

An expert kicker can do with a football what New York Yankees pitching great Whitey Ford could do with a scuffed baseball. It's been said that Ford could take a doctored baseball and make it do just about anything but whistle "Dixie." Likewise, Cox, an expert at any type of kick, had great control over footballs.

He remembered the time Grant approached him one day and asked, "Is there any chance that you could kick the ball low, driving [the ball] down into the corner?" Cox explained, "His idea was to get the ball down on the ground so the other team couldn't make a long return. I told him, 'No problem. I played soccer. If you want me to, when I kick off I will kick the ball like I'm kicking a soccer ball.'

"We were the first one in the NFL to do that. After that a lot of teams started doing that. I would literally use a soccer-style kick and [boot] a line drive that probably never got over eight feet high. The idea was to kick it hard and get it to roll and bounce—hopefully it would take crazy bounces so people had a hard time picking it up."

Cox elaborated further on his field goal kicking craft. "There was never a word said when I walked on the field to attempt a field goal. The guys knew how I was. I was a guy that when I walked on that field the only thing I ever said to myself was, 'Keep your head down and follow through. Just like the golfer.' After that, my whole aim was total concentration on kicking the ball and everybody knew that so, consequently, nobody ever said a word to me."

After breaking huddle there was still no need for conversation. "There was no snap count. The snap was whenever Mick Tingelhoff wanted to snap it. Early on they used to use a snap count, but then we never did that. Paul Krause would open his hand up, and once he did that it was up to Mick whenever he was ready to snap the ball. That's the most logical way to do it. All I was doing was watching Paul's finger—he would put his finger on the ground where he was going to hold it, and I was actually looking down. I didn't know when the ball was snapped until it came into my peripheral vision. As soon as it did, I would start to move toward where his finger was, that spot, to kick the ball. And when Krause put it down, I was staring at a spot on the ball which was just below the middle of the ball. From when it was snapped to when I kicked it, I had 1.5 seconds or it would get blocked."

Krause held for every single one of Cox's kicks. "Not only did he never get hurt," said Cox, "but he only mishandled two snaps, and believe it or not, they were both in the same game against Pittsburgh in Pittsburgh. He literally dropped two consecutive snaps and I thought he was going to commit hara-kiri. It was just not possible for him to do that; he couldn't believe that he did it."

Further, Cox, in an almost scientific analysis, pointed out that "weather was huge in how the ball would carry." A ball travels for greater distances when it's humid or in venues where the air is thin, such as in Denver. "It was like they had helium in the ball there. I can remember warming up in Denver and kicking them against the brick wall behind the end zone on kickoffs. It was absolutely inconceivable how the ball would fly in Denver."

Cox theorized that big time players make big time plays. "My mentality is that to be a great kicker or a great quarterback, you're going to play much better against the great teams." Cox certainly excelled in that department.

As a side note, Cox presents a good case for one of his pet peeves—he contends there should be more kickers in the Pro Football Hall of Fame. Through 2016 there were only three kickers enshrined in football's Hall of Fame and one of them, George Blanda, gained a great deal of fame for his quarterbacking, not just his kicking. The other two are Lou Groza, who was also an offensive tackle, and Jan Stenerud, the only pure placekicker in the Hall—in that kicking was his sole job. Several other stars who handled some kicking chores such as Bobby Lane and Paul Hornung are Hall of Famers, but were *much* better known for playing quarterback and halfback respectively.

"I'm OK with it, because I understand what the situation is—it's really simple: most people don't consider kickers football players. It's a

6

THE NFL THEN AND NOW

Football is a constantly evolving sport. Watch footage of a play or two from its earliest days then switch to a game from, say, 2017. The contrast is so stark, so striking, it's almost as if two different sports were being played. The noticeable differences from the 1950s to now aren't *quite* so extreme, but the game has vastly changed over the last five decades or so.

Nothing stands still for too long in the world of sports. Football, naturally, has evolved and, in some ways devolved, over the years. Mike Ditka observed, "The game has changed. Now, Johnny Unitas changed the game a lot when he started throwing the ball. He was a terrific player and he was put into the right system—he had a great tight end in Mackey, he had great receivers in Jim Mutscheller and Raymond Berry.

"John Unitas was a special guy. If you ever met him personally, he was a sweetheart. I mean nobody deserves success more than him. He worked hard for it. He had nothing, he started with nothing, he was well-known, but he climbed that ladder pretty well."

While football relied upon the run game virtually 100 percent of the time long, long ago (at one time the forward pass wasn't even a legal play), when Unitas showed how the air attack could ravage opponents, things did change. Still, as Ditka stated, a winning team must have more than a splendid quarterback. "You have to understand, for quarterbacks to succeed, you've got to have a team around you. I mean, you can have a great quarterback sometimes and if you put him with a bad team, it's hard to look good."

Sam Havrilak said, "It's more of a wide open passing game now. Back in the fifties, sixties, the philosophy was establish a running game and then go to your passing game. Well, nowadays they come out and they just pass. Now it's the other way around—you set up your running game with the passing game."

John Isenbarger agreed. "You listen to the people in the NFL now and the running backs are kinda third down the line. I mean, they'll pay more for an offensive left tackle if the quarterback is a right-handed guy than a running back because you've got to protect that quarterback."

Myron Pottios said back in the early 1960s college players still had to play on both offense and defense, something nobody does today. It was grueling, and moving on to the NFL actually meant players got to rest much more than they did in their college days, although certainly quite a few players did go both ways in the 1950s. Pottios said that managing to play on both sides of the ball wasn't a real big deal, though. "As long as everybody's doing it, nobody has an advantage over the guy unless you're in better shape. It's not like you were the only guy out there playing both ways.

"We only had a couple substitutions, so the majority of guys had to play. So the team that was in the best physical shape usually was going to come out on top. If you weren't in shape, playing 50, 60 minutes— that's a long afternoon."

Compare that, he said, to today's norm. "Sometimes you play three plays and you're out. Sometimes a drive goes against you where you might be in there playing for five, six minutes straight. But there's a big difference [because] then you come out and sit on the bench and regenerate and freshen up.

"The game was altogether different. Now players are a lot faster and more physical, but also they're fresher."

Even the linebacker position, for example, is played differently today than before. Marchetti said, "In the old days, the linebackers were strong on the run and on pass plays they were pretty good coverage guys, and good at punishing a receiver coming across. They had a little more responsibility."

So how are linebackers different now? "Speed. Speed," Marchetti emphasized. "The whole game is faster now because of things that defensive teams can't do, like holding up an end. It used to be you could beat them up until the ball was in the air. All those guys running those patterns did was try to stay away from a linebacker, particularly, until the ball was thrown—then you had to lay off."

Lenny Moore chipped in, saying, "Different guys had different stylings in the way that they handled themselves. During our day, because they didn't have all these rules and regulations—that you can only hit a certain way, and you can only tackle a certain way—all bets were off. You had to know how to manhandle somebody, but sometimes if you over-manhandled, you may lose what was the strategic [advantage]. Physically, you may want to overwhelm them, but sometimes it may take away from your ability to be able to complete the task." Thus, he feels linebackers of his era had to sometimes decide whether to go for tackles that would really hurt a runner or go with a less physical, but surer tackle.

The terminology and the play of defensive backs has also changed over the years. Volk said his position was called right safety as opposed to simply a "safety" because back then the two safeties "didn't flip flop. I was always on the right side and if the tight end would come out on my side, I'd be the strong safety. Most of the time tight ends went to the left side and that was Jerry Logan's side so I became more of a weak safety, I called it."

George Belu said, "In the fifties and sixties, it was more of an in-close, physical game, one-on-one type of inside contact game. It still is physical, but it was real, get-down-in-the-dirt type of football. It was blocking and tackling that were really emphasized. Now, it's more of a spread, open thing—wide receiver type of game, offensively."

In any case, Chuck Finder, a veteran sportswriter for the *Pittsburgh Post-Gazette*, says changes in the way the game is played have made comparisons of players throughout the years virtually impossible.

While many records (and rules) of major league baseball are long-standing, carved in stone, football's records (and rules) are more akin to something scrawled on an Etch-A-Sketch or drawn in sand near a shoreline. Finder said, for instance, one cannot even determine, say, the top ten quarterbacks of all time. "You can't compare yardage," Finder began. "The field is still a hundred yards long, but the game has changed so much. It's easier for quarterbacks to get four hundred yards as opposed to days when two hundred fifty and three hundred yards were considered phenomenal. And somebody throws for thirty touchdowns and only nine interceptions, but their team could still be 8-8 and they don't get to the playoffs."

Trying to compare the stats of a Johnny Unitas and a Peyton Manning is as deceiving as it is futile, considering other factors such as the length of the NFL schedule. Throughout the 1950s, players built up their stats over a twelve-game schedule. That expanded to fourteen games in 1961, and then in 1978, the schedule began to run sixteen games. An extra four games per season over a lengthy career makes a huge statistical difference. Consider Jim Taylor, whose eighty-three rushing touchdowns stood number two behind only Jim Brown when Taylor retired. Through 2015, those scores rank at number sixteen. Likewise, his 8,597 career yards on the ground also once trailed only Brown, but now are only number thirty-nine all-time.

The schedule has certainly changed over the decades. Doug Crusan said that in the late 1960s teams not only went through eight weeks of training camp, but squads played six exhibition games. "There was also a rookie scrimmage and another one-versus-one [first-team offense against first-team defense] scrimmage we played in the Orange Bowl before the exhibition games—talk about being with people for a long time!"

Of course, a huge change to the NFL took place with expansion—there are more teams in the NFL now than ever before. Raymond Berry believes expansion from the twelve teams the NFL had in his day to today's league of thirty-two teams has resulted in a dilution of talent. "I can think of one year there may have been six future Hall of Fame quarterbacks competing, a 50 percent ratio."

One season it seemed as if every one of the Colts' opponents had a great quarterback. In fact, 80 percent of the quarterbacks they faced were future Hall of Famers. That, said Berry is something which would never happen today. Likewise, he argued further that, "With so many teams in the league, I don't think you face a quality defense every week or face a top line defensive corner every week."

However, Rick Volk disagrees somewhat. While fans of a few of the league's perennial losers such as the Browns of late, might think Volk is dead wrong, he contends that all NFL teams have some great players. He says that lousy players simply don't make it to the highest level of football.

"Everybody in the NFL has good personnel, let's put it that way," Volk asserted. "It's just whether you make a mistake or two that hurts your team, and then you lose—a tipped ball or a runback on a punt return or kickoff return, that kind of thing can change a game around. Then, if you're trying to catch up and score touchdowns, sometimes you're playing a little bit above what you can do all the time [normally] and you make a bad throw, or whatever." And that can make matters even worse, of course.

Even the kicking game has changed in many ways since the Glory Years. Marchetti came up with yet another contrast between the old days and now. He pointed out that in his day many position players doubled as kickers, but many were lacking when it came to field goal accuracy, especially compared to today's kickers.

"Nowadays," said Marchetti, "a field goal kicker, all he does all week long is practice kicking. Therefore, they're probably more relaxed and are able to handle it more than, say, Steve Myhra [the Colts kicker]. I can visualize Steve kicking the late field goal that tied the 1958 championship game, but we didn't have much confidence in him making it."

The main reason so many kickers played other positions back then was that NFL teams carried just thirty-three players. Marchetti listed several kickers of his era who played other positions. "Lou Groza was probably one of the better field goal kickers, and he was also a pretty damn good offensive tackle for the Cleveland Browns. He did two things to help his football team win ballgames. Lou Michaels was our field goal kicker and a defensive player—if something happened to me, he would take my position at defensive left end. I wouldn't say he was the most accurate field goal kicker, but he had the guts to do it."

Several others who had such dual roles include Bert Rechichar, who played four other positions; linebacker Wayne Walker; fullback Sam Baker; halfback Paul Hornung; guard Jerry Kramer; and Bobby Layne, a quarterback.

"In those days," Volk said, "it was more straight-on kicking, too. They didn't have the soccer style. I think they felt at that time soccer style kickers didn't get the ball up in the air right away—they could get their kicks blocked. But that's changed a lot, for sure. They're weapons out there now, and they're almost all automatic."

Today a kicker using the old method would be considered as peculiar as a dodo bird. Traditional kickers tended to be rather untrustworthy, especially the further out they got from the goalposts. Attempting, say, a field goal of fifty-plus yards was virtually unheard of long ago, but such kicks were sometimes successful. In 1953, in just his second NFL season, safety/kicker Bert Rechichar of the Colts set a record when he boomed a fifty-six-yarder. The most amazing thing about the kick is that it was Rechichar's first-ever pro field goal attempt. Plus, the historic kick was accomplished without the use of a special kicking toe—he simply kicked with his normal soft-toed shoe. His field goal broke a record set nineteen years earlier, and it established the new record, which stood until Tom Dempsey let loose on a sixty-three-yard field goal in 1970, just his second NFL season.

Long-range field goal attempts today are far from being oddities for soccer style kickers, especially at the end of a half or fourth quarter, for example. The switch to such kickers began with a few pioneers, including Hungarian imports, the Gogolak brothers, All-Pro Pete first in 1964 then his brother Charlie two years later. The trend surely caught on.

A further change to the kicking game is that today when a team is about to attempt a kick, a new "kicking ball" is put in play. That wasn't the case long ago, says Fred Cox, and that did impair the kicking game at least somewhat back then.

As the placekicker for Minnesota, Cox and his center and holder had to cope with frigid conditions quite a bit. He said a lot of what it took to combat the cold was psychological and he was fine with it, but he added, "The guy who had it the hardest was Tingelhoff. It was a lot harder to snap that ball when it was cold because those balls, when we were playing and didn't have a kicking ball, had so much rosin, man, they were like glass when you snapped them. They were really slippery. We played numerous games when the windchill was well lower than fifteen or twenty degrees below zero."

Weather can still be horrible, of course, but now there are more domes for cold-weather franchises. Plus, as Cox recalled about a game he played against the Green Bay Packers, as soon as workers uncovered the field before the game, it froze, so everybody was ice skating. Lambeau Field has heat under it now, but back then it didn't."

Cox said he wished he could have done his kicking in domes. "I can remember the first time I ever played in Detroit when they got a dome, the Silverdome. I went up there and, of course, it was much like the dome that they built in Minnesota, where the air held the ceiling up. I mean, you thought you died and went to Heaven, the ball flew so far."

Many old-timers gripe that there is way too much arm tackling in the league nowadays, and critics have cited some more modern players such as Deion Sanders for shunning contact. Belu said good tackling correlates to "the amount of time you put into something. I have watched NFL and college practices and teams are spending more time with formations, routes, and motions and trying to trick a defense rather than spending a little time on the basics and techniques of how to block and tackle.

"Defensively, you still have to block, to tackle, but I can see where tackling has changed. But it's coming back to where it was in the fifties and sixties where you put your face to the football and you tackled, shooting your arms. For a number of years it was defensive backs and linebackers who were coming in and trying to knock people down by just rolling them."

In a 2015 interview, Belu said that defenders aiming high and leading with the head, trying more to dole out devastation than make textbook tackles was in vogue "the last few years. But now, take Seattle and a few other teams, and they're teaching tackling the way it was taught years ago."

Berry feels that tackling skills have definitely deteriorated, and that today's defenders are more concerned about using their head gear and otherwise trying to "do damage," to punish ball carriers and to become head hunters, as opposed to making conservative, textbook tackles. "I am totally against how defenders go about taking down the man with the football now." The goal today seems to be to put the big hit on someone, to maul the ball carriers.

Chuck Mercein said the NFL of the 1950s and 1960s featured "some real stickers in those days. The tackling was much better than it is today." Even "little guys" like Pat Fischer and Larry Wilson would put a hurt on ball carriers.

Pottios had a mixed take on the subject, saying some of today's players are actually better at tackling than some of his peers. "But, then again," he began, "with all these restrictions and what's going on [with newer rules], it's tough today to play the game all out. You have to be conscious about hitting the guy.

"Say a guy is running around the end and all of a sudden he's coming at me and I'm coming at him. I know one thing—I have to hit him with force; I want to deliver a blow to him. I don't want to take the blow. If I take the blow, I hurt, I feel the pain and I don't want that. I want him to feel the pain. Now this guy's coming over and, all of a sudden, he drops his shoulder and I want to hit him in the chest. But he bends down and I hit him in the helmet. Penalty.

"I can't come in there under control at full speed where I have to deliver a blow and then stop if I see, 'Wow, he's bending over. I got to get lower.' You just go in there and deliver the blow as hard as you can. You don't have time to see he's going to drop his head.

"There *was* a lot of good tackling back when I played, but also there was a lot of arm tackling." Overall, then, "I think that the ball game today is a lot better than when we played because you've got better athletes, and more of them. And the process evolves, but the game is better today all around than it was when I played."

Moore, like Pottios, said that one thing which really strikes him deals with "where you put your head. Now you have to watch where your head is in reference to tackling. I mean, your head is a part of you, how do you stop from leading and sometimes hitting with it? How do you tackle somebody when you can't put your head in it? How do you take your head out? That's kind of difficult." It seems unfair to men like Moore that a tackler can get hit with a stiff penalty for simply trying to do his job.

Moore continued, "Our thing was, give them a blow that makes sure that they don't want to come back and get another blow like that, that they don't want to come back in this area any more. That was our game plan.

"The forearm you could use. I know that when I used to go out for passes and try to make some of the inside cuts, I had to look out for those linebackers with those forearms. That's what it was about."

Marchetti agreed, saying in his time most defenders would take a shot at a receiver even if he didn't catch the ball with the idea of future intimidation in mind. "In those days, a defensive back could hit a receiver as long as the ball wasn't thrown. He was live. Today, after they go five yards, they can run around all afternoon and not worry about being hit. If they hit you, it's a fifteen-yard penalty." Long ago, defenders could continue to bump and disrupt would-be receivers farther down-field.

Moore added, "Now you've got to watch the helmet, then you've also got to watch how you grab the face mask. See, all that didn't matter—if you twisted his head all around or grabbed the face mask or whatever, it wouldn't be called a penalty. They think that they're trying to stop someone from getting concussions and those kinds of things—it may ease up on that, but during our day all bets were off."

Speaking of face masks, Joe Walton said he never had one until his senior year at Pitt, 1956. "It was just a small bar across the face. I went to the Redskins and Kelly Miller had been the equipment manager with them since my dad was there. When I went to get my helmet, he asked me what size face mask I wanted. I told him, 'I don't really need one. I wore one at Pitt and didn't like it.' He said, 'Well, I'm just advising you, you ought to learn to use one, but if you want to wait, it's all right with me.'

"We played the Los Angeles Rams in our first preseason game and guess what happened? A player broke my nose. The next week I went into Kelly and I said, 'Give me one of those things.'"

An argument can be made that the NFL was tougher in those days simply because the rules were so lax concerning deadly defensive moves. Another one of those tools for blockers was the leg whip. Bob St. Clair said he brought down many a defender by hitting them with, say, a heel to the groin or chest. He even wore his shin guards back-wards to protect his calf muscles for the times he used such takedown tactics.

Many old timers believe rule changes which handcuff the defense and boost the offense have come about simply to increase fan-pleasing, explosive scoring, not necessarily to make the game better. Rules today regarding what constitutes holding by offensive linemen are very len-ient compared to what used to be, aiding those linemen tremendously. Long ago, offensive linemen pretty much had to tuck their arms close to the body or risk seeing a penalty flag fly.

With holding so prevalent now by offensive linemen, it follows that today's quarterbacks have a seemingly endless amount of time to find and hit a receiver. Mike Lucci says that quarterbacks of old, not having so much time, had to do things differently. "I can remember playing against Unitas. You always thought, 'He's going to make you pay if you make a mistake.' You had to do your job, and you had to be where you're supposed to be. They were more precise. They had great timing back then."

Lucci realizes that the rules during his time period made it tougher to pass and tougher to rack up big offensive numbers. "You could not only grab [receivers], you could hit again at eight yards or ten yards as long as the ball wasn't in the air. It was more disruptive. The whole game has changed tremendously from that standpoint."

Even the very definition of what a tackle is has changed. Art Donovan stated that when he first came into the NFL a player's run wasn't considered over until his forward progress was fully stopped. Therefore, he said, "During the fifties, you used to see guys clawing for that extra yard with tacklers sitting on top of them trying to smash in their skull." That led to ball carriers having to adapt and to "give as good as they got." By way of contrast, Donovan said today's ball carriers are down when, say, a knee touches the ground due to a tackle or when an opposing player simply touches the runner when he's on the ground.[1]

Joe Walton added, "Guys used to be able to get back up and run after they were knocked down. Guys were getting hurt. Now, if you're touched, you're down." Then, he said the rule seemed to be if you were knocked down but not pinned down or not in contact with the tackler, you could still advance the ball.

Walton and Marchetti were correct. Prior to the introduction of a new rule which began in 1955, a play didn't come to an end due to a runner being tackled until the referee felt the runner had been stopped, which would then cause him to blow his whistle. It was his subjective decision all the way.

The new rule came into existence after an incident on the last day of October in 1954 when San Francisco runner Hugh McElhenny was injured while crawling for an extra yard or two after being taken down to the ground. He had been on a pace good enough to set a new single season rushing record, but with his shoulder separated on the play, his season was through. The new rule, referred to as the "McElhenny Rule," states that a runner is stopped and the whistle is to blow once a man carrying the football makes contact with the ground with any part of his body (with the exception of his hands or feet) after being tackled by a defender.

Marchetti said the definition of a sack has also changed over the years. "Today, suppose I'm getting blocked on the line and Fatso [Art Donovan] is rushing the passer. If he puts pressure on and the quarterback runs to my left, away from the blocker so that the blocker is blocking me away from the passer, and Artie's chasing him out towards me—now if he gets around and I make the tackle, I'll get credit for a 'miss.' The line coach will mark me as I didn't do my job—the quarterback got around me.

"So, a sack was when you actually got a quarterback in the pocket or you initiated the rush and you chased him around and you made the tackle, not three, four guys jumping on and they get, I don't know, one-fifth of the tackle [sack]. It was one of the most important parts of the game, but it wasn't [hyped] like it is today."

Pottios, who was with the Rams from 1966 to 1970, said although sacks are glamorized now, that was not the case in the 1950s. "The pass rush wasn't the big thing until the middle 1960s when Deacon Jones played for George Allen with the Rams. Prior to that, the only guy that was really physical and would destroy the quarterbacks was Doug Atkins.

"The publicity for the big pass rush began with the Fearsome Foursome when George Allen came to Los Angeles in 1966. *Then* they emphasized the sacks. Before that, nobody talked about sacking the quarterback or kept records—that came later.

"What we linebackers, Maxie Baughan, Jack Pardee, and myself, did was let the front four rush, go destroy." Of course, the Fearsome Foursome of the 1960s, huge by the day's standards, featured more than four players: Merlin Olsen, Lamar Lundy, Rosey Grier, who was replaced by the three-hundred-pound Roger Brown, and Jones.

The rules governing jersey numbers, albeit an issue not as important as, say, what defines a tackle, have also undergone a change. For example, George Belu recalled that fullback/linebacker Marion Motley wore number 76 and Otto Graham, a quarterback/defensive back was number 60. Later, said Belu, the number a player wore was tied in with the position he played. "I think Motley then had to switch to number 36, and his final number was 14 or 16, I believe." Nowadays, then, no runner would wear, say, number 55.

The rules now mandate that certain numbers be worn by players of specific positions. For instance, running backs and defensive backs have to wear a uniform number between 20 and 49. In 2015, a new rule allows teams to assign numbers 40–49 to linebackers. Previously, under a 1973 rule, those men were restricted to numbers from 50 through 59.

Over the years, other rule changes dealing with how many teams make the playoffs have changed the landscape of the NFL. In one regard, players of the 1950s and into the 1960s had it easier than today's players, simply because it was a much shorter trip to make it to the title game. Once the league began to allow more teams to participate in the postseason, the road to the title became rougher and much longer. Teams such as the dynastic Packers of the Glory Years knew that once they won their division, they were rewarded with a nonstop trip to the championship game. Just one playoff win and they would win it all. That was true of their titles in 1961, 1962, 1965, and 1966.

Now, the NFL champ requires surviving several rounds to win it all and wild card teams have it even tougher. The wild card system officially began in 1970, and six of the ten wild card teams to make it to the Super Bowl have won it all, but it takes four postseason victories to claim the NFL championship.

The way fumbles are dealt with has also undergone a change. Pottios said nowadays there are times when a team is awarded a loose ball simply because one of its players wins a wrestling match for the ball. "It wasn't as prevalent when I played. Today you'll see one guy make a tackle and the other guy go for the ball. When we played, everybody was concerned about making the tackle. Then somebody got smart and said, 'Hey, we can rip the ball out,' and it started to grow from then on." He thinks around the mid-1970s that trend began and "defensive players started practicing taking the ball away."

As far as fumbles occurring under a pile of bodies goes, Pottios said, "If you've got, say, two guys on the ground, and one's a big guy, a lot stronger, and he's got a better grip on the ball, he can rip it away." That can happen even though a player had actually secured the ball initially and, technically, should be awarded the football. "Those officials can't see if you've got guys on top on you—they don't know who has the ball until the pile is emptied, and whoever has the ball, it's their ball."

One side note regarding hard hits: Obviously, there are many observers who say the players of yesteryear were more likely to really lay someone out than today's players. One story, supposedly true, that gives a modicum of support to that assertion is worth telling. One of the

THE NFL THEN AND NOW

game's toughest players ever was the aptly nicknamed Mean Joe Greene, a key member of the Pittsburgh Steelers who played the bulk of his career in the 1970s. Andy Nelson was told a story about a time the hulking Greene was prepared to tackle an aging Joe Namath when a Pittsburgh teammate, new to pro football, joined in and was ready to tee off on Namath. The tale has it that Greene shouted out to the rookie to lay off a bit, to tackle Namath, but not forcefully. Nelson, who believes his era was not a forgiving one, chuckled and said, "I don't think that went on in our day. They didn't pull any slack—they hit Unitas as hard as they could hit him. I didn't see anybody ever pulling up."

Back in the 1950s and 1960s, many great quarterbacks, and not their coaches, called their own plays. Mike Lucci said, "I think there was a different generation if you go back to, say, the Blandas—it was more of an instinctive kind of thing. It was more of a street football, and they excelled because they had that inner toughness or that ability to adapt.

"The game has evolved. I mean, it's like now you watch Peyton Manning and some [other quarterbacks], and they have made it so that it's not quite as instinctive. It's like, 'I'm going to read this, and if this happens, I'm going to do that.' He may be the greatest quarterback, he may not be, but I think that back with Blanda, the game was a little different.

"Today you can't touch a receiver after he goes five yards. In the old days you could knock the shit out of him all over the field. So if you really thought about it, routes weren't as precise. They had to throw to an open space, but they had to read to see, 'Well, is the linebacker going to clothesline this guy and knock him off or grab him and impede his route?' It was more instinctive, rather than—I don't know if you want to say reactive—but the game is different, let's put it that way."

Coaches have had their players study film seemingly since the days of Thomas Edison, but even that aspect of coaching and individual prep work has changed. It's impossible to measure with 100 percent accuracy, but there may well be a contrast between the amount of *individual* prep put in by the average player of today versus those of yesteryear through film study.

Raymond Berry stated he believed that when he first began to study game film of opponents in order to analyze the men who would be guarding him in upcoming games, there was just one other man who did the same, Colt teammate Don Shinnick. Berry wasn't saying players of his day didn't study film at all—they did, but only during the times their coaches made them study as a group, not individually, and not with the zeal of a Berry.

Doug Crusan, who came along after Berry, speculated that today's players study film "a lot more now than we did." Sam Havrilak believes that the really good players of today study film diligently and on their own.

Matte may disagree a bit. "They're calling the plays in with the helmets and all that kind of stuff, but we studied film extensively. In fact, my wife knows more about the game than probably I do right now. She would study film with me. She'd take the strong side linebacker, I'd take the middle and the weak side linebacker. We have the old 16 mm; these kids today can bring a DVD home and study the whole game, run it back and forth, no problem. It was a real chore to be able to do that kind of stuff.

"But the thing that Unitas made me understand—and this is where John was so important to me—is he'd say, 'Tom, what you've got to do is not only understand what you're doing during this play, but you have to understand everybody else's position. So what I want you to do is I want you to learn the centers, guards, tackles, outside receivers, and I want you to understand what the patterns are.

"'For instance, if you're running a closed flare on the weak side, you're clearing it out because Raymond Berry is going to come in right behind you. You're in a clear out mode, so you got to get moving—just don't think, "I'll go out there and I have to get open." That doesn't mean shit. What you've got to do is clear the area out for Raymond to come underneath and I'll hit him.' So he made me learn every position so I could understand what a complete football play was, and that was really important."

Matte said the Colts expected him to know not only what was going on with all his teammates on the offensive side of the football, he was expected to know what opposing defenders were doing and what they probably *would* do. He had to recognize various defenses that could be thrown against the Colts and to know his opponents' tendencies.

"So, what I did was spend an enormous amount of time studying film to be able to understand the complete player, not just my assignment. That's what kept me in the league for twelve years. Running backs don't last twelve years. I bluffed them for twelve years, but the reason why I did last that long was Unitas would go to Shula and say, 'I want Matte in my backfield. I know he's going to be on every play because he understands what the play is. That's probably the main reason I got to play as much as I did and the reason why I lasted so long."

As Berry has pointed out, such dedication in watching film on one's own was rare when he played. It became more widespread and sophisticated as time went on. Pottios feels that film study today is so intense, it reveals virtually everything about teams' tendencies. "Listen, these defensive coordinators today are smart. They sit there and look at film after film after film and if they see a flaw in any person, they try to take advantage of it until you fix it. If you are a poor defender in passing situations, they're going to beat you up until a coach finds out, 'Hey, this guy can't do the job. We've got to replace him.'"

Former head coach Joe Walton said film study is a big aid for teams, but the importance of scouting has waned. "Now you're not allowed to scout the team you're going to play—they passed a rule on that. I used to scout. On Saturdays I'd go to a college game to evaluate kids and on Sunday I'd scout the team we were going to play the next week. I remember those days—I worked very hard at it from up in the press box. I took a lot of notes. You didn't have time to talk to anybody. You were busy the whole game. They depended a lot on the visual scouting.

"I had forms that helped me [know what to look for]. I'd jot down teams' coverages. The Giants were particularly concerned about blitzes. It was personal, hands-on. The Giants staff would rent a hotel room the night after day games. I flew back there, and I'd go to the hotel to help them, to give them what I'd seen.

"The exchange of those 16 mm films was much more difficult to do. Nowadays they just have those discs. They plug them in from their computer in Pittsburgh to get the game somebody else played."

Walton said film study from the era of Berry and Shinnick to nowadays has drastically changed. "It's because of the advantage of the technology today. They're much more available to the players. It used to be those films were like gold—the coaches didn't want to let them go out. Now they just make a disc of what you want and you take it home with you, stick it in your DVD." It's as if, armed with such discs and a DVD, every player is a scout.

Not only that, but a player, say a receiver, can ask for a disc to contain, say, only footage of the man who will be guarding him in an upcoming game. He can specify that he wants only footage from this season, or from every time the two ever faced each other, or, for that matter, just about any specific thing(s) he wants. "We even had this at Robert Morris University," stated Walton. "I could ask one of my coaches for all the short-yardage situations, all on one disc. And they'd have it back to me in fifteen minutes to study exclusively.

"They don't even have scouts anymore that watch the games of teams they're going to play. They just break down and study the 'film' that they have so handy. There's really no need for scouts."

However, Walton believes the scouting of young talent is much more sophisticated than in the old days. "Oh, yes. Definitely. There is not one stone unturned anymore as far as the college kids go. My little school I coached for 20 years was Robert Morris. I had three of my players that went to the NFL. The scouts don't miss anybody. They go to the games, they get tapes, scouting combines will tell you about every little town in the world."

Andy Nelson came from a small school and was therefore probably never going to play in the NFL. He said the only way he did make it to the pros was he once enjoyed a big day against Blanton Collier when he was coaching Kentucky. Collier had coached with Weeb Ewbank in Cleveland and informed Ewbank, then with the Colts, about Nelson. "Otherwise, small schools didn't get looked over in those days—not unless you had somebody to really recommend you. They went by word of mouth back then, coaches telling others, 'This guy's good and he can play.'"

Word-of-mouth sharing of information versus today's widespread scouting is as archaic as Fred Flintstone's automobile. "Like John Unitas at Louisville," continued Nelson. "He went to the Steelers and they cut him, and we picked him up." Mistakes are still made by scouts, but are not as common—more thought goes into acquiring and cutting players than ever before.

A good front office has to be in top shape for success to follow, and that is probably best exhibited by the way players are scouted and drafted. All the teams of the 1950s and 1960s were pretty much on the same level field, but some of the teams had different philosophies when it came to acquiring talent, and some were clearly better than others in making their draft picks and trades. Some teams also had more money to pump into the evaluation of talent.

Volk commented, "We had a good group of guys at that time. I always thought about how the Colts drafted back in those days. I'm thinking that a lot of the guys that they drafted maybe did not have the most physical ability, but they were smart and they could play in a unit, as a team player. It wasn't like, 'It's all about me'; it was about the team.

"So I felt that's how they drafted, and everybody sort of got along and everybody played well together. Maybe we didn't have the fastest guys on the team or the biggest guys in the league, but we were able to play and function as a unit, and that was why I really thought the Baltimore Colts were successful then."

Drafting is more exact now, but mistakes are still made—one glaring whopper was the case of Tom Brady. One of the greatest quarterbacks of all time saw nearly 200 players chosen before him. To be exact, he was chosen in the sixth round of the 2000 draft, with 198 men picked ahead of him. However, more scouting/drafting mistakes were made in days long gone by.

Overall, players' prep for games has truly become much better over the years. More game film (although the use of actual film disappeared ages ago) is available, more and better scouting is done now, training and nutrition of players has become a science, and nobody argues that today's players aren't stronger, faster, and bigger, lots bigger.

The average size of an offensive lineman lately is around six feet, five inches and 310+ pounds. A 2011 report revealed that at that time there were 170 men who started at least one NFL game on the offensive line, and only 28 of the Goliaths weighed in at less than 300 pounds. Another survey stated the average NFL defensive tackle weighed in the neighborhood of 305+ pounds. By way of contrast, in the 1950s the average offensive lineman went around six feet, two inches and around 240 pounds. The Colts of the late 1950s were probably a typical team size wise. Jim Parker played at 270, the rest were in the 255, 260 range.

Pottios pointed out that in his day a 300-pound player was very unusual. "Most of the linemen went 225 to 265 pounds. In all my years with the Steelers we only had one guy who was 300, a defensive tackle, and he was just heavy, not really athletic. He played maybe one year, if he even played that whole year. Most of those guys were just fat, out of shape. Now those guys are in great shape and go six foot seven and their rear ends and shoulders are as wide as can be.

"It's a different game. When we played there was a different system of how you played the game. Today, for instance, Vince Wilfork—the guy who plays over center for the Patriots—goes about 325 pounds and he's there for one reason, to have two or three blockers on him and to plug up the middle. Back in our day, the defense mainly was the 4-3, and you had guys who had to play defensive tackle over guards, so they had to be able to move. Otherwise, the center double-teamed you back over to the guard and there'd be a big hole there. If the other tackle gets beat, man, you're looking at three or four yards across there. Now with the big guys, all you have to do is sit there and hold and keep the guard and the tackle off you and plug up that hole."

Training methods have advanced enormously since the 1960s. Nowadays, for example, weight lifting is a huge part of the football scene from high school on up. However, that wasn't the case long ago, as Pottios explained, and he certainly is qualified to speak on that subject. He played college ball for the Fighting Irish of Notre Dame, where he became a team captain and was named to several All-American teams. He began his NFL days as the nineteenth overall pick in the 1961 draft by the Steelers. Later he played for George Allen with the Rams and Redskins, always holding down the middle linebacker spot.

Pottios said that he can't recall seeing or hearing of any NFL teams really getting into weight lifting until well into the 1960s. Prior to that, training was downright unsophisticated for many athletes. Pottios said his older brother Ray taught him how to train properly back in those dark ages. "He would improvise," said Pottios. To get the effect of lifting weights to build muscles, Ray would "push me around a track in a car to build up his legs, to gain lower-body strength. For squats, he would put me on his shoulders and do the squats. We didn't have the weights. I continued that when I got to high school.

"Even in the NFL, weights weren't mandatory until 1969—that's the first time I ever saw any connected with a football [training facility] on-site. The only reason we got the weights was George Allen traded for Bob Brown, who played for the Philadelphia Eagles as an offensive tackle, and he loved to lift weights. He came from Nebraska.

"We had our first universal gym in 1969 and even then it wasn't [really] mandatory that we lift weights, it was just that when Bob Brown came over he wanted a place to lift weights.

"At Notre Dame they had a weight room that you could go to which was open to all the students. So once I went to Notre Dame I didn't have to push cars," he quipped.

Sam Havrilak noted that Unitas, for one, "didn't even look like a football player. If you look at today's players, obviously they work out, they take supplements, none of that was available back when he started."

Havrilak continued, "These players are just so big, when they run on the field it sounds like the ground vibrates. It's like cattle running. If you take your simple physics formula that force equals mass times acceleration, they hit so much harder because they're bigger and they run faster. And they all work out year-round—the teams make sure that they do—so that's probably another reason why you see guys getting hurt. Their joints can't take year-round pounding with both weight training and playing football. There's a limit because the human joint can only take so much." Ironically, today's better preparation to make players fit to play and to hit hard, can also lead to injuries that force them to sit (or perhaps even *quit*, unable to play.

Walton feels that the biggest difference in the NFL from his time to now is the size and speed of "all the players. When I was playing, I was about 205 pounds at five eleven and a half and the linebackers I played against were 210–215. Now the linebackers are 265 and can run like the wind. The tight ends are all monsters, too. They're all six five and 265 pounds. That also makes for those violent collisions that result in concussions. Not that we didn't have violent collisions, but not with as much speed and size as they've got nowadays."

Once a player is drafted out of college, he reports to training camp with a "rookie" tag figuratively attached to his luggage. Long ago, the prevailing attitude about rookies was the same as what had once applied to small children who were in the company of adults—they were to be seen and not heard.

Resentment among vets for rookies ran high because often the feeling was, "This rook is going to take the job of my best friend on the team." Or take *my* job. When big money hit pro sports, the feeling changed a bit to one of, "At his age and talent level, this kid is an improvement, and he's going to help us win. And when we win, we all make more money."

Chuck Bryant was a rookie in 1962 who, due to playing in All-Star games, wasn't in his St. Louis Cardinals camp very long before the season began. "Oh, I stood on the table and sang for my dinner, and I shined shoes, but it wasn't as involved as if I would have been there for the other three or four weeks. I don't think it's the same now. We used to have a rookie show, where the guys had to get up and perform, sing, or put on little displays." A rookie, at the mercy of veterans, was basically an errand boy and a means of entertainment for veterans.

In 2001, George Belu was on the Arizona Cardinals coaching staff. "All the hazing of the past went aside. When you go to the training tables, during two-a-days, they'll still have a rookie carry a plate or [fetch] a dessert for a vet, or something like that, but it's nothing like it used to be. That's because the rookies have to feel a part of the team so quickly today because they're going to need them." That's in part due to free agency, which allows veterans to leave teams readily, and a rookie may well be brought in to fill a void immediately.

Free agency has led to players becoming figurative carpetbaggers. Havrilak said that in the days before free agency teams stuck together longer than now, "basically, in one place for their whole careers so they got to know each other pretty well. When a rookie would make the team, they would kind of haze him quite a bit. We had rookie shows back then. I don't think they have them, or have them sing their college [fight] song, anymore, but we would have to come up with a show and make fun of either the coaches or players."

Even though things aren't very rough on rookies today, some of them have defied the old, conventional ways that prevail. Dez Bryant, a Dallas rookie in 2010, refused to carry the pads of a veteran, a long-standing tradition. Many of the chores given to rookies are meant to break the ice, let them know veterans deserve respect, and some duties, such as the singing, simply inject humor for all, or *almost* all, of the players.

Bryant did not take things that way. He insisted he was in camp to play football, and not to act as a baggage handler. His reaction came across as a, "Nobody disrespects or tries to humiliate me—I'm Dez Bryant!" Instead of blending in with his teammates, especially his fellow rookies, he was placing himself above them. By the way, the veterans prevailed. Several months after training camp was over, the team ran up a bill for almost $55,000 at a steakhouse and had Bryant pick up the tab.

Contrary to the norm of some teams of yesteryear, the Colts treated their rookies well, wanting them to fit in, improve, and help the team. For example, Volk never felt that, if Unitas burned him for a touchdown in a practice session that he was being picked on, nor did he get reamed if he picked off a Unitas pass. "John had that strong arm, and he was the leader of the team, and it wasn't like you are trying to make him look bad or anything. You were trying to improve yourself playing against the best. So if you knocked the ball down, or if you got beat for a touchdown, that was practice, and you knew that it was going to help you in a regular game situation.

"You get prepared for anything in a game situation because we had great receivers that we were playing against when I was a rookie, but I had a great defensive team that I was with at the time as well. They can sort of hide rookies like me that were playing out there because the other ten guys can make up for maybe some of my mistakes at the time.

"It was just an amazing experience for me to come out of Michigan and go to the Colts and be a part of that whole unit and for me to step into that group right away. I was just honored to be on the football team with John, a legend like he is. We won a lot of games and lost some, and he never really changed any part of his personality. He didn't get mad, he just stayed calm."

Treated well, Volk appreciated it and wanted to help the Colts win. He continued, "I started as a rookie so I felt that, 'Geez, they're letting me play here, I don't want to let them down.' Let Johnny U down? It's a professional game, you're in there to win games, get in the playoffs and win championships, so I better play my best because I don't want them to feel like I'm taking money out of their pocket. You just didn't want to be the one that lost the game for the team. That was one of the things that I didn't ever want to have happen to me. But they prepared us."

Volk played in the College All-Star Game before reporting to the Colts' camp. It was an honor, but it held him back a short time from blending in with his future teammates. "You know, it wasn't like coming to Baltimore and being a part of that team. One thing I thought was a little different about Baltimore than a lot of other teams was that they wanted you to excel, they wanted you to be a part of the team even though you're a rookie or second-year guy. They knew you were going to be a part of their team and they made you feel at home.

"That's what really helps because you can play your games and not worry about making a mistake or whatever because other guys were there helping you out. Like if I got beat, say, a receiver running open on me, and Bubba Smith is rushing the quarterback, you know he put some pressure on them, and they didn't have the time to throw. So even though I might have been beaten by a couple of steps, they didn't have the time to look around and see someone was open and throw by the time Bubba's in on them.

"So it's a team effort and everybody was all for the team, and that's the way you win, the way everybody gets acknowledged then. If you have a winning team the guys on that team are going to the Pro Bowl, make All-Pro and that kind of thing." Even if that guy is a newcomer, the Colts welcomed him.

Volk's admiration and appreciation of his teammates jibes with the belief that most players from his time had a stronger sense of camaraderie than today's players. Some of this can be attributed, of course, to the fact that players back then often stuck with one team for an eon, not having the mobility of today's players, who can leave one team and go to another as a free agent.

George Belu said, "Teams have a lot of fun with one another, and the teams that are really close are the ones that can joke around a little bit. They became close knit. They were together nine, ten years. Now, with free agency, you don't develop anything like that. A guy plays three years, applies for free agency and he leaves, so you don't have that real camaraderie. When those guys get together and tell stories, it is a riot. They had that bond. Now, it seems like they do have a relationship, but, boy, everybody is looking out for Brother Self."

Havrilak says today's players, with the exception of some superstars, wind up playing for multiple teams. "With free agency, they follow the trail of money. They would rather go where the money is, I think, than stay loyal to the team."

Marchetti, like Volk, spoke fondly of his era, "I loved my teammates. We all got along good together—they don't do that today. I remember one time Weeb told me to say something to the team before we went out to play the 49ers, and I said, 'Shit, I'm not used to talking or trying to lift a team up,' and I told the whole team, 'Listen, we're having a party. We're all chipping in, and it's at my house. Let's go out and beat the hell out of them then have a lot of fun.' You didn't want to go to a party as a loser. And we had maybe thirty of the thirty-six ballplayers there, and we had a good time."

One time Tom Matte and Johnny Unitas were playing racquetball and Unitas tore his Achilles tendon. Matte rushed him to the hospital, but not too long after that Matte's appendix ruptured and he ended up in the same room as Unitas. "Everybody was bringing a case of beer for us. We had cases of beer lined up against the wall. Everybody would come in and have a cold beer and we'd sit there and talk with them."

New York Giants player Joe Walton said such camaraderie was not exclusive to small cities such as Baltimore. Asked if New York was too big and sophisticated to foster such an environment, Walton said, "No, *it wasn't*. It was a magical time in New York City. The Giants were celebrities. We could go anywhere and get a table. A lot of places picked up drinks or tabs for us.

"Oh, no. You should have seen the way people came to Yankee Stadium in my years there in the early sixties. Women in their long minks and men all dressed up. It was the place to be on Sunday afternoon. Show business people came. After the games we'd all meet down at P.J. Clarke's, a famous watering hole. They treated us like kings."

After winning the NFL championship in 1967, aka the Ice Bowl, Bob Hyland said, "We went out that night and really celebrated—it being New Year's Eve and one of the most important games of our lives.

"The family guys did spend more time together, usually at someone's home. I was a bachelor and a lot of the younger guys hadn't got married yet. We used to go to this place—with an ironic name for Green Bay—called the Tropics, a nightclub where you could get something to eat and a lot of music. We'd go there and have a few beers. That's where we spent time that night. We had at least ten or twelve of the younger guys."

He went on, "If we were to get together now, so many of us would still have good feelings toward each other. It's amazing what winning a championship together can do. The Packers invite us back occasionally. I was back there a few years ago and it really is a great experience being with the guys.

"Sometimes it's kinda sad—you can see we're not physically what we used to be, sometimes mentally as well. The game really takes its toll, but nobody can ever take the Ice Bowl and the Super Bowl win two weeks later away from us."

Winning as a team really does help players come together. Mike Lucci related, "I played for the Browns when we won the championship in '64 and it was a special team." His connection to that team is still strong enough that he has always looked forward to team reunions. "And I only played there three years, but there's still a camaraderie. Ernie Green got put in the Ring of Honor, and I made a special effort to go back for that because we came in at the same time and we played basketball together in the off-season. Hell, I didn't see him a lot, but when I see him, there's an affinity, there's a friendship. We were joking about playing basketball against the Harlem Magicians and stuff like that, and they're memories that nobody can ever take away from you."

Fred Cox said his Vikings also had great unity and fun as a team. "Tarkenton's pet name among the guys was 'Rag Arm.' Francis did not have a great arm. Grady Alderman, who was a great offensive tackle for us for a lot of years, used to get on him all the time. He'd throw a ball, and because he didn't have great velocity, it would always kind of fall off to the right. And somebody would run downfield and miss a pass because it fell off, and when they came back Grady would be in the huddle and he'd say, 'You know, when "Rag Arm" throws it, it always falls off to the right, so take that into consideration.'

"The one thing about our team which was great was it was not unusual for our players to pick on each other like that and guys never got mad. We had great camaraderie. Francis and I played so long, that by the time we were ready to retire there was only him, Mick Tingelhoff, and I [left from the early years]. Everybody else was in their twenties and we were right in the forty range, so we hung around a lot. When we would go on road trips we ate together. He would pick up the tab, and, of course, we let him know he was making the most money. That was part of us picking on people that we did a lot of, too."

Players of long ago not only bonded with teammates, but with their families as well, and those connections were deep, strong, and long lasting. Matte became close friends with the Unitas family. He golfed a lot with John and said of John's children, "His kids, especially Chad, is like an adopted child for me. Whenever we'd do anything, I'd take him with me as a kid. We were close-knit family.

"All the players were, and everybody stayed here in Baltimore, not too many people were like the players today who, as soon as the season is over, they're going back home. We had a basketball team and we went around and did charity stuff. We were very, very close; the wives were close together, so it was a very close-knit ball club, and I think that's what helped make us a success."

Now success seems to come without teams being so close. Pottios has heard the stories that circulated not long ago about major league baseball clubs that, instead of sticking around the clubhouse and riding the team bus to and from the hotel and the ballpark together or going out as a team after games, take twenty-five taxis for twenty-five men and go their separate ways.

In Pottios's day, players would get together at a little bar and bond, but he says there are several reasons why that's no longer the case. "There is no doubt that today it's changed. Each individual is different, and they can't afford to make a mistake, especially with making big money. They can't afford to be seen out in public drinking to the point where they're obnoxious or drunk. There are sportswriters and other people who are just waiting to get them. Most of the guys today are smart enough that they know they have to do it privately."

Pottios said the media in his day was not at all like that of today. "The sportswriters weren't looking for a 'got-you'-type story. They were part of the guys. They drank with the guys and weren't going to write anything derogatory, to hurt you. Today they're looking for stuff because it's a different situation than when we played and all of us socialized together, And we didn't make the money. Today, you make a million dollars, you're a corporation—you can't afford to go out and ruin your image or take chances that something could go wrong where you could jeopardize your career or your future."

However, while teammates bonded back then, fraternization with opponents was frowned upon—they were the enemy, determined to take money out of your pocket. Cox pointed out that conversations among opponents, perhaps former teammates wanting to catch up with each other, took place after contests, never prior to games.

Mercein added, "There wasn't that much fraternization that went on like there is today. Players really hunkered down with their own teammates. There wasn't a lot of socialization off the field, and on the field during the game you didn't really communicate with each other very much, really."

Not mingling with opponents is one thing, antagonizing them is quite another. Nowadays chest thumping, taunting others, and blatant acts of egoism have become the norm. In fact, NFL histrionics have been prevalent since the days of Billy "White Shoes" Johnson, and grew to ludicrous proportions with the antics of men such as Terrell Owens who, craving attention, put on many over-the-top, premeditated displays.

Once he celebrated a touchdown by pulling a Sharpie marker out of his sock, then signed the football. He also celebrated by lying down in the end zone as if preparing to fall asleep, using the football as his pillow and, after another score, he grabbed a bag of popcorn from a fan and poured it through an opponent's face mask. Such displays drive purists berserk.

Belu said there were some NFL players years ago who also craved attention and acted crazy and wild, but they were actually somewhat phony. "They talked about how vicious they were, and poking guys in the eyes. They wanted to make a name for themselves, just to get attention. They weren't the true, hard-nosed guys. Some of them knew down deep inside they probably weren't so good, so it was a little bit of a facade they had."

Still, said Belu, the trash talking and theatrics weren't "as animated as it is nowadays. You hate like heck to see that. Some guys make a play and they're beating their chest, pointing to themselves, and I'm thinking, 'You better look at the scoreboard, buddy. You guys are getting beat by 14, 21 points, and you're over here jumping up and down because you made one play?' Come on.

"The guy you really respect is someone who makes a heckuva play or hit, gets up and gets back to the huddle. Anybody watching the game knows that was one helluva hit. You don't have to jump up and point to yourself and all that, but that's this day and age, I guess."

Many of the modern acts of putting oneself above the team are not unlike a small child craving attention, and that didn't fly back in the 1950s and 1960s. In Marchetti's view, there is way too much of the "me, me" attitude in today's game. "Today there's a lot of showboating. I don't understand that. If you're a good ballplayer, your teammates know it. If you're a good ballplayer, fans know it. Now you see those guys pointing their fingers up to Heaven and all that—I mean, there's just no sense in it."

Marchetti also said there wasn't much trash talking in his time. "You're concentrating on what you did, how you did it, and the play that's coming up. You prep yourself for the play that's coming up. You don't have time to look back."

Unlike many of today's spoiled players, Unitas had no delusions of self-importance. His daughter Paige commented, "Dad was still humble and he never thought a thing about who he was or what he had done. To him it was his job. That's how he made money. He didn't need to be out in the public running around shouting who he was."

Volk said the Colts were far from being a self-promoting, egocentric type of team. "John was our leader on offense, and he really was sort of the leader for the whole team, but he wasn't the kind of guy that was a rah-rah type of a player.

"He didn't go out and do a Ray Lewis and get everybody all fired up, that kind of thing. He was just a straightforward person and he told it like it was, 'Let's get ready and go out and play. Let's go.' But those are the kinds of guys that you look up to because they've been through the war, so to speak. They won big games and then got beaten, too."

John Ziemann, a friend of Unitas, said, "John didn't have to get up there and show himself off. John was the type that, the ball would be in mid-air and he'd expect you to catch it, and he'd be walking off the field like, 'My job's done.' You never saw him dance. He never went in for anything like that."

Matte also remembered Unitas's style well. "Many a time I'd come back to the huddle and he would say, 'Great catch,' because the pass would be out of reach, or I'd knock it down then catch it—something like that.

"He was very subtle how he was a leader and he wasn't showy, he wasn't bossy or anything like that. You see some of these guys out there today always screaming at everybody. John just wasn't that kind of guy. But if he wanted to say something, you'd come to the sideline and he'd say, 'Hey, listen, this is what you're going to do,' and he'd explain it because he *totally* understood the game of football. He spent enormous amounts of time studying and dedicating himself to try to win, that was his key objective."

Paige Unitas remembers many times when she and her father were attending events and even though he knew he possessed the status of a legend and it would have been understandable if he sported a big ego, he sublimated himself, downplaying his accomplishments. "He was extremely humble," said Paige, "and he never changed. All the [celebrities] nowadays are so different—they get some money and they go nuts, or not even money, just the fame and they lose their heads. He never, ever, did that."

Unitas remained calm even immediately after the winning touchdown was scored to secure the 1958 championship. When Paige watched film of that game with her father and later commented, "When you watch him at the very last second before they won, after he handed the ball off to Ameche, he is out of there. I asked him what he was doing. He said, 'Getting the hell out of there. If I didn't get out of there they would have killed me.' People were going crazy. He was probably showered and changed before they even got off the field." No wild demonstrations for Unitas.

That same vivid memory of Unitas lingers with a teammate, Andy Nelson. He is fully aware of the contrast between players' reactions to winning the big one between his time period and today.

Nelson called Unitas a cool customer, saying nothing seemed to excite him. As Nelson walked off the field after winning the 1958 championship game, he glanced over at Unitas. "He wasn't turning back flips or jumping up and down. He just casually walked off. His eyes were focused straight ahead. Like it was just another game. I thought, 'This man just played the greatest game of his life and it's like another game to him.'"

After the victory, Ed Sullivan wanted Unitas to appear on his television show, which originated in New York City, but Unitas turned him down—something that today's players (and their agents) would probably never do. Nelson said, "Nowadays there's so much celebration and fuss. It doesn't stop, but that was John: 'I want to be with my gang [teammates].'"

Nelson rode home from the airport with Unitas that night in silence. When Unitas dropped him off, Nelson thanked Unitas for the ride and he replied, "No problem. Good game. See you tomorrow." Nelson continued, "I got out of the car and he said, 'I'll see you tomorrow,' and that was it. It was as if he were saying so long to a buddy, leaving a factory after putting in an eight-hour shift."

According to a close friend of Unitas, when he entered his home he prepared a sandwich for himself, drank a beer and went to bed. No fanfare for Unitas—he had simply done his job.

Still, as far as today's players' behavior goes, Volk, for one, does not feel his era was different from that of the modern game. "You've got some of your characters out there now that sort of make a bad image of what some of the NFL players are. There are some of them that sometimes don't act professionally, but most of them are pretty down-to-earth guys."

Players' feelings about playing in the Pro Bowl seem to have changed since the golden time period. Pottios said players of his day took pride in being in that game. "Oh, yeah. You better believe it. Look, we've all got egos—every one of us, and that's like a pat on the back or somebody saying, 'Nice game.' Going to the Pro Bowl, it makes you feel great. You get recognition; you love it. Yes, it's very important."

Perhaps with all the exposure and recognition via the media and the salaries today's players reap, they don't feel as if they need to concern themselves much with the Pro Bowl.

For players of the distant past the money for playing in those games wasn't the main thing, and it was minuscule compared to today's salaries. Pottios said, "The winners got $1,500. The losers got $750. We played hard, too. You didn't go out there and stand around. You wanted to win. Those guys had egos. They were out there for a whole week practicing, and they're going on television, and they want to do well. You didn't take the attitude of just going through the motions."

Being human, players' attitudes about losing have never changed—it is a most unpleasant feeling and it always has been. Contrary to what some fans think about today's players, they do take pride in what they do, and they desperately want to win. Some even say that money isn't as big of a motivational factor as long ago; winning a Super Bowl ring is.

Pottios reflected on his career. "Disappointments? Yes, you always want to win the Super Bowl and it's disappointing when you don't." He said once a player earns the championship ring, "That's there forever, but I can't go back and say, 'We won.' That would be the ultimate.

"The only other ultimate goal is the Hall of Fame. Those are what the game is all about, and to go through a career and not have it, it doesn't hurt, but if you had it, it would be a big, big, big plus.

"When you are on a winning team, it's the greatest feeling in the world. When you're on a mediocre or losing team, every week just isn't a great week." Further, and it may be unfair, but much of a player's reputation is linked to what team employed him. Being on a winning team seemingly elevates a player's credentials or his overall worth. "A lot depends on how successful your team is," Pottios began. "If you're on a good team and you go to the championship, naturally you're going to get more recognition than a guy who was on a 4-10 team."

Sadly, though, going to the championship game and almost winning it all often isn't good enough for a player's reputation or his pride and contentment. Winning, say, the NFC title but losing the Super Bowl can leave players feeling empty. Plus, in the vast majority of seasons during the Glory Years, after a team won their division all it took to win the title was to win one more game. Now teams must go through seemingly endless rounds of the playoffs before they even try to win the championship. Thus, there are more opportunities for even very good teams to come up short in the postseason, and, again, one thing has remained unchanged throughout the years, losing in big games hurts—a lot. The Minnesota Vikings, the first modern expansion team to make it to the Super Bowl, once had a stranglehold on the NFC title—they made it to the Super Bowl four times over a seven-year span, but there's a big "however" here. Fred Cox lamented, "The only thing that stands out in my career is we lost four Super Bowl games."

When told that just getting there four times was a huge accomplishment, he replied, "Well, I agree with that, I understand that, and it doesn't bother me. To be honest with you, it doesn't bother me as much as it always bothers the Minnesota fans. But when you're playing, you know that you gave it everything you had, and if you lost, you lost. There is nothing much you can do about it. You only have to live with yourself, and I know that we worked hard and we gave it our best shot."

Joe Walton's first four seasons in the NFL with Washington produced a cumulative record of 13-31-4. Traded to the Giants, his team went 33-8-1 over the next three seasons. While they won the East Division title in those years, 1961–1963, they would, like Cox, lose in the big one each time. So which types of seasons hurt more? Walton commented, "Oh, definitely, the Giants' losses. We didn't quite pull it off. The Giants were a little more sophisticated when I got there, as far as their coaching and teaching goes. Certainly, they had good personnel, and if they didn't have it, they'd trade for it."

As much as losing stings, having the tools to become a star in the NFL but never getting the chance due to injuries hurts even more. That scenario leaves the player pondering forever what might have been; and that is another thing that will always hold true.

Chuck Bryant's story is one such sad tale, which many a player with great potential shares. Bryant was a key part of Ohio State's 1961 success (8-0-1). He was drafted by both the San Diego Chargers of the old AFL and the team he signed with, the St. Louis Cardinals. As a junior, he had led the Big Ten in touchdowns on receptions and his average of 19.8 yards per catch ranked first in the entire NCAA. Those feats are especially impressive because they came while playing for Woody Hayes, who much preferred that his Buckeyes run more than pass.

Just off the Ohio State campus, Bryant played in the College All-Star Game and scored a third-quarter touchdown against Green Bay that gave the collegians a 17–14 lead and a shot at an upset—that is until the Packers poured it on to win, 42–20.

Bryant then joined his Cardinals for a week of training camp just before the 1962 season opened. However, an injury sustained in the All-Star Game would soon haunt him. It took place when Bryant hauled in a John Hadl pass and "ran about thirty-five, forty yards down to the 3-yard line where Bob Jeter tackled me. My leg got hurt and they carried me off the field. I wasn't the swiftest tight end in the world, but after that, I couldn't run anymore."

Bryant did put in one season with the Cardinals, playing in thirteen contests. If healthy, who knows what he might have achieved. Tom Matte was the Ohio State quarterback with Bryant. He said, "Chuck was a helluva receiver, a good tight end—he had great hands, great, and was a good blocker." Bryant, by the way, is the son of Clay Bryant, who led the National League in strikeouts in 1938 when he pitched for the Chicago Cubs.

After Chuck's short stint in the NFL, it was a career in education and coaching for him. Again, his is a representative tale, far from being unique.

Many differences between eras deal with off-the-field topics. For example, race relations in football have improved, at least to some extent over the decades. Glancing back on his college days at the University of San Francisco, Marchetti said, "In 1951, we were undefeated, untied, and we had a chance to go to [the Orange Bowl]. But, they wouldn't take us because we had two black ballplayers, Ollie Matson and Burl Toler." At the time there were only eight bowl games each season and the Orange Bowl was one of the biggest.

Bowl officials told USF they would get an invitation if they left the two black players behind, otherwise they would be undefeated, untied, and uninvited. Marchetti looked back, "We said, 'Go shit in your hat.' I'm not leaving them home. They're my friends." Coincidentally, in 1972 Matson and Marchetti shared center stage at Canton, Ohio, as new inductees into the Hall of Fame.

The Dons finished their untarnished season with a win over Loyola, in a game Marchetti recalled sixty-five years later—he recalled the aftermath of that season, too. "We kicked the hell out of them and we felt we were going to the bowl game. They had said if we won, you're going to the bowl game. I mean, we had one helluva team, but we won and that [issue] came up on the way from Los Angeles, where the Loyola game was, back to San Francisco. We said we just aren't going to play. We got off the train in San Francisco, we all went in our cars, and never heard another word about it."

There was no fuss between the university and the football team over the decision and subsequent loss of revenue due to the refusal. Marchetti said that was simply because things didn't get that far. "I don't think it got to the president of the university because if he had his choice we would have played in that game and probably saved the school—right after that they shut down the football program because of money. I think it just went as far as in the locker room."

Marchetti said the Dons were so talented there were nine players who went on from that one team to play pro ball. "And the best football player was Burl Toler. He played offensive tackle and middle linebacker—you had to go both ways then—and, God Almighty, the way he tackled, the way he played. It was absolutely wonderful, and he was the greatest person in the world. He eventually went into being a referee."

Toler was drafted by the Cleveland Browns immediately after he had been on the undefeated USF team, but a knee injury in 1952 ended his playing days. However, he not only became a referee as Marchetti noted; he was, in fact, the first African American game official in league history.

Football fans and players were closer back in the golden age than they are now. Players were much more accessible and approachable, and some say this is largely due to economics. In the 1950s, for example, the gap in salaries between the average fan and a big league baseball player wasn't huge. Now the disparity is astronomical.

Brooklyn Dodgers ace pitcher Carl Erskine observed that when he was in the major leagues from 1948 through 1959, players would walk down the streets of Brooklyn and travel on subways, mingling freely with fans. They certainly did not ride to their home ballpark in a limo or in a luxurious vehicle. In fact, friendly grocers would stop Dodger players as they walked by on the sidewalk and present them with, say, a bagful or two of free food. Fans would also give presents to players. In short, the social schism between the public and sports figures was much narrower back then.

Marchetti recalled, "Baltimore was our town. We enjoyed playing there, we enjoyed the people—it was really the best part of my life, I think. You could walk in a beer joint or whatever on, say, a Saturday afternoon and shoot pool with the neighbors and have a couple of beers—that makes a good time out of it."

Mike Ditka had a great deal of respect for fan-friendly men such as baseball's Stan "The Man" Musial and Unitas. "They identified with the fans so much better then, and they appreciated them. Listen, guys today that play the game, they don't understand when the fans [go to games they are supporting them]. So they got to treat the fans with respect. And if you treat them with respect and a little dignity, then they'll treat you the same way. And if you don't, they'll end up pissing on you, too."

Paige Unitas said her father realized he owed a lot to his fans. He felt an obligation to talk to his fans and to sign autographs for them—free of charge back then, of course. Furthermore, she said he did those things because he wanted to do them "because people loved him and he always respected the fans and the love that they showed for him. He said that without them he, actually he said the team, wouldn't be. He told me once, 'Paige, it only takes a minute to shake someone's hand and make their day.'"

Of course, fans back in the golden era weren't as invasive as the fans (or the media) of today. Chuck Smith, a high school teammate of Joe Montana, stated his old friend told him he had "to sneak in and out of stores to avoid mob scenes. He has been known to put on sunglasses and a hoodie to travel incognito. He must sometimes feel as if he is a prisoner in his own life."

The popularity of the NFL grew at a berserk pace from around the 1960s/1970s on. Baseball no longer could maintain its claim as being the national pastime. The Cincinnati Bengals franchise sold for $7.5 million in 1967. By way of contrast, the average franchise today is valued at a whopping $1.9 billion.

Marchetti said that, unlike today, nearly half of the big games of the 1950–1960 time frame, including the championship contests, would be "played in stadiums which were maybe three-quarters full, but after [the 1958 title game] stadiums were full, people were looking for tickets."

Now, fans cram venues, often for games that are far from being of earth-shaking consequence. And for the Super Bowl, the face value of the "cheapest" ticket was $850 a pop in 2016, although the NFL did make 1,000 tickets available at $500 each through a lottery for fans. The most expensive face-value tickets, for club seats, were $3,000. Keep in mind that a ticket to the first Super Bowl ran $12 (about the same as $88 in today's money). By 2016, people who went through online services paid an average of almost $5,000 for seats, with reported high-water marks in the ultra-ritzy five-digit neighborhood.

Doug Crusan has tickets from the three Super Bowls he appeared in (1972–1974) framed in his office. "They were $15 apiece for Super Bowl VI, VII, *and* VIII. They're the comp tickets that my wife had for the games. I think one guy paid around $35,000 or something like that for a Super Bowl 50 seat." Naturally, the gap between a ticket for a regular-season game now and one for a championship contest is much wider than from the Glory Years.

Of course, as the popularity of the league rose, so did the cost of advertising during games. Crusan analyzed this. From salaries to the price of tickets, he noted, "The sports world has completely changed." Crusan said that someone told him that a thirty-second commercial aired during Super Bowl VII cost $88,000. That same spot in Super Bowl 50 (2016) went for an astronomical $5 million. "That is beyond staggering." He's correct, of course. The 2016 price tag is 125 times more than the cost of such a commercial shown during Super Bowl I.

It is only natural that the lifestyles of pro football players have changed drastically with the NFL empire's growth. "The game is real popular now," continued Marchetti, "that's the one thing. So you have kids with a lot of money. In the off-season I had to take jobs as a bartender, in a factory, anywhere I could to help make it through the winter." In that regard, Marchetti was far from being unique. Players of the golden epoch simply did not earn enough from playing pro football to take time off after the season ended.

Working after the completion of each season did have a payoff on the field for some. Marchetti attributed his incredible hand strength to his work during off-seasons. "Every job I had, I tried to relate it to football—like when I worked in this factory that made these round, carbonated tubes. They might be a foot wide, and you're supposed to pull them out with two hands. I would always try to pull them out with my fingers, that way my fingers and hands got stronger."

Interestingly, Marchetti has a refreshing take on the issue of players of his era versus today's. He says his peers were not necessarily tougher or at least better prepared to play football than the contemporary players. "How could you say that? Let's say today's ballplayer—I'll compare him to me. The season's over. What has Gino got to do? He's got to make a little more money to support his family. I had three children at that time, and I was playing for $7,000. Even though the money was OK and I'm not complaining about that, but I had to work. I worked as an iron worker, I worked in a factory, I worked tending bar. I did all those things to help supplement my income so that when I went back to Baltimore training camp, I didn't have to worry about my family not eating.

"Today, if the same situation happened, I'd have made enough money so I wouldn't have to work so I could spend the time that I spent as an iron worker, keeping in shape. So when I'd go into camp I'd be stronger, faster, and with a little more determination because I've devoted all winter to football, keeping in shape."

Another Baltimore Colt, big Jim Parker, worked making deliveries, including, said John Unitas's son Chad, "delivering the embalming fluid, or whatever it was, to funeral homes." Although he was fearless on the field of play, Parker startled easily. Because of that, he lost his job one day when a prankster had someone pretend to be a sheet-covered corpse laying on a gurney.

Chad Unitas related, "Jim went downstairs in the morgue once to drop some things off and there was [what appeared to be] a stiff lying there. Jim walked in, set everything down, then all of a sudden, that stiff sat straight up. Jim turned around and ran . . . got in his car and took off and never went back to the job again." It's a given, though, that the next day he was out looking for a job again, albeit in a different line of work.

Aside from off-season jobs, there was one way to make money beyond one's regular-season salary, but it was a highly uncertain, irregular source of income. Rick Volk explained, remembering how glad he was to be drafted by Baltimore. "It was a winning program, a winning organization—that was the big thing, the main thing. In those days without free agency, the only way you could make any extra money was to get into the playoffs, and we were able to do that. I was just a lucky person at that point."

The disparity in salaries earned by players of long ago and today is as big as the Mariana Trench is deep. Actually, though, thanks goes to the men of the past for helping the game become popular enough that it grew to the point where salaries skyrocketed.

One time Unitas was on a television show along with Joe Montana and Dan Marino. John's brother Leonard remembered at one point "a remark was made about the money that these guys make nowadays and Marino and Montana both said, 'Thanks, John. You're the one that started it.'"

The escalation has never really slowed down, nor has the enormous amount of television coverage, which surely helps pay the bills for teams and players alike—keep in mind the networks didn't even bother to broadcast the Pro Bowl until 1958.

So, fueled by television money, salaries eventually soared. However, the highest salary of Raymond Berry, arguably the game's greatest receiver of all time, by the time he reached his peak season for earning power, was a mere $42,000, and his base salary in his rookie season was a paltry $8,500.

Alex Karras had been in three Pro Bowls by 1964, when he signed a two-year deal for $25,000 annually. That made the future All-1960s Team member one of the best paid linemen in the NFL. Detroit teammate Lem Barney made the Pro Bowl team as a rookie in 1967, when he led the league with ten interceptions, and again in the following two seasons. His reward? $15,000 for his 1970 (option year) salary.

In 1971, the great Johnny Unitas was old enough to have proven his worth, and was still doing well. For example, in the previous season, at age 37, his team's record with him at quarterback was 10-2-1. Nevertheless, his 1971 salary was, by today's standards, measly, at $125,000. Clearly in the 1950s and 1960s he and almost every player were grossly underpaid.

Pro Bowl linebacker Mike Lucci, who played from 1962 to 1973 recalled that at one point in his career he had done well enough to become the highest-paid defensive player on the Lions. Lucci definitely was good—teammate Bill Malinchak said, "He was an outstanding middle linebacker. I mean, he was just terrific. He didn't get as much notoriety as a Butkus or Nitschke, but he was that good."

Despite Lucci's ability, he certainly never struck it rich. He reflected, "You didn't make life-changing money. I mean, if you're the highest paid defensive player on the team now, you're making 10, 15, 20 million dollars—that's life-changing money. But I'm happy to see these guys get it. The only thing I'm not happy about is I think the league has a little more responsibility to some of the old-time players that are in trouble."

Going even further back into the 1960s and earlier, linemen were receiving virtual slave wages. Doug Crusan estimated that the average salary for a lineman circa the late 1960s was approximately $17,000. "If I told you what I made, you'd fall over because it sure doesn't equate to today's standards whatsoever. I would say that back then [around the late sixties], most of your offensive lineman were probably in the $17,000–25,000 range. How's that?! That's sure unlike today." Some offensive linemen today earn in the $10–$13 million range.

The Sandra Bullock movie *The Blind Side* made even casual football fans aware of the fact that for almost all quarterbacks, except the southpaws, their left offensive tackles are vital to protect them from wicked pass rushers who came at them from their blind side. Crusan, who was the left tackle who protected quarterbacks such as Bob Griese and Earl Morrall, said that today's players at his position "are paid pretty good money."

As a side note, Crusan added that long ago nobody made a big deal out of his position being so vital. "I had no idea, but as time rolled, they

named the left offensive tackle the 'blind side,' but it was never refer-
enced. Looking back at it now, boy, that is a heckuva responsibility
because both Griese and Morrall were right-handed and they don't see
anybody coming. But I really didn't think about it that much. I just did
my job. Sometimes when you were on the strong side you had a tight
end there—you had help if you needed it. It just depended on the
formation."

Raymond Berry said that fans often ask him if he wished he was
playing today, making so much more money than he earned in his era.
His standard joking reply is, "Actually, if you want an ideal situation, I
would like to have played *when* I played, but at *today's* salaries."

Pottios said that like today's athletes themselves, NFL paychecks
today are way bigger and better. Also, in his time the majority of players
had one- or two-year contracts even though his first contract was for
three seasons. "But it didn't make any difference because back then
whether you had a three-year contract or a five-year contract for
$20,000 a year, there were no guarantees. If they cut you after the first
year, all you got was the bonus for signing and for playing that year—
after that you got nothing.

"There were no agents back then—it was you negotiating with the
owner or the general manager, and you know what their purpose was—
to get as much money for themselves as they could; and they had the
hammer, so to speak." The hammer was the ultimatum they could
smash players with: sign and play or go home. On losing clubs a general
manager could toss in, "We came in last with you, and we can do the
same without you."

Players simply had no clout. They might request to be traded, but
ultimately they were powerless. Marchetti said that in his second or
third season he asked to be swapped to the 49ers. "I tried to get the
Colts to trade me, and the general manager Kellett asked me why. I
said, 'I'd like to play in front of the people I grew up with.' He said,
'Well, Gino, I will never trade you. Never. You understand that?'"

Upset and angry, Marchetti protested, staying home during the first
several days of preseason training. "Then I called Kellett and said,
'Have somebody pick me up at the airport. I'm coming in.' So that was
my big holdout."

Nowadays he believes he would have been able to play with San
Francisco at some point. "You couldn't in the early days. You just

couldn't leave one team and play for another because first of all, most of the guys didn't have agents. That cut down on their bargaining power. There was nothing you could do.

"I'll tell you about the biggest raise I ever got. I went in one year to sign, I think it was 1958. I walked in his office and there was a contract which wasn't signed, mentioned no money, whatever. I said, 'Give it to me.' He asked why and I said, 'Just give it to me.' He looked at me strangely as I signed the contract and said, 'Put in what you think I'm worth,' and I walked out of his office. That was my biggest raise, the biggest one on the team that year, but owners had all the leverage. He could have put down whatever he wanted and I would have had to play for it."

Marchetti negotiated his salary for 1966 after he had already retired. He explained, "The guy that was going to take my place didn't pan out, so they wanted me to come back." Colts owner Carroll Rosenbloom asked him to come back. "When he asked how much money I wanted, I did the same thing I did to Kellett. 'I'll sign the contract for whatever it is, I'll play for it, but this is my last year.' When I looked at the contract it was for $4,000 a game, so it was for $56,000." He played in four games, but seems to recall that he was paid the entire sum.

Early on, as great as Marchetti was, he was definitely underpaid, but he believes he ended up all right monetarily "in more ways than one because of Carroll Rosenbloom. He came to me after a game and asked me, 'Gino, what the hell are you going to do with your life?' I asked him, 'What do you mean? I'm playing with the Colts, I'm happy as hell, everything is going nice. What more should I want?' He said, 'I want you to move to Baltimore and open a business there. I'll help you with the financing. The fans love you.' I didn't commit myself.

"Two days later I called him and said, 'I'm moving to Baltimore.' And he kept his word and helped me in so many ways it's unbelievable." Eventually, due to wise investments, Marchetti was set for life.

Rosenbloom intervened another time, just after Marchetti's broken leg in the 1958 title game. Marchetti was unable to play in the Pro Bowl game, but Rosenbloom made sure he still got his share of the money, as if he had played. "He was like that type of guy with people he trusted." Not too many players were fortunate enough to play for an owner like Rosenbloom, however.

Players needed to unite against the more typical, sometimes tyrannical type of owner. Joe Walton remembered the first stirrings of a players' union, not very potent way back when. "In the late 1950s our elective representative was Eddie LeBaron, and Mr. Marshall who was the owner of the Redskins found out about it and traded him the next day to the Dallas Cowboys."

As the sixties drew to a close, the power pendulum began to swing just a bit, as the players' union finally was able to pump up and flex its bargaining muscles somewhat. In 1968, Detroit lineman John Gordy left the playing field and became the president of the NFL Players Association. He was instrumental when the association negotiated its first collective bargaining agreement.

With Gordy gone from the Lions, Malinchak became the new team player rep. He noted that while changes were coming, they didn't take place immediately. "When we threatened to go out on strike," said Malinchak, "Russ Thomas, who was our general manager, he called John and I in individually and said, 'Don't take them out on strike.' I said, 'I'm not going to take them out, they're going to vote.' He repeated, 'Don't take them out on strike.' It was kind of ominous.

"And they voted to go on strike, so we went out. But then I understood what happened. I was naive to the fact that you just didn't do that then—this is 1968. I was a starting wide receiver in 1967. In 1968, they wouldn't let me play at all. They just put me on the bench. That was just the way it was. You just didn't go against them." Some marginal players even got cut, as retribution was swift. Clearly, the lack of players' power contrasts sharply to what the players now have.

Walton picked up his tales of owners' mistreatment in his time period. "I'll tell you another story. It was either the last four or five games when we were out of the chance to make the playoffs. Mr. Marshall used to let some of the players go to save money. We used to have just thirty-two guys at the time, anyway, I think it was. Then we'd be down to twenty-seven guys through the end of the season. In three of those games, I never left the field. I played the whole game. I was defensive corner, offensive receiver, and special teams player. I was on every special team. I didn't know any different—that's what we did in college, played both ways."

Crusan entered the NFL eleven years after Walton and sixteen years after Marchetti broke in, and said salary negotiations were still done directly with general managers. Crusan scoffed when asked if he had an agent, but replied, "When Csonka, Kiick, and Warfield left Miami and went to the USFL, to the Memphis team, I think they got an agent at that time, but that was rare in my time. There were some out there, and you could have a friend or maybe a friend who was a lawyer who would just look over the contract verbiage for you. Most of it was done with direct contact—for me with Joe Thomas, our GM."

Players and general managers basically sat in an office and haggled. Raymond Berry said he never had an agent until shortly before he signed on as the head coach of the New England Patriots in 1984.

Walton stated, "When we went to the training camp in the late fifties, we didn't get paid a dime until we made the team. I think they gave us $10 a week 'laundry money,' that was it. You got your first paycheck after the first league game. That was one of the things we were fighting for. They finally agreed to pay us $50 a game in the preseason, which we got in, I believe, the '59 season. When I got my first paycheck, the preseason games were deducted from my check."

Likewise, players of the 1950s and 1960s received very little money for their appearances in Pro Bowl games and even in championship games. Berry, who played in the first Pro Bowl Game ever to be tele-vised (in 1958), said he believed the winners' share was in the neighbor-hood of $800, and the losers earned around $600.

When the Colts won the NFL title in 1958 and 1959, the winners' share was just short of $4,700, but Berry said there were no complaints on his part because he had only earned about $12,000 per season back then. Members of the winning team, Green Bay, earned $15,000 when they knocked off Kansas City in Super Bowl I. That sum rose to $25,000 just two years later. The winners of the Super Bowl played in 2016 lugged home almost $100,000.

"Right now," mused Pottios, "the main difference is football is more of a business than back when we played because of the money in-volved." With big salaries for today's players, a person is more cautious about doing "something to jeopardize it. You got to be crazy. You never know when your last day playing is going to be. Your career could be over the next game."

Walton reflected, "We didn't make a lot of money, but we had a lot of fun. We had great camaraderie. We had some characters, and a lot of great people."

John Isenbarger, a four-year NFL veteran, pointed out another monetary contrast, and it deals with greed. "Here's a problem with the kids [players] of today. If you would call me today, and I was playing in the NFL and you were writing a book, I'd say, 'How much are you going to pay me? Are you going to pay me $50,000 for what I know?' I mean, it's unbelievable. I just think the numbers they're paying athletes any more is just outrageous. Hey, I'm not jealous, but I'm envious!"

Finally, on a lighter note, even the appearance of players today is different from those of the good old days. Uniforms are flashier and, as Matte tells it, even in his time some clothing styles were considered to be old fashioned. A case in point: he thought the high-top shoes of Unitas were amusing. "He would never, ever wear the low-cut shoes. We thought they were really cool; he said, 'I like my high-tops.' He just felt that when he planted his foot, the lower shoe sort of rolled over so he always wanted to use those high tops, and that was his trademark, so I think he stuck with it."

Of course, Peyton Manning is a throwback, a quarterback very much like Unitas. He even wore black high tops in college because of Unitas, and for his first game after Unitas passed away, Manning declared he would again wear black high-tops as a tribute to Unitas. However, the NFL prohibited that.

While it's true that football has changed enormously over the years, no, over the *decades*, the fundamental reasons millions of fans continue to flock to the sport are the same—football was, and remains, a great game to play, to watch, and to savor. However, it's up to each fan to choose his or her own personal golden age, and to decide if the changes in the game represent devolution or evolution.

Modern football fans may say of the changes in the game: "We've come a long way, baby." However, many readers of this book, no doubt traditionalists, remain adamantly convinced that, "Football was better in the good ol' days—the Glory Years." No argument here.

NOTES

I. THE BEST OFFENSIVE PLAYERS

1. Brad Herzog, *The Sports 100* (New York: Macmillan, 1995), 233.
2. Allan Maki, *Football's Greatest Stars* (Buffalo, NY: Firefly Books, 2008), 33.
3. Maki, *Football's Greatest Stars*, 67.
4. Maki, *Football's Greatest Stars*, 139.

3. FUNNIEST QUOTES AND TALES

1. All quotes and anecdotes in this chapter are from the author's interviews or are widely quoted and can be found in various sources, except for the specific cases where an endnote is provided.
2. Joe Nick Patoski, *The Dallas Cowboys* (New York: Little, Brown, 2012), 238.
3. Patoski, *The Dallas Cowboys*, 238.
4. Lee Green, *Sportswit* (New York: Ballantine Books, 1984), 261.
5. Green, *Sportswit*, 276.
6. Green, *Sportswit*, 307.
7. Brad Herzog, *The Sports 100* (New York: Macmillan, 1995), 289.
8. Herzog, *The Sports 100*, 234.
9. Douglas Martin, "Art Donovan, a Behemoth of Modesty, Dies at 89," *New York Times*, August 5, 2013, http://www.nytimes.com/2013/08/06/sports/football/art-donovan-a-behemoth-of-modesty-dies-at-89.html?_r=0.
10. Green, *Sportswit*, 177.

11. Green, *Sportswit*, 13.

12. Green, *Sportswit*, 1.

13. Gene Strother, "Inglorious Basterds: The 10 Most Underrated Dallas Cowboys of All Time," *Bleacher Report*, December 11, 2009, http://bleacherreport.com/articles/307107-inglourious-basterds-the-ten-most-underrated-dallas-cowboys-of-all-time/page/3.

14. "Walt Garrison Quotes," AZ Quotes, http://www.azquotes.com/author/46554-Walt_Garrison.

15. Richard Whittingham, *Sunday's Heroes* (Chicago: Triumph Books, 2003), 121.

16. Whittingham, *Sunday's Heroes*, 143.

17. Whittingham, *Sunday's Heroes*, 34.

18. Allan Maki, *Football's Greatest Stars* (Buffalo, NY: Firefly Books, 2008), 106.

19. Green, *Sportswit*, 166.

20. Whittingham, *Sunday's Heroes*, 168.

21. "Joe Don Looney, 45, Former Football Star," *New York Times*, September 26, 1988, http://www.nytimes.com/1988/09/26/obituaries/joe-don-looney-45-former-football-star.html.

22. Richard Langford, "Ochocinco and the 20 Most Eccentric Players in NFL History," Bleacher Report, February 15, 2011, http://bleacherreport.com/articles/607846-ochocinco-and-the-20-most-eccentric-players-in-nfl-history/page/21.

4. THE TOUGHEST PLAYERS

1. Michael MacCambridge, ed., *ESPN Sports Century* (New York: ESPN, 1999), 195.

2. "NFL Top 10: Most Feared Tacklers," NFL Network Produced by NFL Films, Original air date August 5, 2008.

3. "Sports Anecdotes: NFL," http://www.speaklikeapro.co.uk/NFL2htm (2015).

4. "NFL Top 10: Most Feared Tacklers."

5. Richard Whittingham, *Sunday's Heroes* (Chicago: Triumph Books, 2003), 137.

6. THE NFL THEN AND NOW

1. Richard Whittingham, *Sunday's Heroes* (Chicago: Triumph Books, 2003), 111.

BIBLIOGRAPHY

BOOKS

Beilenson, Peter., ed. *The Sports Page*. White Plains, NY: Peter Pauper Press, 1989.
Berry, Raymond, with Wayne Stewart. *All the Moves I Had: A Football Life* Guilford, CT: Lyons Press, 2016.
Buckley, James Jr. *The NFL's Top 100*. Berkeley, CA: Thunder Bay Press, 2011.
Carroll, Bob. *When the Grass Was Real*. New York: Simon & Schuster, 1993.
Curtis, Mike, with Bill Gilbert. *Keep Off My Turf*. Philadelphia: J.B. Lippincott, 1972.
Green, Lee. *Sportswit*. New York: Fawcett Crest, 1984.
Hersch, Hank. *Greatest Football Games of All Time*. New York: Time Inc. Home Entertainment, 1997.
Herzog, Brad. *The Sports 100*. New York: Macmillan, 1996.
Jenkins, Dan. *Saturday's America*. New York: Berkley Books, 1973.
Karras, Alex, with Herb Gluck. *Even Big Guys Cry*. New York: Signet, 1977.
Landry, Tom, with Gregg Lewis. *An Autobiography: Tom Landry*. New York: Harper Paperbacks, 1990.
MacCambridge, Michael, ed. *ESPN Sports Century*. New York: ESPN, 1999.
Maki, Allan. *Football's Greatest Stars*. Buffalo, NY: Firefly Books, 2008.
Olderman, Murray. *The Pro Quarterback*. Englewood Cliffs, NJ: Prentice-Hall, 1966.
Olderman, Murray. *The Running Backs*. Englewood Cliffs, NJ: Prentice-Hall, 1969.
Patoski, Joe Nick. *The Dallas Cowboys*. New York: Back Bay Books, 2012.
Smith, Red. *The Red Smith Reader*. New York: Random House, 1982.
Smith, Ron. *Pro Football's Heroes of the Hall*. St. Louis: Sporting News, 2003.
Stewart, Wayne. *America's Cradle of Quarterbacks*. Carlisle, PA: Tuxedo Press, 2014.
Whittingham, Richard. *Sunday's Heroes*. Chicago: Triumph Books, 2003.

TELEVISION SHOWS

Beyond the Game: Green Bay Packers: The Ice Bowl and More. John Vorperean Executive Producer. Directed by Keith Baker. Original air date July 28, 2015.
A Football Life: Dick Butkus and Gale Sayers. NFL Network Produced by NFL Films. Original air date November 28, 2014.

A Football Life: The Fearsome Foursome. NFL Network Produced by NFL Films. Original air date December 20, 2012.

NFL Top 10: Most Feared Tacklers. NFL Network Produced by NFL Films. Original air date August 5, 2008.

WEBSITES

AZ Quotes. "Walt Garrison Quotes." http://www.azquotes.com/author/46554-Walt_Garrison.

Curtis, Mike. *Mike Curtis Football.* http://www.mikecurtisfootball.com.

Langford, Richard. "Ochocinco and the 20 Most Eccentric Players in NFL History." *Bleacher Report.* http://bleacherreport.com/articles/607846-ochocinco-and-the-20-most-eccentric-players-in-nfl-history/page/21.

Martin, Douglas. "Art Donovan, a Behemoth of Modesty, Dies at 89." *New York Times,* August 6, 2013. http://www.nytimes.com/2013/08/06/sports/football/art-donovan-a-behemoth-of-modesty-dies-at-89.html?_r=0.

New York Times. "Joe Don Looney, 45, Former Football Star." September 26, 1988. http://www.nytimes.com/1988/09/26/obituaries/joe-don-looney-45-former-football-star.html.

O'Brien, Stephen. "30 Funniest NFL Quotes." *NFL-Ireland.* http://nfl-ireland.com/nfl/1970-30-funniest-nfl-quotes/.

Speak Like a Pro. "Sporting Anecdotes: NFL." http://www.speaklikeapro.co.uk/NFL2.htm.

Strother, Gene. "Inglorious Basterds: The 10 Most Underrated Dallas Cowboys of All Time." *Bleacher Report.* http://bleacherreport.com/articles/307107-inglourious-basterds-the-ten-most-underrated-dallas-cowboys-of-all-time/page/3.

INDEX

ABOUT THE AUTHOR

Wayne Stewart was born in Pittsburgh and raised in Donora, Pennsylvania, a small town that has produced four big-league baseball players, including Stan Musial and the father-son Griffeys. In fact, Stewart was a member of the same Donora High School baseball team as classmate Griffey Sr. Stewart, who retired from teaching after thirty-one years, now lives in Amherst, a suburb of Cleveland, Ohio.

Mr. Stewart began covering the sports world as a writer in 1978, freelancing for publications such as *Baseball Digest, Beckett Baseball Card Monthly, Baseball Bulletin, Boys' Life*, and for official team publications of ten major league clubs, including the Atlanta Braves, the Baltimore Orioles, the Boston Red Sox, and the Los Angeles Dodgers.

He has interviewed and profiled many stars from several sports including Larry Bird, George Gervin, Robert Parish, Nolan Ryan, Bob Gibson, Rickey Henderson, and Ken Griffey Jr. Among the thirty-two books he has written to date are biographies of Babe Ruth, Stan Musial, and Alex Rodriguez; *Baseball Oddities; Fathers, Sons, and Baseball; You're the Umpire*; and, most recently, *All the Moves I Had*, the autobiography he cowrote for Lyons Press with NFL Hall of Fame wide receiver Raymond Berry.

Stewart has also appeared as a baseball expert/historian on numerous radio and television shows including an ESPN Classic program on Bob Feller, on ESPN radio, and on the Pat Williams radio program. He also hosted several radio shows for a small Lorain, Ohio, station including pre-game reports prior to Notre Dame football games and Cleveland Indians baseball games, and a call-in talk show. He has written for several Ohio newspapers and some of his works have been used in eight anthologies.